MARCUS AURELIUS

MEDITATIONS
OR THE COMMENTARIES
WRITTEN BY HIMSELF
FOR HIMSELF
TWELVE BOOKS

FIRST BILINGUAL EDITION
LATIN & ENGLISH

Latin translation from the Schulzian Greek edition by
Johann Friedrich Dübner

MMXXIII

First Edition

© 2023
DeVela Publishing
ISBN: 9798860287600
Impreso por Kindle Direct Publishing

MARCI AURELII ANTONINI

IMPERATORIS

MEDITATIONES

SIVE COMMENTARIORUM
QUOS IPSE SIBI SCRIPSIT
ΤΩΝ ΕΙΣ ΕΑΥΤΟΝ

LIBRI DUODECIM

EDITIO PRINCEPS

LATINA & ANGLICA

Latina translatio ex versione Graeca Schulziana per
Johann Friedrich Dübner

MMXXIII

DER TEVTSHEN ACADEMIE
ZWEYTEN THEILS
ZWEYTES BVCH VON DER SCVL
TVRA ODER BILDEREY KVNST.

Cum Gratia et Privilegio Sac. Cæs. Majest.

J. De Sandrart del. Richard Collin sculps. Antv. 1677.

TABULA RERUM

AD LECTOREM

Quamquam, VIRI PERILLUSTRES et EXCELLENTISSIMI, non una erat causa, cur hoc quidquid est studii a me in curanda hac Antonini Editione collocatum tantorum Virorum conspectum vereri posset; tamen, omnibus ponderatis rationibus, pudorem et a natura mihi infitum et humanitatis literis excultum vincere atque splendidis VESTRIS nominibus opusculum hoc inscribere decrevi.

Vehementer enim iam dudum optavi, ut summae illius observantiae et reverentiae, quam insigni utriusque VESTRUM in me humanitati debeo, exstaret monumentum; idque splendore VESTRO non omnino indignum.

Although, most illustrious and excellent gentlemen, there was not a single reason why this endeavor of mine, in the care of this edition of Antoninus, might be feared by the scrutiny of such great men; however, after considering all reasons, I decided to overcome the shame inherent in me by nature and cultivated by the humanities and to dedicate this small work to your illustrious names.

For I have long ardently wished that there should be a monument to the highest degree of that observance and reverence, which I owe to the distinguished humanity of both of you; and that it should not be entirely unworthy of your brilliance.

Nolui igitur vehementem animi impetum, quotidie me stimulis agitantem, ut tandem aliquando gratias pro multis magnisque vestris in me collatis beneficiis agerem publiceque declararem, diutius reprimere.

Therefore, I did not want to suppress the vehement impulse of my heart, which daily urged me, so that finally, at some point, I might publicly express gratitude for the many great benefits conferred upon me by both of you.

Etsi enim satis intelligebam, quam levis esset opera et nullo fere loco habenda, quam in Antonino edendo collocavissem, tamen ea visa est ipsius libelli praestantia eaque Divi auctoris maiestas, ut certo considerem, vos non posse pudere, in tanti Principis, esse comitatu.

Although I understood well enough how light and hardly noteworthy the task was that I had undertaken in editing Antoninus, yet the excellence of the very booklet itself and the maiesty of the divine author made it certain for me to consider that you could not be ashamed to be in the company of such a great ruler.

Praeterea quoque iustitiae ratio, qua suum cuique tribuere iubemur, exigebat, ut haec Antonini Editio vobis traderetur.

Furthermore, the principle of iustice, by which we are commanded to give each their due, required that this edition of Antoninus be handed over to you.

Vestrum enim est vestroque debetur studio, quidquid nitoris huic novae Editioni accesserit, vestro in bonas literas amori, vestrae humanitati atque benevolentiae.

For it belongs to you and is owed to your devotion, whatever grace has been added to this new edition, out of love for your commitment to good literature and your humanity and kindness.

Non vero iam loquor de summis vestris in Patriam meritis, non de singularibus animi et ingenii virtutibus, quibus uterque vestrum immortalem illius Viri, quocum aut sanguis aut affinitas vos iunxit, gloriam aemulatur, non denique de egregia illa prudentia et moderatione, qua nobis pacem tamdiu servastis, bellumque ab oris nostris nuper profligastis;

I am not speaking now about your outstanding merits to the homeland, nor about the exceptional virtues of character and intellect, by which each of you emulates the glory of that immortal man to whom either blood or affinity has united you. Nor am I finally speaking about that excellent prudence and moderation by which you have preserved peace for us for so long and recently averted war from our shores.

quae quidem omnia tanta funt, ut nec possint nec velint nisi a laudatis laudari: sed hoc solum publice profiteor, inter tot tantas, quibus premebar, muneris laboriosissimi molestias mihi opus fuisse REVENTLOVIIS ac BERNSTORFFIIS, ut, quod coeperam, demum perficerem.

All of these things, indeed, are so great that they neither can nor would wish to be praised by anyone except those who are esteemed. But I publicly confess only this: among so many and great challenges that weighed upon me, it was necessary for me to rely on the laborious efforts of REVENTLOVIIS and BERNSTORFFIIS in order to finally complete what I had begun.

TU enim, perillustris et generosissime REVENTLOVI, non tantum thesaurum literarium Havniensem mihi, homini obscuro, liberaliter reclusisti, sed etiam singularibus favoris tui atque humanitatis pignoribus animum subinde vacillantem roborasti ad opus continuandum et demum, ut poteram, conficiendum;

For you, most illustrious and generous REVENTLOVI, not only generously opened the literary treasure of Copenhagen to me, a humble individual, but also with the tokens of your special favor and humanity, you strengthened my wavering resolve to continue the work and finally bring it to completion;

Tu vero, perillustris et generosissime BERNSTORFFI, eximia tua liberalitate ac munificentia aditum mihi aperuisti ad fontes literarios, quibus Italia superbit, atque inter medios terrores belli funestissimi, quod foecundissimas atque amoenissimas Europae partes devastabat, supellectilem literariam, quae ad Antoninum meum comparata erat, incolumem atque intactam ad me adferendam curasti.

and you, most illustrious and generous BERNSTORFFI, with your outstanding generosity and munificence, you provided me access to the literary sources that Italy boasts of, even amid the midst of the direst horrors of the devastating war, which was ravaging the most fertile and delightful parts of Europe, you ensured that the literary collection, which was intended for my Antoninus, arrived to me unharmed and intact.

Tantum igitur quum fuerit utriusque vestrum in me et Antoninum meum studium: quis est, quin videat, quidquid boni novae huic Editioni infit, id vestro praecipue studio deberi, quidquid autem paevorum, id meae folius culpae tribuendum esse?

So, as much as both of your dedication to me and my Antoninus has been, who can fail to see that whatever good is found in this new edition, it is primarily owed to your dedication, and whatever shortcomings exist, they should be attributed solely to my fault?

Multos vero atque magnos adhuc paevos residere, qui essent tollendi, facile largior, et hoc tantum opto, ne tot atque tanti remanserint, ut vos unquam poeniteat, studia mea adiuvisse.

There are indeed still many great shortcomings that could be removed, and I readily acknowledge this. My only wish is that there are not so many and so significant that you would ever regret supporting my efforts.

Quod reliquum est, vobis, comites perilustres atque generossimis vestris gentibus res fecundissimas, et quidquid verorum bonorum obtingere potest mortalibus, precor.

For the rest, to you, most illustrious companions and to your most generous families, I wish the most abundant blessings and all that can befall mortals in terms of true goodness.

NOMINIBUS VESTRIS PERILLUSTRIBUS
GENEROSISSIMIS EXCELLENTISSIMIS

In the illustrious, most generous, and excellent names of yours.9

DEVOTE ADDICTUS

Devotedly dedicated,

IOANNES MATTHIAS SCHULTZ

PRAEFATIO NOVI EDITORIS

Tria omnino esse, quorum is, qui in vetere aliquo Scriptore edendo operae pretium facere velit, rationem habere debeat, recte monuit Clarissimus WYTTENBACH in erudita Praefatione Moralibus Plutarchi praefixa:

To sum up, there are three things to consider, of which he who wishes to engage in the editing of some ancient author, as rightly pointed out by the distinguished WYTTENBACH in the scholarly Preface prefixed to Plutarch's Morals:

primum scilicet, utrum liber dignus fit, qui edatur:

Firstly, whether the book is worthy of being published;

Alterum, digna auctore editio utrum exstet, an desideretur:

Secondly, whether a worthy edition by a reputable author exists or is desired;

Tertium, an ipse perficiundae editioni idoneus fit editor.

Thirdly, whether the editor himself is suitable for the task of completing the edition.

His igitur tribus explicandae cum omne praefandi munus absolvatur, de unoquoque horum trium et mihi pauca erunt dicenda.

Thus, when all the duties of the preface are fulfilled with these three things being explained, a few words will be spoken by me about each of these three.

Ad primum igitur quod attinet, neminem facile reperiri puto, qui neget, Marci Aurelii Antonini Commentarios, qui Τὰ εἰς ἑαυτόν inscripti ad nostra pervenerunt tempora, dignos esse, qui ab omnibus literarum humanarum studiosis saepissime legantur, ne dicam, ediscantur, atque igitur et optime et quam emendatissime edantur.

Regarding the first point, I think there is hardly anyone who would deny that the Commentaries of Marcus Aurelius Antoninus, which are titled "To Himself" and have come down to our times, are worthy to be frequently read, not to mention memorized, by all students of human literature, and therefore should be edited both excellently and with utmost accuracy.

Possem hic quidem, quum res ipsa ita ferre videatur, in Antonini mei laudes exspatiari:

quo minus tamen hac opportunitate utar ad Scriptorem, cuius edendi curam suscepi, celebrandum, eius rei plures, et, ut opinor, idoneas habeo causas.

Primam, quod Clarissimus MEINERS in Commentatione de Marci Aurelii Antonini ingenio, moribus et scriptis, quae Commentariorum Regiae Societatis Literarum Goettingensis Tomo VI. inserta est, tam erudite et eleganter de hac re disputavit, ut omnis mihi materia praerepta videatur.

Alteram, quod neminem eorum, quorum in manus haec nostra Editio venerit, tam rudem omnium literarum futurum arbitror, quin sciat, Antoninum Imperatorem, eundem et Philosophum.

Praestantissimum, in aureolo hoc libello gravissima quaeque tractasse argumenta, sibique sanctissima illius scholae decreta inculcasse, quae omnes omnium temporum homines in admirationem fui vel invitos rapuit:

tertiam, quod sufficere censeo ad Antonini laudes celebrandas Testimonia scriptorum veterum et recentiorum, quae ad calcem huius Praefationis ex Gatakeri Editione repetere visum est.

Ad alterum vero quod attinet, utrum iam talis existet huius libri Editio, ut nova fine damno carere possimus, eo brevior hic ero, quod in iis, quae sequuntur, Prolegomenis prolixius de singulis Editionibus disputavi:

ex quibus apparebit, non talem nos habere eius libri Editionem, quae et parabilis et usui apta fit.

I could indeed, when circumstances seem to allow it, expound at length on the praises of my Marcus Aurelius:

However, I shall refrain from taking this opportunity to celebrate the author whose editing I have undertaken, and I have several, as I believe, suitable reasons for this:

Firstly, because the distinguished MEINERS, in his essay on the character, morals, and writings of Marcus Aurelius, which is included in Volume VI of the Literary Commentaries of the Royal Society of Göttingen, has discussed this matter so eruditely and elegantly that it seems to me all material has been preempted.

Secondly, because I believe that no one among those into whose hands this edition of ours will come will be so unlearned in all literature as not to know that Marcus Aurelius was both an Emperor and a Philosopher.

Most outstandingly, to have treated the weightiest subjects in this precious little book, and to have impressed upon oneself the holiest precepts of that school, which has captivated all people of all times, whether willingly or unwillingly, with the deepest admiration.

Thirdly, because I consider it sufficient for celebrating the praises of Marcus Aurelius to reproduce the testimonies of ancient and modern writers, which have been decided to be included at the end of this Preface from Gataker's Edition.

Regarding the second point, whether such an edition of this book already exists that we can do without a new one, I will be brief here because I have discussed each edition more extensively in the following Prolegomena."

From which it will become apparent that we do not have such an edition of this book that is both suitable and convenient for use

Optima enim, quae Th. Gatakeri studio debetur, Editio cum perrara repertu est, saltem in nostris regionibus, tum non omnino talis, qualem optare fas est.

> The best edition, which is owed to the diligence of Thomas Gataker, is indeed very rare, at least in our regions, and still not entirely as one might wish.

Eorum vero, qui post Gatakerum hunc librum evulgarunt, nemo probabilis subsidiorum apparatu ad Antoninum recensendum, et a naevis, quibus scatebat, perpurgandum accessit, praeter Gallicum Editorem De Foly:

> However, among those who have published this book after Gataker, no one with a credible arsenal of resources for reviewing Marcus Aurelius and purging him of the blemishes that were rampant, except for the French editor De Foly.

quem tamen in hac opera non eam, quam par erat, adhibuisse diligentiam inter omnes constat.

> However, it is universally acknowledged that even De Foly did not apply the diligence in this work that was expected.

Ad tertium denique, quod attinet, utrum ego is sim, abs quo parari possit probabilis Antonini Editio, de eo penes alios iudicium esto! Equidem, quamquam omni studio in id incubui, ut diligentiae certe laude non omnino indignus viderer, tamen opere perfecto probe intelligo, multa huic Editioni desse, quae ad probam requirantur atque omnibus numeris absolutam, immo multa inesse;

> "As for the third point, whether I am the one from whom a credible edition of Marcus Aurelius can be prepared, let others be the judge of that! Indeed, though I have devoted all my zeal to it so as not to appear entirely unworthy of the praise of diligence, I clearly understand, with the work being completed, that many things are lacking in this edition, which are required for a good one and complete in all respects. Indeed, there are many things present.

quae iure merito reprehendi possint.

> Which can rightly and deservedly be criticized

Ne vero ab aequis lectoribus bonique consulentibus nimiae temeritatis in Editoris munere suscipiendo arguar, liceat mihi, qua occasione in hanc cogitationem devenerim, quid consilii ceperim, et qua ratione id exsequi studuerim, prolixius exponere.

> And, lest I be accused by fair-minded and prudent readers of undertaking the editor's task with excessive rashness, allow me to explain more elaborately on the occasion that led me to this thought, what plan I have adopted, and in what manner I have endeavored to carry it out.

Quum ante septem annos, et quod excurrit, in Historia Philosophiae maximo cum studio versarer, nulla inter Graecorum Philosophorum scholas me magis capiebat, quam Stoica, cuius igitur monumenta, quae supererant omnia, conquirere et tractare constituebam.

> When seven years and the time that has elapsed before that, I was deeply engaged in the study of the history of philosophy, no school among the Greek philosophers captivated me more than the Stoic school. Therefore, I decided to collect and study all the remaining monuments of it.

Inter alios vero disciplinae Stoicae scriptores Antoninus mihi ita eminere videbatur, ut saepe mirarer, libellum eius a nostri temporis Criticis omnino negligi, dum alii veterum auctorum libri elegantiore habitu prodirent, Antoniniano illo si non inferiores, at profecto non praestantiores.

Intelligere ergo mihi visus sum, operae pretium esse facturum, qui in hoc Antonini libro emendando et illustrando operam navaverit, atque, ut est iuvenilium animorum fervor, ipse de eo cura mea qualicunque perpoliendo cogitare coepi.

Erant quidem multae et gravissimae rationes, quae ab hoc consilio me deterrere et potuissent et debuissent nam omnibus fere carebam, quibus opus est ei, qui tanto labore feliciter defungi cupiat.

Deerat non solum illa ingenii felicitas, quae paucis cuiusvis saeculi hominibus peculiari naturae beneficentia conceditur, sed deerat etiam idonea accuratae et exquisitae doctrinae copia, deerat supellex literaria et libros nanciscendi opportunitas, deerant opes criticae, deerat denique, quo plerique iuvenum, qui ad talem laborem accedunt, frui possunt, qui rem consilio et opera adiuvet.

Verum is, qui me impulerat, aetatis fervor, his omnibus neglectis, animum semper ad agendum stimulavit.

Comparandus igitur erat, quo aliquid saltem pretii Editioni meae adferri posse arbitrabar, Apparatus criticus, quo qui destituitur, de idonea veteris scriptoris Criticis neglecti Editione cogitare non potest.

Among the various authors of Stoic philosophy, Antoninus seemed to me to stand out so prominently that I often marveled at how his little book was completely overlooked by the critics of our time, while the works of other ancient authors were being published in a more elegant form, which, if not inferior to the work of Antoninus, certainly were not superior.

Therefore, I thought that it would be worth the effort for anyone who devoted themselves to correcting and elucidating this work of Antoninus, and, as is the fervor of youthful minds, I began to contemplate personally taking care of it to some extent.

There were indeed many weighty reasons that could and should have deterred me from this plan, for I lacked almost all the resources needed by someone who wishes to successfully undertake such a laborious task.

I lacked not only that intellectual aptitude which is granted by the peculiar kindness of nature to only a few individuals of any era, but I also lacked an abundant supply of accurate and exquisite learning, literary resources, and opportunities to acquire books. I lacked critical resources, and, finally, I lacked the support that most young people who embark on such a task can enjoy, which could assist in planning and carrying out the work.

But the enthusiasm of youth, despite all these shortcomings, always spurred me on to action.

Therefore, I believed that I should at least provide something of value to my edition, and this was to be a critical apparatus, without which one cannot even think of producing a suitable edition of a neglected ancient author.

Neque possum dignis laudibus praedicare Virorum Illustrium, Clarorum et Doctorum benevolentiam, quae me hominem obscurum in apparatu hoc colligendo adiuvit.

I cannot praise enough the kindness of the illustrious, eminent, and learned individuals who, by assisting me in collecting this apparatus, supported an obscure individual like me.

Editionum scilicet antiquarum, quae in Bibliotheca Augustissimi nostri REGIS Havniensi adservantur, notitiam mecum communicavit Vir Summe Venerabilis MOLDENHAWER, Theologus Havniensis Clarissimus ac Doctissimus.

Specifically, the most venerable and learned gentleman, MOLDENHAWER, a theologian of the highest order in Copenhagen, graciously shared with me his knowledge of the ancient editions that are preserved in the library of our most August king.

His porro Editionibus ut mihi uti easque per otium excutere liceret, facile impetravi a studio, quo in bonas literas fertur, qui huic Bibliothecae praest.

Furthermore, in order to use these editions and examine them at my leisure, I easily obtained permission from the librarian, who is known for his devotion to the fine arts, and who oversees this library.

Illustris COMES de REVENTLOV, Augustissimo Nostro REGI ab interiore administratione reipublicae.

The illustrious Count de REVENTLOV, in charge of the internal administration of our most august king's realm.

Ex eadem porro Bibliotheca Regia eorundem Virorum de Patria ac literis optime meritorum studio ac benevolentia accepi coniecturarum Reiskianarum fasciculum, quem olim cum aliis MSS.

From the same Royal Library, I received, through the kindness and scholarly efforts of these same men distinguished for their contributions to their homeland and literature, a bundle of Reiskian coniectures, which I had once deposited there along with other manuscripts.

Reiskianis emerat magnum illud Daniae decus, P. F. SUHM, cuius praestantissimam atque optimis libris refertam Bibliothecam non auctione distractam, sed cum Regia illa coniuncta esse gaudent nobiscum omnes, qui literas amant.

Suhm, the great pride of Denmark, had acquired those Reiskian treasures, and his outstanding library, filled with the best books, is not only a source of pride for us all who love literature but also a part of our royal heritage, not sold at auction but rather joined with the Royal Library.

Editionibus autem his diligenter excussis intellexi parum esse in iis subsidii ad naevos, quibus laborabat Antonini textus, tollendos, atque varias, quae mihi ex iis enotatae erant, lectiones nihil fere esse, nisi aut errores operarum, aut correctiones, ne dicam depravationes, ex Editorum ingenio profectas.

However, upon careful examination of these editions, I realized that there was little help in them for removing the blemishes that afflicted the text of Antoninus, and the various readings I had noted from them were mostly either errors in the works or corrections, not to say perversions, originating from the ingenuity of the editors.

Maximo igitur studio flagravi, Lectionis Varietatem ex Codd. MSS. excerptam mihi comparandi:

Therefore, I burned with great zeal to obtain a collection of textual variations from manuscript codices.

quod etiam, quamvis in mediis belli crudelissimi furoribus, mihi contigit.

ADLERO enim Viro Summe Venerabili, Theologorum Slesvicenlium Praeside, quae eius erat humanitas, me commendante, adii per literas Virum Humanissimum:

et supra laudem meam quamcunque elatum SILVESTRE de SACY, insigne Gallicarum Musarum decus, eumque rogavi, ut, si inveniri possent in Bibliotheca Nationis Franco-Gallicae variantes lectiones, quas olim in usum De Ioly ex Codicibus Bibliothecae Vaticanae excerptas curavisset Assemanus, De Ioly vero Bibliothecae Regis Galliarum tradidisset, in usum meum denuo describendas curaret.

Haud longo tempore post me certiorem fecit Doctissimus SILVESTRE de SACY, se reperisse inter Codd. Bibliothecae illius variantes lectiones, Assemano curante, collectas, qua in re etiam Viri Doctissimi FRANC.

LAPORTE du THEIL et MERCIER de Saint LEGER nonnullam ipsi praestitissent operam.

Docuit me quoque, praeter illam Lectionis varietatem, in eadem Bibliotheca fervari Aegidii Menagii Notas in Antoninum ineditas, quas, si vellem, in usum meum transscribendas curare esset paratus.

Denique mihi et Antonino meo gratulandum erat de eo, quod Vir Doctissimus atque exquisitae linguae Graecae cognitionis laude florens DIAMOND.

CORAIL se non indignum haberet, illas chartas in usum meum describere.

Quin etiam ultro mihi obtulit exquisitas in Antoninum coniecturas, quae ipsi inter legendum in mentem venerant.

This also happened to me, even in the midst of the cruelest ravages of war.

I approached the highly venerable man, the President of the Theologians of Schleswig, namely ADLER, with a letter of introduction, and he, with his characteristic kindness, welcomed me.

Above and beyond my meager praise, I approached SILVESTRE de SACY, the distinguished ornament of the French Muses, and I asked him if it were possible to find in the National Library of France any variant readings that Assemanus had once extracted from the Codices of the Vatican Library for the use of De Ioly, and which De Ioly had then entrusted to the Library of the King of France. I requested that he undertake the task of retranscribing them for my use.

Not long after, the highly learned SILVESTRE de SACY informed me that he had found among the codices of that library the variant readings collected by Assemanus, in which matter also the very learned FRANC.

LAPORTE du THEIL and MERCIER de Saint LEGER had themselves contributed some effort in this regard.

He also informed me that, in addition to those textual variations, there were unpublished notes by Aegidius Menagius on Antoninus preserved in the same library, and he was willing to have them transcribed for my use if I so desired.

Finally, it was a reason for congratulating both myself and my Antoninus that the very learned and highly renowned scholar of Greek, DIAMOND, who excelled in his knowledge of the Greek language, was involved.

CORAIL considered it worthy of himself to transcribe those pages for my use.

He even voluntarily offered me his exquisite coniectures on Antoninus, which had come to mind while he was reading.

Varias quoque lectiones a Francisco Barberini olim Patre Purpurato Translationi Italicae additas sua manu transcriptas SILVESTRE DE SACY, Vir mihi nunquam non cum laude nominandus, cum alio apparatu ad Antoninum meum pertinente misit.

Interea et AUGUST. MAR. BANDINIUM, Doctissimum Bibliothecae Mediceo Florentinae Praefectum, rogaveram lectiones Codicum Antonini Florentinorum, quas quidem curante Viro illo Doctissimo, a BENCINIO et BONIO,

Viris Intelligentissimis, collectas accepi, adiutus in ea re summa, munificentia et liberalitate Perillustis COMITIS DE BERNSTORFF, qui etiam tempore eo, quo maxime in Italia belli saevitia furebat, chartas ex Italia incolumes ad me deferendas curavit.

His ergo subsidiis ad novam Antonini Editionem parandam instructus, iterum iterumque textum, quem vocant, qualis Gatakeri opera erat nobis traditus, diligenter et ex omni parte cum Editionibus antiquioribus et varietate lectionis ex Codicibus MSS. excerpta comparavi.

Quo vero maiorem cum Antonino meo familiaritatem contraherem, et melius intelligerem, ubi obscuritatis aliquid in hoc scriptore lateret, ere esse putavi, Antonini Commentarios in linguam vernaculam transferre:

SILVESTRE DE SACY, a man never to be mentioned without praise, also sent me various readings added to the Italian translation by Francisco Barberini, the former Cardinal in Purple, which he had transcribed with his own hand, along with other material related to my edition of Antoninus.

In the meantime, I had also asked AUGUST. MAR. BANDINIUM, the most learned Prefect of the Medicean Library in Florence, to provide me with readings from the Codices of Antoninus in Florence, which, with the assistance of that very learned man, were collected by BENCINIUS and BONIUS.

With the assistance of these most intelligent gentlemen, I received the collected readings. I was greatly aided in this endeavor by the great generosity and liberality of the Most Illustrious COUNT DE BERNSTORFF, who even during the height of the war's devastation in Italy arranged for the safe transport of documents from Italy to me.

Equipped with these resources to prepare a new edition of Antoninus, I diligently compared the text, which is known as Gataker's work, with older editions and with readings excerpted from manuscript codices to capture every aspect of textual variation.

In order to develop a deeper familiarity with my Antoninus and better understand any hidden obscurities within this author, I believed it would be worthwhile to translate Antoninus' Commentaries into the vernacular language.

cuius quoque studii fructum, Translationem theodiscam postea typis exscribendam tradidi eo inprimis consilio, et ut doctorum virorum iudicia de eo cognoscerem, utrum in opere coepto mihi esset pergendum, an totum Editionis munus deponendum, et ut, si fortasse consilium meum non omnino improbarent, eorum monitis ad opus rite instruendum adiuvaretur et regeretur studium meum de literis bene merendi.

I also entrusted the fruit of this effort, a German translation, to be later printed, with the primary intention of seeking the judgment of learned individuals on whether I should continue with the project or abandon the entire task of the edition. I hoped that if they did not entirely disapprove of my plan, their advice would assist and guide my efforts in properly preparing the work and in meriting recognition for my contributions to literature.

Iam vero, quid ex hoc labore profecerim, ingenue profitebor.

Now, I will candidly confess what progress I have made with this labor

Intellexi scilicet, subtiliorem literarum cognitionem et ingenium in aliorum Scriptorum Crisi probe exercitatum requiri in eo, qui Editionem Antonini probabilem parare vellet;

I realized that a more profound knowledge of literature and a well-exercised intellect in the critical examination of other authors are indeed required for someone who wishes to prepare a credible edition of Antoninus.

praesertim in ea apparatus critici penuria, qua multis in locis, et iisque admodum corruptis, et obscuris ad coniecturam artificium confugiendum.

Especially in the absence of a critical apparatus, which, in many places, and those often extremely corrupted and obscure, necessitates resorting to the art of coniecture.

Et quamquam a Censore, qui in Ephemeridibus literariis, quae Ienae prodeunt, de Translatione illa sententiam ferebat, candido sane et aequo iudice, confilium, quod coeperam, non improbari videram, tamen non semel in eo fui, ut laborem hunc deponerem.

And although I had seen that the plan I had initiated was not disapproved of by a fair and impartial iudge, who expressed his opinion on that translation in the literary iournals published in Iena, I was not once in a situation where I considered abandoning this labor.

Quod quo minus facerem, prohibuit pudor, ne fidem datam fallerem, Virorumque humanissimorum, qui studium meum adiuverant, operam prorsus inutilem redderem.

What prevented me from doing so was a sense of honor, lest I break my commitment and render the efforts of the most kind-hearted individuals who had supported my endeavor entirely in vain.

Praeter pudorem hunc etiam alia accedebant, quae me ad consilium meum exsequendum adhortarentur in quibus praecipuum erat hoc.

In addition to this sense of honor, there were other factors that encouraged me to carry out my plan, among which the foremost was this.

Specimine Editionis meae in Ephemeridibus Lipsiensibus, quae Allgemeiner Literarischer Anzeiger inscribuntur, proposito, Vir humanissimus et de literis optime meritus LANGER, Bibliothecae Guelferbyterianae Praefectus, ultro ad Virum Illustrem et Celeberrimum HEYNE scripsit, eumque meo nomine rogavit, ut mecum communicaret Lectionis Varietatem, quae inest Codici Guelferbyteriano;

With a sample of my edition presented in the Leipzig Journal, known as 'Allgemeiner Literarischer Anzeiger,' the most gracious and highly deserving scholar LANGER, the Prefect of the Guelph Library, voluntarily wrote to the illustrious and renowned HEYNE on my behalf. He asked him to share with me the textual variations present in the Guelph Codex.

qui et Philostirati quaedam continet et tunc temporis in HEYNII manibus erat.

The Guelph Codex also contains certain works of Philostratus and was in HEYNE's possession at that time.

Neque Goettingensis ille Philologorum Nestor, quae singularis eius est humanitas, huic negotio se subduxit, adeoque ipse lectiones variantes ex hoc Codice descripsit.

The renowned HEYNE, the Nestor of philologists at Göttingen, with his exceptional kindness, did not shy away from this task and, in fact, transcribed the variant readings from this codex himself.

Denique liberaliter me monuit de iis, quae in Specimine illo displicere possent, atque, quid mihi in primis agendum esset, si Editoris probabilis officio defungi cuperem, sapientissime docuit.

Finally, he generously advised me on what might be displeasing in that sample and, most wisely, taught me what I should primarily focus on if I desired to fulfill the role of a credible editor.

Tot igitur tantisque quum obstrictus tenerer Virorum de literis bene meritorum in me studiis, nolui spem, quam de me conceperant, prorsus irritam reddere, quamvis multa erant, quae prohiberent, quin hanc Spartam, ut decebat, exornarem.

Thus, bound by the support and encouragement of so many and such distinguished individuals in the field of literature, I did not wish to entirely thwart the hope they had conceived of me, even though there were many obstacles preventing me from adorning this task, as it should be.

Denuo igitur ad Antonini opusculum emendandum et illustrandum accessi, quod quum iam in eo fit, ut me Editore in publicum prodeat, paulo copiosius de consilii mei ratione disputandum est.

Therefore, I once again approached the task of correcting and illustrating the work of Antoninus, which, as it is now becoming a public endeavor with me as the editor, requires a slightly more detailed discussion of my plan.

Prima quidem cura posita erat in nova textus, quem vocant, recensione quam principem Editionis bonae partem intelligentes literarum humanarum cultores uno ore prositentur.

The first concern was focused on a new revision of the text, which is considered the principal part of a good edition, as all lovers of the humanities will agree.

Diligenter igitur primum perlegi singulos, quibus opusculum constat, libellos, eaque eorum loca enotavi, quae emendatione indigere viderentur

Quo facto omni, quam collegeram, critica materia usus sum ad novam operis recensionem, seu potius recognitionem adornandam:

non enim tanta est in hoc libro materiae criticae copia, ut sufficiat ad iustam eius recensionem.

In textu vero constituendo hanc mihi scripsi regulam, ut solam Editionum antiquiorum et Codicum Manuscriptorum fidem sequerer, nec nisi rarissime, et in iis quidem locis, ubi certa videbatur emendatio, coniecturas ope depravata emendarem.

Satius enim duxi, de vitiis, quae temporum iniuria Antonini textum deformarunt, in Notis contextui subiectis lectores monere, et varias, quas Viri docti tentarunt, emendandi rationes proponere, quam coniecturis nimium indulgendo textus integritatem in discrimen adducere.

Cum enim omnis, quae coniectando nititur, emendatio dubia est, tum in Scriptore, qualis noster, brevitatis admodum studioso, omnium difficillima.

Accedit, quod in Antonini orationis serie, quippe saepe interrupta, nihil fere inest adiumenti et praesidii ad certam et indubitatam emendandi rationem reperiundam.

Ad Orthographiam porro quod adtinet, omnia intacta reliqui, praeter interpungendi rationem passim, ubi sensus hoc postulare videbatur, emendatam, et diligentiorum duplicis, qua Sigma indicatur, figurae usum, quem aliquid adferre posse putabam ad expeditiorem libelli lectionem.

Therefore, I carefully read through each of the booklets that constitute the work, and I marked those places that seemed to require correction.

Having done this, I used all the critical material I had gathered to prepare a new revision, or rather a re-examination, of the work.

For there is not such an abundance of critical material in this book that would suffice for a proper revision of it.

In establishing the text, I set this rule for myself: to follow only the authority of older editions and manuscript codices, and to make emendations through coniecture only very rarely and in those places where a certain correction seemed necessary.

For I thought it better to inform readers in the accompanying notes about the errors that have marred Antoninus' text due to the ravages of time and to present various methods of emendation attempted by learned individuals, rather than risking the integrity of the text by indulging too much in coniectures.

Since every emendation that relies on coniecture is doubtful, it is especially challenging in the case of an author like ours, who is very concise.

Furthermore, in the series of Antoninus' discourse, which is often interrupted, there is scarcely anything to provide assistance and support for finding a certain and indisputable method of emendation.

As for orthography, I left everything untouched, except for punctuation, which I corrected here and there when it seemed necessary for clarity. I also corrected the use of the double form of Sigma, which I believed could contribute to the easier reading of the booklet.

Neque tamen spondeo, Sigmatis figuram ubique loco suo collocatam esse, quamquam voluissem.

However, I do not guarantee that the figure of Sigma has been placed in its proper place everywhere, although I would have wished for it.

At restant plura, inprimis in spiritibus atque tonis et in his inclinandis, quae mutata velim.

But there are still many things remaining, especially in the accents and musical tones and in those that need adiustment, which I would like to change.

Consulto autem hanc boni Editoris partem omisi, non quod eam indignam putabam diligentia, sed quod verebar, ne eam rite possem tueri, quum non ad eam huius rei cognitionem me pervenisse sentirem, quae ad eam certius constituendam sufficeret.

However, I intentionally omitted this part of a good editor's work, not because I considered it unworthy of attention but because I feared that I might not be able to properly defend it, as I did not feel that I had acquired the necessary knowledge in this matter to determine it more accurately.

Caeterum exemplar Editionis Wollianae typis transcribendum tradidi, prius quanta per oculorum, qua tum temporis laborabam, infirmitatem licuit, diligentia a sphalmatis typographicis et aliis, quae eam obsidebant, depravationibus correctae;

Moreover, I entrusted the copying of the Wollian edition to be transcribed into print, correcting as many typographical errors and other corruptions as I could with the diligence that my eye's weakness, which I was suffering from at the time, allowed.

et quum nihil sumtus pepercerit redemtor huius Editionis, Vir honestus, quin accuratissime impressa et correcta prodiret, spero fore, ut inde saltem nitoris aliquid huic Editioni accedat.

And although the purchaser of this edition spared no expense, I hope that an honest person, having ensured that it is printed and corrected with the utmost care, will contribute at least some splendor to this edition.

Si quae tamen insunt, in primis in Notis Contextui subiectis, quae et minori literarum charactere, quem vocant, a me exaratae et formis minoribus stanneis impressae sunt eius rei veniam a lectore aequi bonique consulente peto, quum per locorum distantiam mihi non licuerit, operis corrigendis praeesse.

However, if there are any mistakes, especially in the notes included in the text, which were written by me in smaller lettering and printed in smaller brass types, I request the reader's forgiveness, considering that I was unable to oversee the correction of the work due to the distance between the locations.

Gravissima etiam operarum sphalmata ad finem voluminis indicabo.

I will also point out the most serious errors in the works at the end of the volume. So far, I have discussed the revision of the text.

Hactenus de textus recensione: restat, ut de interpretatione latina et Commentario pauca dicam.

It remains for me to say a few words about the Latin translation and commentary.

Interpretationem latinam addendam putavi, quum paranda esset Editio in usum lectorum omnis fere generis, atque igitur et eorum, "qui in graecis literis, non, ut ita dicam, habitant, sed peregrinantur potius, eamque e Xylandri, Casauboni et Gatakeri translationibus adornavi.

I thought it necessary to add a Latin translation since the edition was being prepared for the use of readers of almost all kinds, including those who, to put it in this way, do not dwell in Greek literature but rather journey through it. I adorned it with translations from Xylandri, Casauboni, and Gatakeri.

Quo autem in labore qua diligentia versatus sim, alii iudicent:

As for the diligence with which I have engaged in this work, let others judge.

Hoc tantum addere lubet, me inprimis perspicuitati consuluisse;

I would like to add only this: I have primarily aimed for clarity.

Eamque ob causam non dubitasse, sermonis latini elegantiam, passim et puritatem, negligere qua in re et Gatakerus et Xylander me exemplis praeiverunt.

For this reason, I did not hesitate to occasionally neglect the elegance and purity of the Latin language, in which both Gataker and Xylander set examples for me.

Sunt tamen in Translatione nostra, quae nunc mutata velim.

However, there are some things in our translation that I now wish to change. I, 18 has been retained, guided by some kind of superstitious reverence.

Sic nescio qua superstitiosa religione ductus retinui I, 18.

Thus, guided by I know not what superstitious reverence, I retained I, 18.

Gatakerianum usum particulae quod praecedente formula perspectum habere, ibidemque falsum pronominis suus usum ex Translatione Casauboni ductum.

I followed Gataker's use of the particle "quod" with the preceding formula and borrowed the incorrect use of the pronoun "suus" from Casaubon's translation in the same place.

Sic porro cum Gatakero verbum eniti cum Infinitivo construxi I, 13, ubi ut rectius adhiberetur, et id generis alia.

In this way, I also constructed the verb with the infinitive, following Gataker, in I, 13, where it would be more appropriate, and in similar cases.

Neque vero tot tantosque naevos superesse arbitror, quin emendatior et castigatior merito dici possit Translatio nostra cum Xylandrina et Gatakeriana comparata.

I do not think there are so many and so great defects remaining that our translation, when compared with Xylander's and Gataker's, cannot be rightfully considered more improved and corrected.

Ad Commentarium denique quod adtinet, notas criticas a philologicis et historicis secernere, et ipsi Contextui subiicere visum est.

As for the commentary, it seemed appropriate to separate the critical notes from the philological and historical ones and place them beneath the text itself.

In has igitur retuli non solum varias lectiones, quae proprie dici possunt, sed etiam manifesta librariorum et typothetarum vitia.

So, I have included in these not only various readings, which can properly be called so, but also the evident errors of scribes and printers.

Neque vehementer metuo, ne propterea in reprehensionem incurram apud aequos et intelligentes lectores, quamquam fortasse erunt, qui hoc factum vituperent.

I do not greatly fear that I will incur reproach from fair and intelligent readers on account of this, although there may perhaps be some who will criticize this action.

Non enim nullum usum habere videtur ad certum de Editionum indole iudicium ferendum et ad iuvandam artis criticae, quae in coniectando cernitur, copiam, si tales errores colliguntur.

For it does not seem to have no use at all to provide a certain judgment about the nature of the editions and to assist the abundance of the critical art, which is observed in coniecture, if such errors are collected.

Cui et hoc accedit, quod saepe videmus, in iis lectionibus, quae aliis haud indoctis stupendi librariorum errores videbantur, alios his acutiores viam ad veras Emendationes indagandas reperisse.

To this is added that we often see, in those readings where some not unlearned scholars seemed to have astonishing errors of scribes, others, sharper than these, have found the way to seek true emendations.

Quanto minorem igitur ingenii critici vim in me inesse sentiebam, tanto magis in hoc incumbendum putavi, ut quantum fieri poterat, omnia colligerentur, quibus acutiores adiuvarentur ad Antoninum meum emendandum.

Therefore, the less critical genius I felt within myself, the more I believed that I should focus on gathering as much as possible to aid those with sharper wits in correcting my Antoninus.

Quod vero praeter lectionis varietatem etiam omnes, quae mihi innotuerunt, Virorum doctorum coniecturas adieci, plures fortasse erunt, qui reprehendant.

However, in addition to the variety of readings, I have also included all the coniectures of learned scholars that came to my knowledge. There may be many who criticize this decision."

Habeo tamen, quo me defendere possim:

Nevertheless, I have a defense at hand.

consilium enim erat talem Editionem parandi, quam qui possideret, aliis omnibus carere facile possit, nisi ipse vellet Antonini librum edere.

The plan was to prepare an edition that anyone possessing it could easily do without, unless they wanted to publish the book themselves.

Quam vero in Commentario philologico et historico instruendo rationem ingressus sum, eam non ignoro et improbari posse, et a multis iisque magni nominis viris improbari solere.

However, I am aware that the approach I adopted for the philological and historical commentary can be disapproved of by many, especially by those of great renown.

Gatakeri scilicet commentarios, additis quibusdam Casauboni et Xylandri notis, ita repetii, ut ea refervarem, quae ad doctrinam tantum ostentandam, non ad Antoninum illustrandum facere videbantur.

Multa enim profecto erudite et subtiliter disputata in Notis Gatakerianis insunt, ut religioni mihi ducerem, haec negligere, quibus excitari et ali possent ingenia literarum graecarum studiosa.

Sunt vero etiam, quorum nullus fere usus est, quae igitur, ut sumtibus lectorum parcerem, omittere visum est.

Quum denique multis in locis Gatakerus in errore versaretur, in aliis iisque admodum obscuris nihil adnotaret, quo proclivior fieret aditus ad sensum explicandum, illud corrigere, hoc vero, quantum per virium imbecillitatem licuit, supplere studui.

Talis vero veterum commentariorum repetitio novis curis aucta curare adeo improbanda sit, sane non video, atque gaudeo, Philologos nostri temporis summos in hac commentandi ratione exemplo praevivisse, quamquam ab ea arrogantia longe absim, ut putem, me in omnibus eorum vestigia legisse.

Haec sunt, quae priusquam primus Editionis meae tomus in publicum emitteretur, praefari volui.

Eum excipient, et singulis nundinis Lipsiacis, si Deus vitam valetudinemque concesserit, prodibunt Tomi duo paullo minores, quorum prior notas ad octo libros priores, posterior notas ad reliquos libros, decreta philosophiae Antoninianae fecundum artis regulas in unum corpus collecta, Indices porro Graecitatis, Nominum propriorum, et Auctorum in Notis laudatorum continebit.

I, of course, followed Gataker's commentaries, with the addition of some notes from Casaubon and Xylander, in such a way that I preserved what seemed to be for the display of learning, not for the illumination of Antoninus.

Indeed, there are many erudite and subtle discussions in Gataker's notes that I considered it a disservice to neglect, as they could stimulate and nurture the minds of those enthusiastic about Greek literature.

There are, however, some notes that were hardly of any use, and thus, to save the expenses of the readers, I decided to omit them.

When Gataker, in many places, was in error, and in others, especially obscure ones, made no annotations to facilitate the understanding of the text, I endeavored to correct the former and supplement the latter to the best of my ability, considering my own limitations.

The repetition of such ancient commentaries, enhanced with new care, should not be so strongly criticized, in my view. I am glad to see that the greatest philologists of our time have set an example in this method of commentary, although I am far from being arrogant enough to think that I have followed in their footsteps in all respects.

These are the things I wished to say before the first volume of my edition was published.

It will be received, and at each Leipzig book fair, if God grants me life and health, two slightly smaller volumes will be published. The first will contain notes on the first eight books, and the second will contain notes on the remaining books. The decrees of Antoninian philosophy, according to the rules of art, will be collected into one body. Furthermore, there will be indices of Greek words, proper nouns, and authors mentioned in the notes.

Caeterum si videro, Editionem in gratiam iuvenum literarum Graecarum studioforum, et aliorum, qui maiora volumina fastidiunt, adornatam desiderari, atque operam hanc meam qualemcunque non omnino improbari, aliam minoris voluminis Editionem curabo.

However, if I see that an edition designed to benefit young enthusiasts of Greek literature and others who find larger volumes cumbersome is desired, and if this modest effort of mine is not entirely disapproved, I will prepare another edition of smaller size.

Selecta lectionis varietate, brevi adnotatione et indice idoneo instructam:

It will be equipped with a selected variety of readings, brief annotations, and a suitable index.

Quo quidem confilio rogatos velim humanissime Viros doctos atque harum rerum intelligentes, ut, quae observaverint a me in Antonini libris sive explicandis sive emendandis errata et peccata, de iis me aut publice aut privatim admoneant.

With this advice in mind, I kindly request that learned individuals who are knowledgeable about these matters, whether publicly or privately, bring to my attention any errors and mistakes they may have observed in my editions of Antoninus, whether in terms of explanations or emendations.

Maxima enim flagro cupidine de literis bene merendi, ideoque et spondere audeo, me in posterum meliora et curatiora daturum,

For I am burning with the greatest desire to earn merit in literature, and therefore, I dare to promise that I will produce better and more carefully prepared works in the future,

si licuerit otio honesto frui et literato, cuius quidem in spe fuavissima animus, multis magnisque molestiis iamiam fessus, iucunde requiescit.

if it is possible for me to enioy honorable and learned leisure. Indeed, my spirit is now resting in the sweet hope of this, fatigued as it is by many and great troubles.

Dabam Slesvici, Nonis Ianuariis Anni post R.S.

I was giving [this], in Schleswig, on the Nones of Ianuary, in the year [of the foundation of Rome] after the consulship.

MDCCCII.

1802

I. M. Schultz

LIBER I

GRATITUDO ET INFLUENTIA

1. **Avi Veri *exemplo operam me dare oportet,* ut suavibus sim** moribus neque irae indulgeam.

I ought to follow the example of my grandfather Verus, to be of sweet manners and not indulge in anger.

2. Existimatione et recordatione genitoris mei ad verecundiam et animum viro dignum *excitari debeo.*

By the estimation and remembrance of my father, I ought to be aroused to modesty and a character worthy of a man.

3. In matre *exemplum habui,* pietatis in Deos et liberalitatis; abstinentiae non solum a malo perpetrando, verum etiam cogitando;

In my mother, I had an example of piety towards the gods and generosity; of abstinence not only from committing evil but also from thinking about it;

tum frugalitatis in victu, quae ab opulentorum vita et consuetudine longissime abeat.

Then he advised me to practice frugality in my food, which is far from the lifestyle and habits of the wealthy.

4. A proavo *habui,* quod publicos litterarum ludos non frequentavi, et domi bonis praeceptoribus usus sum, atque intellexi, in talibus rebus non parcendum esse impensis.

From my great-grandfather, I learned that I did not attend public literary games, and I made use of good teachers at home, and I understood that in such matters, expenses should not be spared.

5. Ab educatore, ne *in circo spectator* Prasianus aut Venetianus neve parmularius aut scutarius fierem, ut labores sustinerem, paucis indigerem, ipse operi manus admoverem, rerum alienarum non essem curiosus nec facile delationem admitterem.

From my educator, I learned not to become a spectator in the circus, neither a Prasianus nor a Venetianus, nor a shield-bearer or spearman, so that I could endure hardships, be content with few things, contribute with my own hands, not be curious about other people's affairs, and not easily accept gossip.

6. Diognetus *me monuit,* ne studium in vanas res conferrem neque iis fidem haberem, quae a praestigiatoribus et impostoribus de incantationibus et daemonum expulsione aliisque eius generis rebus narrantur; neque coturnices alerem, neve insana talium rerum admiratione tenerer;

Diognetus warned me not to devote my studies to vain things and not to believe in the stories told by illusionists and impostors about enchantments, exorcisms, and other such things; not to raise quails, nor to be captivated by the foolish admiration of such matters.

Ut libere dicta aequo animo ferrem, philosophiae me addicerem et primum quidem Bacchium, deinde vero Tandasidem et Marcianum audirem; ut dialogos puer adhuc scriberem, ut grabatum et pellem et eius generis omnia, quae ad Graecam disciplinam pertinent, expeterem.

So that I could bear freely spoken words with a calm mind, I devoted myself to philosophy and first listened to Bacchius, then to Tandasis and Marcianus; so that, as a young boy, I wrote dialogues and sought after a bed, a fur rug, and all other things related to Greek studies.

7. Rustico *debeo,* quod in cogitationem veni, mihi morum emendatione et curatione opus esse; quod neque ad aemulationem sophisticam declinavi, neque de theorematis commentatus sum, aut exhortatorias oratiunculas declamavi, aut virum strenue exercitia subeuntem munificumve me ostentando homines in admirationem mei rapere studui; quod a rhetoricae, poesis et elegantioris dictionis studio abstinui;

I owe it to Rusticus that I came to the realization that I needed improvement and care in my character; that I did not indulge in sophistical competition, nor did I engage in discussions about theorems, deliver declamatory speeches, or seek to impress people by presenting myself as a virtuous man actively involved in exercises or displaying my generosity; that I refrained from pursuing studies in rhetoric, poetry, and refined language.

Quod non elegantiore veste indutus domi incedo; quod epistolas simpliciter scribo instar eius, quam is ipse Sinuessa ad matrem meam dedit;

That I do not walk at home dressed in elegant attire; that I write letters simply, similar to the one that he himself wrote to my mother in Sinuessa.

Quod, si qui me irritaverint aut aliquid deliquerint, iis placabilem et ad reconciliandum facilem me praebeo, simul atque in gratiam redire volunt;

That if anyone irritates me or makes a mistake, I am easily approachable and willing to reconcile with them as soon as they seek to make amends.

Quod diligenter legere soleo, non contentus sum maria rei intelligentia, neque garrulis properanter assentior; quod commentarios Epicteti legi, quorum mihi ipse copiam fecit.

I am accustomed to reading diligently, and I am not satisfied with merely superficial understanding. I do not hastily agree with gossips. I have read the commentaries of Epictetus, from which he himself provided me with ample material.

8 . Apollonii *exemplo didici* liberum esse et sine dubitatione cautum et circumspectum, neque aliud quidquam vel minimum respicere, nisi rationem; mei similem semper esse in doloribus acerrimis, in prolis amissione, in morbis diuturnis;

I learned from the example of Apollonius to be free and cautious without any doubt, not looking at anything else, not even the least thing, except reason; to always be similar to myself in the most intense pains, in the loss of children, and in prolonged illnesses.

Eidem acceptum refero , quod mihi contigit, ut in vivo exemplo perspecte viderem, eundem et constantissimum esse posse et remissum;

I give the same credit to Apollonius for what happened to me, as I had the opportunity to clearly see in a living example that he could be both extremely steadfast and gentle.

In eo vidi studium in enarrandis philosophorum scriptis a morositate alienum atque conspexi hominem, qui peritiam ac sollertiam qua in tradendis theorematis pollebat, manifesto bonorum suorum minimum existimabat; *ab eo* didici, quomodo beneficia, quae putantur, ab amicis sint accipienda, ut neque propterea addicti fiamus, neque ea sine *grati animi* sensu praetermittamus.

In him, I saw a passion for explaining the writings of philosophers, free from pedantry, and I observed a person who greatly undervalued his own possessions despite his expertise and skill in conveying the theorems. From him, I learned how to receive favors, which are thought to be from friends, in such a way that we do not become enslaved by them, nor do we neglect them without a sense of gratitude in our hearts.

9 . In Sexto *suspexi* benevolentiam et exemplum domus paterno affectu administratae, et intelligentiam vitae secundum naturam institutae, et gravitatem non simulatam item sollicitam in explorandis amicorum necessitatibus diligentiam;

In Sextus, I admired his kindness and the example of a household managed with parental affection. I also noticed his understanding of living in accordance with nature and the sincerity of his concern in diligently exploring the needs of his friends. His seriousness was genuine and unwavering.

Tolerantiam erga imperitos et temere opinantes studium eius ad omnes se accommodandi, ita ut consuetudo eius omni adulatione gratior esset, eodemque tempore iisdem maxime venerandus videretur;

He cultivated tolerance towards the inexperienced and hastily opinionated, making an effort to adapt himself to everyone, so that his behavior would be more pleasing, gaining favor through constant affability, and at the same time, he appeared highly respectable to those very same people.

Artem per notiones claras et perspicuas via ac ratione praecepta ad vitae usum necessaria reperiendi et ordine collocandi:

He possessed the skill of discovering and arranging the necessary principles for practical living through clear and transparent concepts and reasoning.

Idem neque umquam neque alius cuiusquam perturbationis indicium dedit, sed simul et affectibus maxime immunis et amantissimus fuit, bonae famae studiosus, idque sine strepitu, et eruditus sine ostentatione.

The same person never showed any sign of disturbance, nor did anyone else; he was both highly immune to emotions and very loving, devoted to a good reputation, and he did so without any fuss, and he was educated without ostentation.

10. Alexandrum Grammaticum *observavi* ab increpationibus sibi temperare, neque probrose vituperare, qui barbarum aut soloecum aliquid vel absonum proferunt, se dextre id modo, quod dici debet, proponere, aut respondendi aut confirmandi aut de re ipsa, non de verbo, deliberandi specie usum, aut alia eiusmodi scita commoneatione.

I observed Alexander the Grammarian to refrain from harshly reproaching those who utter something foreign or incorrect in grammar, but rather, he skillfully puts forward what should be said, using the occasion for responding, affirming, or discussing the matter itself, not just the word, and engaging in other such instructive conversations.

11. A Frontone *didici* intelligere, qualis sit tyrannorum et invidentia et versutia et simulatio; eosque, qui a nobis patricii appellantur, ut plurimum a genuino paterni animi affectu alieniores esse.

From Fronto, I learned to understand the nature of tyrants, their envy, cunning, and deceit. Moreover, I discovered that those who are called "patricians" by us are often quite distant from genuine paternal affection.

12. Ab Alexandro Platonico, ne saepe nec nisi necessitate coactus alii dicerem vel in epistola scriberem, me esse occupatum, neque hac ratione continuo recusarem officia quae rationes ad eos, quibuscum viverem, exigerent negotia urgentia praetendens.

From Alexander the Platonist, I learned not to frequently speak or write to others unless compelled by necessity. I avoided using this as a constant excuse to refuse duties that living with others might demand, pretending to be busy with urgent matters.

13. A Catulo, ne parvi facerem amicum aliquid culpantem, etiam si forte temere culparet, quin etiam periculum facerem eum in pristinum statum restituendi;

From Catulus, I learned not to take offense at a friend who criticized something minor, even if they did so impulsively, and not to hesitate to help them return to their former state of friendship.

Item ut libenter praeceptorum laudes celebrarem, quemadmodum de Domitio et Athenodoto memoriae proditum est; ut liberos meos sincera pietate prosequerer.

Similarily, I learned to gladly praise the virtues of those who are my mentors, just as it is remembered about Domitius and Athenodotus. I also learned to treat my children with genuine affection and devotion.

14. A fratre meo Severo, propinquorum et veritatis iustitiae studiosum esse:

Per eundem Thraseam, Helvidium, Catonem, Dionem, Brutum cognovi et animo concepi imaginem reipublicae liberae, in qua aequis legibus et eodem iure omnia administrentur, et regni, quod civium libertatem omnium maximi aestimet;

Praeterea ab eodem, aequalem et constantem esse in studio philosophiae;

Benefacere et impense largiri, bene sperare et neutiquam dubitare de amicorum amore:

Is quoque non usus est dissimulatione erga eos, qui vituperandi videbantur, neque amicis eius opus erat, ut quid vellet aut nollet, coniectura assequerentur, sed id apertum fuit.

15. In Maximo *cognovi* illud, sui compotem esse neque ulla re transversum abripi;

Animo esse bono, tum in aliis rebus adversis, tum in morbis; moribus uti et suavitate et gravitate bene temperatis;

Negotia, quae impendent, non gravate perficere.

Quidquid ille dixit, id ex animi sententia eum dicere, et quidquid egit, id consilio non malo eum agere, omnes persuasum habebant.

Porro nihil admirari et ad nihil obstupescere nec festinare neque cunctari neque consilii expertem aut deiectum esse, neque nunc hilarem esse et rursus irasci et suspiciosum esse; liberalem esse et promptum ad ignoscendum;

I learned from my brother Severus, my relatives, and my dedication to truth and justice.

Through them, I came to know and conceive in my mind the image of a free republic, where all things are administered under just laws and the same rights, and a government that values the liberty of its citizens above all else.

Moreover, I learned from him to be equally committed and steadfast in the pursuit of philosophy,

to do good deeds and be very generous, to have good hopes and not doubt at all about the love of friends.

He did not employ deception towards those who seemed worthy of criticism, nor did his friends need to guess what he wanted or didn't want, as he was always open and transparent about it.

In Maximus, I discovered that he was self-aware and never swayed by external influences.

He possessed a good temperament, both in facing adversity and dealing with illnesses. He conducted himself with well-balanced manners, combining charm and dignity.

He managed his responsibilities with ease, even in challenging situations.

Whatever he said, it was believed to be his sincere opinion, and whatever he did, it was considered the result of wise deliberation, not malice.

Furthermore, to admire nothing and be amazed by nothing, to neither hurry nor hesitate, to not be lacking in judgment or disheartened, to be neither cheerful nor angry and suspicious at times; to be generous and ready to forgive.

Mendacium fugere, atque hominis non eversi potius, quam erecti specimen exhibere neque quemquam ab eo contemptui se habitum existimasse, neque ausum esse se illi praeferre; denique honeste urbanum esse:

To shun lies, to display the example of a man who is not broken but upright, and to never think of anyone as beneath him, nor dare to consider oneself superior to others; in short, to be gracefully courteous.

16. A patre mansuetudinem et immotam in iis, quae diligenter csunt, perseverantiam, vanae gloriae ab opinatis honoribus quaesitae contemptum, amorem laborum et assiduitatem, animum promptum ad audiendos eos, qui aliquid, quod ad publicam utilitatem spectat, afferant, firmam constantiam in tribuendo cuique, quod eius dignitas postulat, peritiam, ubi intentione opus sit, ubi remissione:

From my father, I learned gentleness and unwavering perseverance in diligently pursued matters. I also acquired contempt for empty honors sought after by vain glory. I embraced a love for labor and diligence, and I developed a readiness to listen to those who bring something beneficial for the public good. I have a firm constancy in giving each person what their dignity demands, and I know when to be exacting and when to be lenient.

Coercere amores puerorum; civilitati morum studere; amicis concedere, ut neque coenae semper adsint neque in itineribus sese necessario comites praebeant;

To control the affections of young boys; to cultivate civilized behavior; to allow friends not to be always present at dinners and not to necessarily accompany him on journeys.

Semper similem sui deprehendi ab iis, qui necessitate aliqua impediti ab eo abfuere; in consiliis diligenter inquirere atque constanter, neque vero "destitit ab indagatione contentus obvia rerum specie."

I have always found him consistent with himself by those who, due to some necessity, were unable to be present with him; in deliberations, he would diligently and persistently investigate, never content with merely the obvious appearance of things.

Amicos retinendi studiosum esse, eos nec fastidio mutantem nec perdite amantem; contentum esse in omnibus et vultu serenum; e longinquo prospicere et etiam ad minima administranda parari sine strepitu; acclamationes et omnem adulationem sub eo repressam esse;

To be eager to retain friends, not changing them out of disdain nor excessively loving them to the point of losing oneself. To be content in all things and maintain a serene countenance. To look far ahead and be prepared even for the smallest tasks without making a fuss. To suppress applause and all forms of flattery under one's rule.

opes reipublicae necessarias semper conservare, sumptus publicos parce erogare et aequo animo ferre quorundam his de rebus reprehensiones;

To always preserve the necessary resources of the state, to spend public funds sparingly, and to accept with equanimity the criticisms of some regarding these matters.

Neque circa deos superstitiosum esse, neque circa homines popularem auram captantem, blandientem, plebem demerentem, sed sobrium in omnibus et constantem, nusquam ineptum nec novitatis studiosum;

and to not be superstitious about the gods, nor to seek popularity with the people by flattery, pandering, or ingratiating, but to be sober and steadfast in all things, neither inappropriate nor eager for novelty;

Rebus, quae ad vitae cursum faciliorem reddendum faciunt, quarum copiam uberrimam affert natura, sine fastu pariter atque sine excusatione uti, ita ut praesentibus sine affecta tione frueretur, absentibus non indigeret;

to use the things that make life easier and are abundantly provided by nature without arrogance or excuses, so that one can enjoy them without affectation when present and not be in need of them when absent.

Dicere posse quemquam, sophistam eum fuisse aut vernam aut scholasticum, sed virum maturum, perfectum, adulatione superiorem, qui et suis et aliorum rebus praeesse posset.

It could be said of such a person that he was not a sophist, a slave, or a mere scholar, but rather a mature and accomplished individual, free from flattery, capable of leading both himself and others.

Praeter haec vere philosophantes colere, ceteros neque probro afficere neque tamen ab iis transversum abripi; porro suavem esse in vitae consuetudine et festivum nec vero ad fastidium usque;

Besides genuinely cherishing true philosophy, neither to censure others nor to be swayed by them in the wrong direction; furthermore, to be pleasant in one's way of life, cheerful, yet not to the point of excess.

Corpus suum cum temperantia quadam curare, non ut vitae avidum, aut ad ornatum luxumve, neque tamen negligenter, quo factum est, ut propter suam diligentiam in paucissimis arte medicorum remediisve internis et externis opus haberet.

To take care of one's body with a certain moderation, not for the pursuit of excessive indulgence or luxury, but also not negligently, which led to the result that due to his diligence, he rarely needed the services of physicians or remedies, both internal and external.

Potissimum autem sine invidia loco cedere, si qui maiore quadam facultate pollebant, eloquentia aut doctrina iuris morumve aut aliarum rerum cognitione, et simul cum iis operam dare, ut singuli propriis, quibus quisque excellebat, facultatibus, existimationem consequerentur;

But most importantly, to yield one's place without envy, to those who excelled in some greater ability, whether it be eloquence, legal knowledge, moral understanding, or expertise in other matters, and at the same time, to work together with them, so that each person could achieve recognition in their respective areas of excellence;

Omnia more maiorum agere, ne illud quidem ipsum affectantem, ut morem maiorum servare videretur;

To conduct oneself in all things according to the customs of our ancestors, even without appearing to deliberately imitate the customs of our ancestors.

Tum porro non facile moveri et huc illuc iactari, sed in iisdem et locis et negotiis immorari; post vehementissimos capitis dolores statim iuvenilem ac vegetum ad consueta negotia redire;

Moreover, not being easily agitated and tossed here and there, but remaining steadfast in the same places and pursuits; after severe headaches, immediately returning to my usual tasks youthful and vigorous.

Non multa habere arcana, sed paucissima ac rarissima, eaque tantum ad res publicas spectantia prudentiam ac moderationem in muneribus edendis, operibus exstruendis, congiariis largiendis et eiusmodi rebus, quae sunt hominis id ipsum quod agi oportet nec vero laudem e rebus gestis efflorescentem spectantis;

To possess few and very rare secrets, particularly those pertaining to the welfare of the state, which require wisdom and moderation in the discharge of duties, in the construction of public works, in the distribution of gifts, and similar matters. They focus on what truly matters for fulfilling their responsibilities and do not seek excessive praise for their accomplishments.

Non intempestive balneis uti, non de aedibus exstruendis laborare, non de cibariis curiosum esse neve vestimentorum textura et colore neve de servitiorum specie;

They do not excessively indulge in baths at inappropriate times, nor do they overly concern themselves with building luxurious houses or being overly particular about food and clothing choices. They do not obsess over the texture and color of their garments or the appearance of their servants.

Vestem e Lorio, villa inferius sita, et Lanuvinis villis ei plerumque in usu fuis erga portitorem Tusculanum deprecantem quomodo se gesserit, et qualis fuerit omnis sic agendi ratio.

They wear clothing from Lory, a village situated below the villa, and for the most part, they often practice this custom towards the Tusculan porter, asking him how he has been and what manner of conduct they should adopt in all their actions.

Nihil immite nihil inverecundum, nihil vehemens, neque ut dixeris usque "ad sudorem":

Nothing harsh, nothing rude, nothing forceful, nor as they say, "to the point of sweating,"

Sed omnia singulatim sumpta esse perpensa, quasi per otium, sine perturbatione, ordine constantia, convenienter inter se.

but all things are taken with careful consideration, as if in leisure, without agitation, with a calm and constant order, and in harmony with one another.

Conveniret in eum quod de Socrate memoriae traditum est, eum et abstinere et frui potuisse iis, quibus plerique nec abstinere per infirmitatem nec frui sine intemperantia possunt;

It would be fitting to apply to him what is handed down in memory about Socrates, that he was able both to abstain and to enjoy those things which most people cannot abstain from due to weakness, nor enjoy without excess.

posse autem in altero robustum, in altero temperantem ac sobrium se praestare, id vero viri est firmo animo invictoque praediti, qualem se in Maximi morbo praestitit.

17. A Diis bonos avos, bonos parentes, bonam sororem, bonos praeceptores, bonos familiares, necessarios, amicos, omnes fere habui:

iisdem debeo; quod in neminem eorum temere quidquam deliqui, quamquam ita animo affectus ut, si res tulisset, utique eiusmodi aliquid admisissem, sed deorum benevolentia non ita ceciderunt res, ut in reprehensionem incurrerem;

Quod non diutius apud pellicem avi enutritus sum, et quod aetatis florem indelibatum servavi nec ante iustum tempus virilitatis specimen dedi, sed ultra etiam distuli;

Quod principi ac patri subiectus fui, qui mihi omnem fastum demeret et ad intelligentiam adduceret, posse in aula ita degi, ut nec satellitio nec vestitu insigniore nec facibus nec statuis et simili ornatu opua sit;

Posse *principem* ita contrahere sese, ut proxime ad privati vitam accedat, nec tamen propterea demissius vel remissius negotia publica imperatorie administrare;

Quod mihi contigit frater, qui moribus suis me ad curam mei excitaret, honore autem et suo in me affectu me exhilararet;

To be strong in one aspect and temperate and sober in another, that is truly the mark of a man endowed with a firm and invincible mind, just as he demonstrated in the case of Maximus's illness.

I have had good grandparents, good parents, a good sister, good teachers, good relatives, necessary acquaintances, and almost all good friends, blessed by the good gods.

I owe the same to them; that I have not wronged any of them rashly, although I was so inclined in mind that if circumstances had demanded it, I might have committed such an act, but the kindness of the gods did not lead events to a point where I would deserve reproach.

That I was not raised any longer with my grandfather's mistress, and that I preserved the unblemished bloom of my youth and even delayed showing the proper sign of manhood until the right time.

That I was subject to a prince and father who taught me to remove all arrogance and to understand that it is possible to live in the court without needing attendants, extravagant clothing, torches, statues, and similar adornments.

That a ruler can conduct themselves in such a way as to come very close to the life of a private individual, yet still manage public affairs imperially without becoming too humble or lax in their duties.

That I had a brother who, through his character, motivated me to take care of myself, and through his esteem and affection, made me happy.

Quod liberi mihi neque ingenio tardi neque corpore distorti nati sunt; quod non longius progressus sum in rhetorica, poetica et reliquis studiis, quae me fortasse plane detinuissent, si me feliciter in iis proficere sensissem; quod eos a quibus educatus sum, ad honores, quos expetere ipsi mihi videbantur, evehere festinavi, nec spe eos lactavi, me, quum iuvenes adhuc essent, id in posterum facturum;

That my children were born neither with slow intellect nor deformed bodies; that I did not advance further in rhetoric, poetry, and other studies that might have completely detained me if I had sensed successful progress in them; that I hurried to elevate those who raised me to the honors they seemed to desire for themselves, nor did I deceive them with false hope that I would do it in the future when they were still young.

Quod cognovi Apollonium, Rusticum et Maximum; quod imago vitae secundum naturam institutae, qualis esset, clare et frequenter animo meo obversata est; ita ut, quod ad Deos ac dona, auxilia et consilia ab iis mihi oblata attinet, nihil obstiterit, quominus iam pridem naturae convenienter viverem;

That I have known Apollonius, Rusticus, and Maximus; that the ideal image of a life in accordance with nature has been clearly and frequently present in my mind; so that, regarding the gifts, support, and guidance offered to me by the gods, nothing has hindered me from living in harmony with nature for a long time.

Quod vero nondum id assequutus sim, id mea culpa atque inde quod Deorum submonitiones et tantum non clarissima praecepta neglexi, acciderit;

But indeed, that I have not yet achieved this, is my fault, and it happened because I neglected the admonitions of the gods and almost the most illustrious teachings.

Quod in vita, qualis ea fuit, corpus mihi tamdiu perduravit;

Because in life, as it was, my body endured for so long

Quod nec Benedictam nec Theodotum attigi, sed etiam postea affectibus amatoriis correptus ad sanitatem redii;

I have not only met Benedicta and Theodotus, but I have also returned to health after being struck by amorous affections later on

Quod, quamquam Rustico saepe succensui, nihil ultra admisi, cuius me poeniteat; quod mater mea, quum mature decessura esset, mecum tamen ultimos aetatis annos transegit;

That, although I often got angry with Rusticus, I have committed nothing that I regret; that my mother, even though she was destined to die soon, spent the last years of her life with me.

Quod, quoties pauperi aut alius rei indigo opitulari statuebam, nunquam audivi, mihi deesse pecuniam, unde id facerem, et quod non ulla mihi umquam talis necessitas obtigit, ut ab alio sumere cogerer;

That, whenever I decided to assist a poor person or someone in need, I never heard that I lacked the money to do so, and that I have never been in such a situation where I would be forced to take from another.

Et quod talis mihi uxor contigit, tam obsequens, tam amans, tam simplex;

Quod abunde mihi suppetiverunt viri ad liberos educandos idonei;

Quod per insomnia mihi remedia data sunt cum alia tum adversus sanguinis excretionem et capitis vertiginem, idque Caietae tanquam chresae;

Quod, quum animum ad philosophiam adiecissem, non in sophistam incidi, neque in scriptoribus et syllogismis resolvendis tempus deses contrivi, neque coelestibus curiose perscrutandis detentus sum.

Haec enim omnia Deorum auxilio et fortuna, indigent.

Also, that such a wife came to me, so obedient, so loving, so straightforward;

and that I had more than enough suitable men to raise children

That remedies were given to me through dreams, both against bleeding and dizziness, and this happened at Caieta, as if they were divine gifts.

That when I turned my mind to philosophy, I did not fall into sophistry, nor did I waste my time on solving puzzles with writers and syllogisms, nor did I get caught up in overzealously investigating celestial matters.

All these things require the help of the gods and fortune.

LIBER II

Rationem et Virtutem Amplexans

I . Mane sibi praedicere: incidam curiosam, ingratum, contumeliosum, fraudulentum, invidum, insociabilem: omnia ista vitia iis ex ignorantia bonorum et malorum evenerunt.

To admonish oneself in the morning: I might encounter someone curious, ungrateful, insulting, deceitful, envious, unsociable: all these vices have befallen them because of ignorance of good and evil.

Ego vero, qui perspectam habeo naturam boni, honestum id esse, ac mali, turpe id esse, porro naturam ipsius qui peccat, eum mihi esse cognatum, non sanguinis aut seminis eiusdem, sed mentis ac divinae particula participem.

Indeed, I, who have a clear view of the nature of good, consider it to be honorable, and of evil, I consider it to be shameful. Furthermore, the person who sins, I consider him to be related to me, not by blood or the same seed, but as a fellow partaker of the mind and the divine.

Nec a quoquam eorum laedi possum: in id enim quod turpe est, nemo eorum me coniiciet.

Nor can I be harmed by any of them: for into that which is shameful, none of them can cast me.

Neque ei, qui mihi cognatus est, succensere possum eumque odio persequi: nam ad mutuam operam nati sumus.

I can't be angry with him, who is my relative, nor can I pursue him with hatred: for we are born for mutual help.

Ut pedes, ut manus, ut palpebrae, ut ordines superiorum et inferiorum dentium: itaque invicem sibi adversari contra naturam est, adversantis autem est indignari et aversari.

Just as the feet, the hands, the eyelids, and the rows of upper and lower teeth work together, so it is against nature for them to be in conflict with one another. It is the mark of one who is in conflict to be resentful and turn away.

2 . Hoc quicquid tandem sum, caruncula est et animula et animi principatus. Missos fac libros: noli amplius distrahi.

Whatever I am at last, it is a little piece of flesh and a tiny soul and the rule of the mind. Send away the books: do not be distracted any longer.

Sed ut iam moriens caruncula contemne: cruor est ossicula et reticulum, ex nervis, venulis et arteriis contextus.

But as you die, despise this little piece of flesh: it is merely blood, bones, and a network, woven from nerves, veins, and arteries.

Quin etiam animam contemplare, qualis sit: spiritus, nec semper idem, sed quod singulis momentis evomitur et resorbetur. Tertia igitur pars est animi principatus.

Moreover, contemplate the soul as it is: a spirit, not always the same, but that which is breathed out and inhaled at every moment. Therefore, the third part is the rule of the mind.

Ad hunc igitur animum intende: senex es.

So, focus your mind on this: you are old.

Noli pati, ut ille amplius serviat, aut amplius impetu insociabili raptetur aut amplius fatum vel praesens inique ferat vel futurum horreat.

Do not allow him to serve any longer, or be carried away by violent impulses, or bear fate unfairly in the present, or dread it in the future.

3 . Deorum opera providentia plena.

The works of the gods are full of providence.

Quae fortuna accidunt, non seiuncta a natura seu complexu et implexu rerum, quae a providentia administrantur. Inde omnia fluunt. Accedit autem id, quod necessarium est et id, quod universo mundo, cuius tu pars es, conducit.

The things that happen by chance are not separate from nature or the interweaving and interconnectedness of things that are governed by providence. From there, everything flows. Moreover, what is necessary and what contributes to the whole world, of which you are a part, is added.

Unicuique vero parti bonum, quod natura universi fert et quod ad hanc conservandam facit.

To each part, indeed, comes the good that the nature of the universe brings and that which it accomplishes to preserve this world.

Conservant autem mundum ut elementorum ita etiam concretarum rerum mutationes. Haec tibi sufficiant, semper decreta sunto: librorum autem sitim pelle, ne murmurans moriaris, sed vere placidus Diisque ex animo gratias agens.

They maintain the world, including both the elements and the changes in concrete things. Let these things be enough for you; always be determined: dispel your thirst for books, so that you do not die complaining, but rather, be sincerely peaceful and give thanks to the gods from your heart.

4. Memento, quamdiu haec distuleris, et quoties a diis opportunitates nactus iis non usus sis. Oportet tandem aliquando sentias, cuius mundi pars sis et abs quo mundi rectore delibatus substiteris.

Remember, for as long as you have deferred these things, and how many times you have missed opportunities given by the gods. It is necessary, finally, that you realize of what part of the world you are and from whom you have received the gift of existence by the ruler of the world.

Tum vero, circumscriptum tibi esse terminum temporis, quo nisi ad serenitatem usus fueris, id abibit et tu abibis.

But indeed, you have a limited time set before you, and if you don't use it for tranquility, it will pass away, and so will you.

Neque unquam tibi redibit.

And it will never come back to you.

5. Singulis horis animo in id incumbe, ut firmiter, quemadmodum decet Romanum et virum, id quod in manibus est, cum diligente nec ficta gravitate, pietate, liberalitate et iustitia peragas tibique otium ab omnibus aliis cogitationibus redimas.

Every hour, direct your mind to perform with steadfastness, as befits a Roman and a man, the task at hand, with diligence and sincere gravity, piety, generosity, and iustice, and free yourself from all other distractions.

Redimes autem, si quasi ultimam vitae quamcunque actionem peregeris procul remotam ab omni temeritate et animi commoti aversione ab imperante ratione et simulatione et nimio tui studio et aegritudine suscepta ex iis quae a fato tribuantur.

And you will redeem yourself if, as if it were the last action of your life, you act far removed from all rashness, and turn away from emotions that conflict with reason, from pretense, and from excessive self-love and grief arising from things determined by fate.

Vides quam pauca sint, quae si quis tenet, leniter fluentem et divinae similem vitam degere potest.

You see how few things are required to live a tranquil and god-like life.

Etenim Dii nihil plus requirent ab eo, qui haec observat.

For the gods ask nothing more from the person who observes these things.

6. Ignominia, ignominia te ipse affice, anime! honorem autem tibi vindicandi tempus non amplius habebis: fugit enim vita unicuique.

Haec autem tibi tantum non exacta est nullam tui ipsius reverentiam habenti et in aliorum animis felicitatem tuam collocanti.

Disgrace, disgrace, inflict it upon yourself, oh soul! But you will no longer have the time to claim honor for yourself, for life is swiftly fleeing from each one.

But this is not for you alone, unaccomplished, having no regard for yourself, and placing your happiness solely in the minds of others.

7. Distrahunt te quae extrinsecus incidunt. Otium tibi concede ad discendum boni aliquid et desine in gyrum circumagi. Iam vero etiam alia circumcursatio cavenda.

Nam ii quoque nugantur, qui labore in vita defatigantur nec scopum habent, quo omnem impetum omninoque mentem dirigant.

You are distracted by external events. Allow yourself leisure to learn something good and stop wandering in circles. Moreover, you should be cautious about other pursuits as well.

For those who also toil in life without having a goal to which they direct all their effort and their entire mind, they too are wasting their time in vain.

8. Idcirco, quod non animadvertit ea, quae in alius animo aguntur, non facile quisquam repertus est infelix.

Illos autem, qui sui animi motus non percipiunt, necesse est infelices esse.

Therefore, anyone who does not pay attention to the things happening in the minds of others is not easily found to be unhappy.

However, those who do not perceive the movements of their own minds must necessarily be unhappy.

9. Horum semper oportet memorem esse, quae sit rerum universitatis natura, quae mea, quo pacto se haec ad illam habeat et qualis pars universitatis sit.

Et neminem esse, qui te prohibeat, quominus ea, quae naturae, cuius pars es, consentanea sunt, et facias et loquaris.

One should always bear in mind the nature of the universe, the nature of oneself, how they relate to each other, and what part one plays in the universe.

And there is no one who prevents you from doing and speaking those things that are in accordance with the nature of which you are a part.

10. Subtiliter Theophrastus in comparandis peccatis, prout quis populari quadam ratione haec inter se contulerit, dicit, graviora esse, quae ex cupiditate committantur, quam quae ex ira.

Iratum enim cum dolore quodam et occulta animi contractione rationem aversari, manifestum est.

Subtly, Theophrastus, in comparing sins, as one might assess them with a common sense, says that those committed out of desire are more serious than those committed out of anger.

For it is evident that when someone is angry, they turn away from reason with a certain pain and a hidden contraction of the mind.

15

Qui antem ex cupiditate peccat, a voluptate victus, intemperantior quodam modo et effeminatior apparet in peccatis.

However, the person who sins out of desire, being overcome by pleasure, appears in sins to be somewhat more intemperate and effeminate.

Recte igitur et philosophiae convenienter dixit, maiori crimini esse, quod cum voluptate peccetur, quam quod cum dolore.

Therefore, rightly and in accordance with philosophy, it is said that the sin committed with pleasure is a greater offense than the one committed with pain.

Omninoque alter ei magis similis videtur, qui antea iniuriam passus et dolore ad irascendum coactus est, alter sua sponte ad laedendum accedit, cupiditate ad aliquid faciendum ductus.

And indeed, the one who has suffered iniury before and is forced by pain to become angry seems more similar to the other who, of their own accord, approaches to harm, led by desire to do something.

11. Quasi fieri possit, ut confestim e vita exeas, ita singula agere et dicere et cogitare te oportet.

As if it were possible for you to depart from life immediately, you should act, speak, and think as if each moment were your last.

E vivis autem discedere, si quidem Dii sunt, non est quod quis timeat.

And if indeed the gods exist, there is no reason to fear departing from life while you are still alive.

Nam in malum te non coniicient.

For they will not cast you into evil.

Sin vero sut non sunt aut non curant res humanas, quid mea refert vivere in mundo vacuo diis aut providentia vacuo?

But if indeed the gods do not exist or do not care about human affairs, what does it matter to me to live in a world empty of gods or providence?

Verum et sunt et curant res humanas, atque ne in ea, quae vere mala sunt, ineidat homo, prorsus in ipsius potestate collocarunt.

Indeed, they both exist and care about human affairs, and to ensure that man does not fall into those things that are truly evil, they have entirely placed it within his own power.

reliquorum si quid esset malum, id quoque providis sent, ut omnino penes ipsum esset, ne in id incideret.

And if there were any evil among the rest, they foresaw it as well, so that it would entirely rest within the person himself not to fall into it.

Quod autem hominem non deteriorem reddit, quomodo id vitam hominis peiorem redderet?

And whatever does not make a man worse, how could that make his life worse?

Neque vero ex ignorantia, neque id intelligens, quoniam impotens erat ad hoc cavendum sut emendandum, universitatis natura id neglexisset.

Indeed, neither out of ignorance nor understanding, because the nature of the universe, being unable to guard against or correct this, would have overlooked it.

Non tantum peccasset aut ex impotentia aut ex artis defectu, ut bona et mala pariter bonis hominibus atque malis sine discrimine evenirent.

He would not have sinned merely out of impotence or a lack of skill, so that good and evil would happen to both good and bad people indiscriminately.

Iam vero mors et vita, honor et ignominia, dolor et voluptas, divitiae et egestas, haec omnia pariter bonis hominibus atque malis eveniunt, quippe quae neque honesta nec turpia sint. Itaque nec bona nec mala sunt.

Indeed, death and life, honor and disgrace, pain and pleasure, wealth and poverty, all these things happen equally to good and bad people, since they are neither honorable nor dishonorable. Therefore, they are neither good nor bad.

12 Quomodo omnia celeriter evanescant, in mundum ipsa corpora, in aevum memoriae eorum, qualia sint omnia, quae sub sensus cadunt?

How quickly everything vanishes: the physical bodies into the world, their memories into the age, and all that falls under the senses.

Et potissimum quae aut voluptate alliciunt aut dolore terrent aut fastu celebrata sunt, quam vilia et contemptu digna et emortua, rationalis facultatis est intelligere: quinam sint ii, quorum opiniones et voces nominis claritatem largiuntur.

Especially those things that either attract through pleasure, terrify through pain, or are celebrated with pride. A rational faculty can understand how cheap, worthy of contempt, and dead they are. It can discern who those are whose opinions and voices grant them fame.

Quid sit mori, et, quando quis id per se solum spectet et cogitatione ab eo separaverit quae simul cum eo concipiuntur animo, eum nihil aliud id esse habiturum, nisi opus naturae.

What death is, and when someone looks at it solely in itself and separates from it the thoughts that are conceived together with it in the mind, they will consider it to be nothing other than an operation of nature.

Naturae autem opus si quis timeat, eum esse puerulum.

If someone fears the work of nature (i.e., death), they are like a little child.

Hoc tamen non solum naturae opus esse, verum etiam naturae prodesse.

However, this is not only the work of nature but also beneficial to nature.

Quo pacto homo deum contingat, et qua sui parte, et quando certo quodam modo ita se habeat illa hominis pars.

In what way a human being can touch the divine, and in what part of oneself, and at what time, that part of the human can be in a certain manner.

13   Nihil miserius est eo, qui omnia undique circumit et quae subter terram sunt, ait ille, rimatur, eaque, quae in aliorum animis sunt, per coniecturas indagat, non autem sentit sufficere, si quis cum eo, quem intra se gerit, genio versetur et hunc sincere colat:

There is nothing more miserable than someone who roams around everywhere, as he says, exploring things even below the ground and investigating what is in the minds of others by coniecture, but does not feel content if someone does not engage with and sincerely cherish their own inner self (genius).

Huius autem cultus in eo cernitur, ut purus servetur a perturbatione animi, et temeritate et aegritudine propter ea, quae a Diis et hominibus fiunt:

However, the practice of this (self) consists in preserving oneself pure from disturbances of the mind, from rashness and grief due to those things that happen from gods and men.

Nam quae a diis proficiscuntur, venerabilia sunt virtutis nomine quae ab hominibus, cara cognationis ratione, interdum etiam miseratione digna propter ignorantiam bonorum et malorum:

For the things that originate from the gods are worthy of reverence in the name of virtue, and the things that come from humans are dear due to the bond of kinship, and sometimes worthy of pity due to their ignorance of good and evil.

Haec caecitas haud minor est illa, quae nos privat facultate alba et nigra discernendi.

This blindness is not much less than the one that deprives us of the ability to distinguish between white and black.

14.   Etiam si ter mille annos victurus esses, et insuper tricies mille, memento tamen, neminem aliam amittere vitam, quam ipsam eam, quam vivat, neque aliam vivere quam eam, quam amittat.

Even if you were to live for thirty thousand years and even more, remember nevertheless that no one loses any other life than the one they are living, and they do not live any other life than the one they are losing.

Eodem igitur redit longissimum vitae tempus cum brevissimo: nam praesens par, etiam si id quod perit non par sit, et id, quod amittitur, ita instar puncti videtur:

Therefore, the longest time of life returns to the same point as the shortest time, for the present is equal, even if that which perishes is not equal, and that which is lost seems like a mere point.

Neque enim quod praeteriit aut quod futurum est ut quis amittat, fieri potest: quomodo enim eo, quo caret, quis eum privabit?

For what has passed or what is yet to come cannot be lost by anyone. For how can someone be deprived of something they lack?

Horum igitur duorum memini oportet: alterius, omnia, ex aeterno eiusdem speciei esse et in orbem relabi, nec differre, utrum centum annis ducentis aut infinito tempore eadem aliquis sit visurus.

Therefore, one must remember these two things: first, that everything is of the same eternal essence and flows back into the cosmic cycle, and it makes no difference whether someone will see the same thing after a hundred, two hundred, or an infinite number of years.

Alterius, et eum, qui diutissime vixerit, et eum, qui celerrime obierit, par amittere.

Secondly, that we will all equally lose the other person, whether they live for a long time or die swiftly.

Nam praesens solum est, quo privari poterit, si quidem id tantum habet et, quod quis non habet, id non amittat.

Indeed, the only time in which one can be deprived is the present, because it has only that much, and what someone does not have, they cannot lose.

15   Omnia in opinione sita: manifesta enim sunt, quae a Monimo Cynico dicuntur.

Everything is based on opinion: for what is said by Monimus the Cynic is evident.

Manifesta quoque utilitas dicti si quis vim eius salutarem nec tamen ultra veritatem admittit.

The utility of the saying is also evident if someone accepts its beneficial power without going beyond the truth.

16   Contumelia se afficit animus hominis potissimum tum, quam, quantum per ipsam stat, abscessus et quasi tuber mundi sit:

The human mind is most affected by insults when it deems itself to be significant and departs from its proper place as if it were the center and prominent part of the world.

Nam aegre ferre aliquid eorum, quae fiunt est desistere a natura, cuius in parte uniuscuiusque aliarum rerum natura continetur.

For to bear with difficulty something that happens is to depart from nature, in which the nature of each individual thing is contained as a part.

Tum vero, quando hominem aliquem aversatur aut adeo ei nocendi consilio adversatur, quales sunt irascentium animi.

But indeed, when someone detests a certain person or opposes them with the intention of harming them, it is the nature of an angry mind.

Porro se ipse contumelia afficit, quando voluptati aut dolori succumbit.

Furthermore, a person afflicts themselves with insult when they yield to pleasure or pain.

Item quando simulat ac ficte et fallaciter aliquid vel facit vel loquitur.

Likewise, when they pretend, act, or speak something in a deceptive and false manner.

Denique, quando actionem aliquam suam aut conatum ad nullum scopum dirigit, sed temere et inconsulto quantillum id est exsequitur, quum etiam minima quaeque ita agi oporteat, ut ad finem referantur.

Finally, when they direct any of their actions or endeavors towards no goal, but rather, they carry it out hastily and without thought, even the smallest things should be done in such a way that they are directed towards an end.

Finis autem animalium ratione praeditorum est, urbis et civitatis antiquissimas rationi et legi obsequi.

The end, however, of animals possessing reason is to obey the reason and law of the oldest city and state.

17 ·   Vitae humanae tempus, punctum.

The time of human life is a like a dot.

Materia fluens.

Flowing matter.

Sensus obscurus.

Obscure sense.

Totius corporis compages ad putredinem vergens.

The entire structure of the body tending towards putrefaction.

Animus, turbo.

The soul, a whirlwind.

Fortuna, res perplexa.

Fortune, a perplexing thing.

Fama, iudicii expers: ut paucis dicam, omnia corporis, fluvius.

Fame, devoid of judgment: to say it in a few words, everything is of the body, a river.

Omnia animi, somnium et fumus.

All things of the mind are like a dream and smoke.

Vita, bellum et peregrini commoratio.

Life, war, and dwelling in a foreign land.

Fama posthuma, oblivio.

Posthumous fame, oblivion.

Quid igitur est, quod deducere potest?

What, then, can lead to a meaningful life?

Unicum et solum, philosophia.

The one and only thing, philosophy.

Haec autem in eo cernitur, ut eum, qui intus est, genium a contumelia et laesione immunem serves, voluptatibus et doloribus superiorem, nihil temere facientem nec ficte simulateve, non indigentem, ut alius quid faciat aut non faciat, porro ea, quae obveniunt et attribuuntur, accipientem ut quae inde veniunt, unde ipse venit, post omnia autem mortem placido animo opperientem, quippe nihil aliud.

Indeed, philosophy consists in preserving the inner self, the genius, immune from insult and iniury; being superior to pleasures and pains; acting neither rashly nor deceitfully; being self-sufficient and not dependent on others for their actions or non-actions; accepting what comes and is attributed to them as what comes from where they come from; and facing death after all with a tranquil mind, for there is nothing else.

Nisi solutionem elementorum, e quibus singula animalia sunt composita.

Except for the dissolution of the elements from which each individual animal is composed.

Quod si ipsis elementis nihil timendum est ex eo, quod unumquodque eorum perpetuo in aliud mutatur.

However, if there is nothing to fear from the elements themselves because each of them is perpetually changing into another.

Quam ob causam quis suspectam habeat omnium rerum mutationem et in partes dissolutionem? nam naturae conveniens est.

Nihil autem malum, quod naturae convenit.

For what reason should anyone suspect the change and dissolution of all things? It is natural and in accordance with nature.

Indeed, nothing that is in accordance with nature is evil.

LIBER III

STOICAE PHILOSOPHIAE INVESTIGANS

I

Non hoc solum reputari oportet, vitam in dies absumi minoremque eius partem relinqui, verum etiam illud reputandum est, etiamsi quis diutius victurus sit, tamen obscurum esse, an mens ipsius pariter posthac idoneam habitura sit vim ad intelligentiam rerum ac doctrinae eius, quae ad scientiam rerum divinarum humanarumque spectat.

This should be considered not only that life is being consumed day by day, and a lesser portion of it remains, but also that it should be considered whether, even if someone were to live longer, it remains uncertain whether their mind will have the same capacity for understanding and learning about matters pertaining to the knowledge of divine and human things.

Nam si delirare coeperit, perspirari quidem et nutriri et visis impelli et impetum capere et quae id genus alia sunt non deficient.

For if someone begins to wander in their mind, indeed they may still perspire, be nourished, be affected by things seen, and be moved by impulses, and all other similar functions may not be lacking.

Sed se ipso uti et officii numeros diligenter ediscere, et quae apparent articulatim explicare et de eo, num sese iam hinc educat, deliberare et quae, huiusmodi sunt, quae iudicandi facultatem bene subactam requirunt, ea vero ante exstinguuntur.

But to use oneself and diligently learn the duties, and to explain in detail what is evident, and to consider whether he is now training himself from here, and to deliberate about those matters which require a well-subdued faculty of judgment, indeed these are extinguished beforehand.

Festinandum igitur est, non solum idcirco, quod mors in dies propior imminet, verum etiam idcirco, quod intelligentia et perceptio rerum ante desinit.

Therefore, there is a need to hasten, not only because death approaches closer day by day but also because intelligence and perception of things cease before that.

2. Oportet etiam talia observari, ea quoque, quae per consequentiam iis, quae natura fiunt, adnascuntur, suavitatis aliquid et illecebrarum habere: ut, panis quum coquitur, diffinduntur quaedam eius partes.

It is also necessary to observe such things that arise as a consequence of natural processes, which have a certain sweetness and allure: for example, when bread is baked, certain parts of it are divided.

Haec igitur sic hiantia et quodammodo contra professionem artis pistoriae comparata decoris quid nescio quo modo habent et singulari quadam ratione cupiditatem edendi movent: porro etiam, ficus, quum maturuerunt, dehiscunt, et in maturissimis olivis id ipsum, quod prope ad putredinem accedit, propriam quandam amoenitatem baccae conciliat.

Therefore, these things, gaping in a way and somehow contrary to the profession of the baker's art, possess a certain attractiveness and, in a unique manner, arouse a desire to be eaten. Moreover, even figs, when they ripen, split open, and in the ripest olives, that very aspect that comes close to decay imparts a certain charm to the fruit.

Spicae autem deorsum nutantes, et leonis supercilium et aprorum ex ore profluens spuma et multa alia, quae, si quis separatim spectat, a pulcritudine longe absunt, tamen, quoniam ea, quae natura fiunt, sequuntur, ad ornatum et delectationem pro sua quaeque parte conferunt.

Moreover, the nodding ears of corn, the eyebrow of a lion, the froth flowing from the mouths of boars, and many other things, which if observed individually are far from beauty, yet, since they follow the course of nature, each contributes to the overall adornment and delight in its own way.

Ita ut si quis interiorem sensum habeat et profundiorem intelligentiam eorum, quae in universo fiunt, ei propemodum nihil non etiam eorum, quae per consequentiam accidunt, grata quadam ratione cum aliis concinnatum videri debeat.

Thus, if someone possesses an inner sense and a deeper understanding of the things that happen in the universe, almost nothing, even the things that occur as a consequence, should appear to him out of harmony with others but rather gratifying in a certain way.

Hic etiam veros belluarum rictus non minore cum voluptate spectabit, quam quos pictores et fictores imitando exhibent, atque et vetulae anus et senis florem quendam ac decus et puerorum venustatem modestis suis oculis intueri poterit.

Here, he will also behold the true jaws of wild beasts with no less pleasure than those which painters and sculptors represent by imitation. Moreover, he will be able to gaze upon the charm and beauty of an old woman and the gracefulness of an elderly man, as well as the loveliness of children, all with his modest eyes.

Atque eius generis multa non cuivis probabilia occurrent, sed ei tantum, qui cum natura eiusque operibus intimam quandam familiaritatem contraxerit.

And many things of this kind will not be probable to just anyone but only to those who have developed an intimate familiarity with nature and its works.

3 · Hippocrates postquam multos morbos sustulit, ipse morbo correptus obiit.

After Hippocrates cured many diseases, he himself was afflicted by an illness and passed away.

Chaldaei multorum mortes praedixere, postea etiam ipsos fatum intercepit.

Indeed, the Chaldeans foretold the deaths of many, but later, fate itself intercepted them as well.

Alexander et Pompeius et Caius Caesar quum totas urbes toties funditus evertissent et in acie multa millia equitum peditumque interfecissent, et ipsi vita excesserunt.

Alexander, Pompey, and Gaius Caesar, after having completely razed many entire cities and killed many thousands of cavalry and infantry on the battlefield, themselves passed away.

Heraclitus quum rerum naturam scrutatus tam multa de conflagratione mundi disseruisset, aqua intercute distentus et stercore bubulco oblitus interiit.

Heraclitus, after scrutinizing the nature of things and discussing so much about the conflagration of the world, died by being distended with dropsy and covered in cow dung.

Democritum pediculi, Socratem alii pediculi sustulerunt. Quorsum haec? Conscendisti, navigasti, ex alto in portum devectus es.

Democritus was killed by lice, while others killed Socrates. What is the purpose of these examples? You have boarded, sailed, and from the deep, you have been carried to the harbor.

Exscende! si in aliam vitam, nihil diis vacuum, ne ibi quidem, sin vero in conditionem sensu privatam, desines labores et voluptates tolerare et inservire vasi tanto deteriori, quanto praestantius est, id quod servit: hoc enim mens et genius, illud terra et sanies.

Ascend! If to another life, nothing is void of gods, not even there; but if to a state devoid of sensation, you will cease to endure labors and pleasures and to serve a vessel so inferior as it is, the more excellent that which serves. For the former is of the mind and intellect, the latter of the earth and decay.

4 · Id quod relinquitur vitae noli conterere in cogitationibus de aliis, nisi si ad communem utititatem spectas.

Do not dwell on what is left of life in thoughts about others, unless it pertains to common utility.

Nam profecto alio negotio privaris hoc est, cogitans, quid ille agat et quam ob rem, quid dicat, quid cogitet, quid moliatur et quae alia sunt huiusmodi, quae faciunt, ut ab animi principatu diligenter observando divageris.

Indeed, by engaging in such thoughts about others, you deprive yourself of attending to more important matters. Pondering on what someone else does, why they do it, what they say, what they think, what they plan, and other similar things leads you to stray from diligently observing the rule of your own mind.

Oportet igitur vanitatem quoque et temeritatem in serie cogitationum declinare, omnium autem maxime curiositatem et malitiam, teque adsuefacere, ut ea tantum cogites, de quibus interrogatus, quid nunc mediteris, libere statim respondeas "hoc vel illud," ita ut ex iis confestim appareat, omnia *in te* esse simplicia et benevola et animalis communi utilitati prospicientis, despicientis cogitationes, quae voluptatem omninove oblectationem spectant, itemque aemulationem quandam aut invidentiam aut suspicionem aut aliud quidlibet, quod si animo te agitasse fatearis, pudore te suffundi oporteat.

Therefore, it is necessary to avoid vanity and rashness in the course of your thoughts, especially curiosity and malice. You should accustom yourself to only think about things for which you can freely answer when asked, "What are you currently meditating on?" Respond promptly with "this" or "that," so that it immediately becomes apparent that you possess simple and benevolent thoughts, looking out for the common welfare of all living beings and disregarding thoughts that aim solely for pleasure and amusement, as well as any kind of envy, resentment, suspicion, or anything else that, if you were to admit having entertained in your mind, would cause you to feel ashamed.

Nam profecto vir talis, non amplius differens, quin in optimorum numero sit, sacerdos quasi quidam est et minister Deorum, numine quoque, quod in pectore gerit, familiariter utens, quod hominem praestat incontaminatum omnibus voluptatibus, omni dolore illaesum, nulli contumeliae obnoxium, omnisque malitiae sensu carentem, certaminis maximi, ne ab ulla animi perturbatione prosternatur, luctatorem, iustitiae colore bene tinctum, ex toto animo quae eveniunt sibique tribuuntur amplectentem, non saepe neque sine magna et ad publicam utilitatem spectante necessitate cogitantem, quid tandem alius loquatur aut agat aut meditetur.

Indeed, such a man, not hesitating to be counted among the best, is like a kind of priest and minister of the Gods, intimately utilizing the divinity that resides within his heart. He becomes like a person uncontaminated by all pleasures, untouched by any pain, not susceptible to insult, and devoid of all malice. He is like a contestant in a great struggle, determined not to be overthrown by any disturbance of the mind, a champion colored with the essence of justice, wholeheartedly embracing whatever events and outcomes are given to him, not often and only with great necessity considering what others may say, do, or think, always focusing on the public good.

Sola enim sua sunt, in quibus operam collocat atque ea, quae sibi ex universi natura destinantur, assidue contemplatur, atque illa quidem honesta praestat, haec autem bona esse habet persuasum: quae enim cuique adsignata est sors, convenienter infertur et infert.

For he alone values his own affairs, and he constantly contemplates those things which are assigned to him by the nature of the universe. He regards honorable actions as superior, and he holds the conviction that these are true goods: whatever lot is assigned to each person, it is fittingly presented and accepted.

Meminit autem, cognatione contineri quidquid rationis sit particeps, et omnibus hominibus prospicere naturae hominis esse consentaneum.

He remembers that everything endowed with reason is connected, and it is consistent for all humans to act in accordance with human nature.

Gloriae autem non ei, quae ab omnibus proficiscatur, esse studendum, sed ei tantum, quae ab iis, qui naturae convenienter degant.

However, one should not strive for glory that comes from everyone, but only for the glory that comes from those who live in harmony with nature.

Qui non ita vivunt quales sint domi et foris, noctu et interdiu, quales cum qualibus volutentur, semper memor est.

Those who do not live in such a way as they are at home and abroad, at night and during the day, or as they are when they are with various individuals, always keep this in mind.

Proinde nihili pendit laudem ab iis profectam, qui ne sibi quidem ipsi placent.

Therefore, he places no value on praise that comes from those who don't even please themselves.

5. Noli invitus agere, neque a communione generis humani alienus, neque re non explorata, neque animo in diversa tracto: ne urbanitas animi tui sensum lenociniis exornet.

Do not act unwillingly, nor be estranged from the fellowship of humankind, nor act without proper investigation, nor let your mind be pulled in different directions, lest the urbanity of your mind be adorned with the allurements of deception.

Ne sis multorum verborum, neque multorum negotiorum.

Do not be a person of many words, nor of many tasks.

Praeterea Deus, qui in te residet, sit praeses animalis masculi, aetate maturi, rei publicae studiosi, Romani, principis, ita compositi, quasi qui exspectet classicum, facile e vita discessurus, qui neque iureiurando opus habeat neque hominis cuiusquam testimonio. Inest vero serenitas, et neque externo ministerio indigere, neque tranquillitate, quam alii praestant.

Furthermore, may the God who resides within you be the guardian of a mature male individual, devoted to the state, a Roman citizen, a leader, well-balanced as if awaiting the trumpet call, ready to depart from life without needing oaths or the testimony of any person. He possesses serenity and requires neither external service nor the tranquility that others provide.

Rectum igitur esse oportet, non erectum.

It is necessary to be upright, not arrogant.

6. Si quid in vita humana deprehenderis praestantius iustitia, veritate, temperantia, fortitudine, denique animo tuo sic affecto, ut in iis, quae sanae rationi convenienter agentem te praestat, se ipso, fato autem in iis contentus sit, quae sine nostra optione attribuuntur.

If you find anything in human life more excellent than justice, truth, temperance, and fortitude, in the end, let your mind be so disposed that in those things which make you act in accordance with sound reason, you consider yourself sufficient, and in things assigned by fate without our choice, be content with fate itself.

Si quid, inquam, praestantius hoc deprehenderis, eo toto animo fac te vertas, eoque, ut bono praestantissimo, quod inveneris, fruaris.

If, I say, you discover anything more excellent than this, with your whole soul turn yourself towards it, and so that you may enjoy it as the most excellent good you have found.

Sin nil praestabilius offenderis eo, qui in te collocatus est, genio, qui et omnes suos motus sibi subiecit et visa quaeque diligenter explorat et a sensuum affectionibus, ut dicebat Socrates, se abduxit, et Diis se submisit et hominum curam gerit.

But if you find nothing more excellent than the divine spirit that resides within you, which has subjected all its movements to itself, carefully explores all that is seen, and, as Socrates said, has withdrawn itself from the influences of the senses, and has submitted itself to the Gods and cares for the welfare of humanity.

Si animo sic affecto inferiora vilioraque cetera omnia deprehenderis, nulli alii rei cuiquam locum concede, quo si semel inclinaveris animo devergente, non amplius bonum proprium ac tuum sine distractione omnium maximo colere poteris.

If, with your mind so disposed, you perceive other things as inferior and less valuable, do not grant a place to anything else, so that if you once incline your mind towards a deviation, you will no longer be able to cultivate your own true good without being distracted by various concerns.

Nefas enim est, ullam aliam rem quamcumque diversi generis bono illi rationali et efficienti ex adverso consistere, ut imperitae multitudinis laudem, magistratus, divitias, voluptatum fructum: quae omnia, si vel tantulum coavenire visa fuerint, confestim praevalebunt et *te* abducent.

For it is wrong for anything of a different nature to oppose that good which is rational and efficient, such as the praise of the ignorant multitude, positions of power, wealth, and the enioyment of pleasures. If any of these seem even slightly attractive, they will immediately gain the upper hand and lead you astray.

Tu vero, inquam, quod praestantius est, id simpliciter et libere elegito, eique strenue adhaerescito.

Indeed, I say, choose that which is more excellent, choose it with simplicity and freedom, and adhere to it vigorously.

Praestat autem, quod prodest. Si *conducere tibi* videtur, quatenus ratione praeditus es, retine.

Indeed, what is beneficial is preferable. If it seems advantageous to you, considering your rationality, then hold onto it.

si vero quatenus animatus es, repudia.

But if it is advantageous only in terms of your animality (i.e., your basic animal instincts), then reiect it.

et a fastu ahenum serva iudicium.

And preserve a bronze judgment against pride.

Modo ut tuto rerum examen instituas!

Indeed, proceed with examining things carefully and safely!

7 · Cave, unquam quidquam tibi prodesse putas.

Beware, never think that anything is beneficial to you.

Quod te aliquando compellat, ut fidem fallas, verecundiam deseras, oderis aliquem, suspectum habeas, diras impreceris, appetas aliquid quod parietes et velamenta desideret.

What may sometimes prompt you to betray trust, abandon modesty, harbor hatred, entertain suspicions, utter curses, or desire something that requires walls and veils, avoid succumbing to such impulses.

Qui enim suae ipsius menti et genio et sacris virtutis eius primas defert, tragoedias non excitat, gemitus non edit, non solitudine, non frequentia indiget.

Indeed, he who gives priority to his own mind, genius, and sacred virtues does not stir up tragedies, does not utter groans, and does not depend on solitude or the company of others.

Et, quod maximum est vivit, neque appetens *vitae*, nec fugiens.

And, what is of the greatest importance, he lives, neither desiring life nor fleeing from it.

Utrum autem longiore an breviore temporis spatio anima sua corpore circumdata utatur, ne tantillum quidem curae habet:

However, whether the soul makes use of its body for a longer or shorter period of time, it does not concern itself even in the slightest.

Nam si statim demigrandum est, non minus promptus discedit, quam si ad aliam aliquam rem peragendam se conferat, quae salva verecundia et decore peragi potest.

For if it is time to depart immediately, it leaves just as readily as if it were engaging in some other task that can be carried out with dignity and decorum, preserving its integrity.

Hoc unum per totam vitam cavens, ne mens in ullo deprehendatur conatu, qui animal rationale et sociale dedeceat.

Throughout life, being mindful of this one thing: to avoid any effort of the mind that would dishonor the rational and social being

8. In mente hominis castigati et purificati nihil purulenti, nihil impuri, nihil subdoli offendes.

In the mind of a disciplined and purified person, you will find nothing putrid, nothing impure, nothing deceitful.

Neque vitam eius fatum unquam abrumpit imperfectam, perinde ac si tragoedum dixerit aliquis ante fabulam finitam ac peractam scena cessisse.

Nor does fate ever cut short the life of such a person prematurely, as if someone had announced before the tragedy's conclusion and the play's completion that the actor had left the stage.

Porro nec servile quidquam, neque affectatum, neque addictum, neque abscissum, nec poenae obnoxium, nec latebrosum.

Furthermore, there is nothing servile, affected, addicted, severed, subjected to punishment, or hidden in such a person.

9. Facultatem, e qua opiniones nascuntur, diligenter cole. In ea omnia insunt, ut menti tuae nulla innascatur opinio, quae vel naturae sit contraria vel animalis ratione praediti constitutioni: cuius haec est promissio, ut a temeritate in assentiendo alieni, et hominibus benevoli atque diis obsequentes reddamur.

Cultivate the faculty from which opinions arise with great care. In it lies everything, so that no opinion contrary to nature or the constitution of a rational being may be born in your mind. Its promise is to make us free from hasty agreement with others and to become benevolent towards people and compliant with the gods.

10. Missis igitur omnibus, haec pauca tantum retine: praeterea memento, unumquemque praesens tantummodo temporis spatium, quod puncti instar obtinet, vivere: reliquum aut exactum aut in incerto. Exiguum igitur est quod unusquisque vivit.

Exiguus quoque terrae in quo vitam agit angulus, exigua denique, quae vel longissime propagatur fama posthuma, eaque per successionem homunculorum tradita celerrime moriturorum, ac ne se ipsos quidem cognoscentium, nedum eum, qui iam pridem fato concessit.

11. His, quae dixi, decretis unum adhuc addendum est, visi cuiusvis, quod se offerat, definitionem vel descriptionem esse faciendam, ut quale sit ex natura sua et per omnes ac singulas eius partes spectatum, clare intelligas, et quodnam sit proprium eius nomen, quae item nomina eorum, e quibus conflatum est et in quae resolvetur, tecum possis disserere.

Nihil enim tantam vim habet ad animi magnitudinem gignendam, quam posse singula, quae in vita occurrunt, via ac ratione explorare eaque semper sic intueri, ut simul tecum reputes, quali mundo qualem usum haec res praebeat, quam habeat existimationem et universitatis rerum et hominis respectu, utpote civis supremae illius civitatis, cuius quasi domus sunt ceterae civitates.

Having dismissed all else, retain only these few things: furthermore, remember that each person lives only in the present moment, which is like a point in time, the rest is either in the past or uncertain. Thus, the life of each individual is brief.

Indeed, the tiny corner of the earth where one lives, and the small bit of fame that may spread furthest after death, is transmitted through the swift passing of short-lived individuals, who don't even know themselves, let alone the person who long ago departed by fate.

To the decrees I have mentioned, one more thing must be added: whenever anything presents itself to you, you should make a definition or description of it, so that you can clearly understand what it is by its very nature and by examining all its parts individually. Also, understand its proper name and the names of those things from which it is composed and into which it can be dissolved, so that you can discuss them with yourself.

For nothing has such power to engender greatness of mind as being able to explore each individual thing that occurs in life through method and reason, and to contemplate them in such a way that you simultaneously consider the purpose of each thing in this world, the estimation it holds in the universe and in relation to humanity, just as a citizen of that highest city, of which all other cities are like dwellings.

Quid sit ex quibus compositum et quamdiu ut permaneat a natura comparatum sit id quod nunc mihi visum obiicit: quanam ad id virtute opus sit, ut mansuetudine, fortitudine, veritate, fide, simplicitate, moderatione, reliquis.

What it is composed of, how long it is destined to remain as arranged by nature, what virtue is required for it, such as gentleness, fortitude, truth, faith, simplicity, moderation, and others.

De singulis igitur rebus dicendum est: haec divinitus venit.

It must be said about each individual thing: this has come from the divine.

Haec per complexum et fati serie connexa et contexta, et tali rerum concursu ac fortuna: haec a contribuli et cognato et sodali.

These things are connected and woven together in a complex and interconnected series of fate, with such a concurrence and fortune of events: these are from our fellow human beings, relatives, and companions.

Qui tamen nescit, quid naturae suae sit consentaneum. At ego non ignoro.

Yet, there are those who do not know what is in accordance with their nature. But I am not ignorant of it.

Ideoque secundum societatis legem a natura sancitam benevolum et iustum me praesto. Neque tamen non in mediis illis rebus eius pro aestimatione rationem habeo.

Therefore, in accordance with the law established by society and sanctioned by nature, I conduct myself as benevolent and iust. However, even in those intermediate matters, I do not disregard reason for the sake of evaluation.

12. Si rectae rationi obsecutus id quod instat, sedulo, strenue et placide peregeris, non opus aliquod accessorium, sed genium tuum purum integrumque servaveris, quasi illum statim esses redditurus.

If, following right reason, you diligently, vigorously, and peacefully perform what is at hand, you will not need any external accessory, but you will preserve your own pure and unblemished character, as if you were about to return it immediately.

si hoc indesinenter egeris, nihil exspectans aut fugiens, sed praesente actione naturae consentanea et heroica in singulis dictis ac vocibus veritate contentus, prosperam ages vitam.

If you consistently act in this manner, without expecting or avoiding anything, but engaging in each action with the harmony of nature and heroism, content with truth in every word and utterance, you will lead a prosperous life.

quod quin facias, nemo est, qui te impedire possit.

Indeed, there is no one who can prevent you from doing this.

13. Quemadmodum medici ad subita mala sananda in promptu habent instrumenta et ferramenta.

Just as doctors have instruments and tools at hand for treating sudden illnesses.

Sic te in promptu habere oportet decreta ad res divinas humanasque cognoscendas et ad omnia, etiam minima, ita agenda, ut memineris utrorumque inter se vinculi.

Likewise, you should have at hand principles for understanding divine and human affairs and for acting in all matters, even the smallest, so that you remember the connection between both.

Neque enim rem ullam humanam recte perficies, nisi simul eam ad deos retuleris, neque contra.

For you will not accomplish any human matter rightly unless you also relate it to the gods., nor the other way around.

14. Noli amplius evagari.

Do not wander further.

Neque enim futurum est, ut commentarios tuos perlegas aut priscorum Romanorum et Graecorum res gestas et ex variis scriptis excerpta, quae tibi in senectute [tractanda] reposuisti.

For it will not be possible for you to read your own commentaries or the deeds of ancient Romans and Greeks, or the various writings you have compiled for yourself to be used in your old age.

Festina igitur ad finem, et si qua tibi tui cura est, dum licet, missa spe vana, tibi ipse consule.

Therefore, hasten towards the end, and if you have any concern for yourself, while it is still possible, abandon empty hopes and take care of yourself.

15. Non intelligunt, quam multiplicem vim habeant vocabula haec, furari, serere, emere, quiescere, videre quid factu opus sit.

They do not understand, how manifold power these words have, to steal, to sow, to buy, to rest, to see what needs to be done.

quod non oculis fit, sed alio aliquo visu.

What is done not by the eyes, but by some other sight.

16. Corpus, anima, mens: corporis sensus, animae impetus, mentis decreta. Visorum imaginibus imprimi, etiam pecudum est: interno impetu quasi fidiculis agitari, ferarum quoque est et effeminatorum hominum et Phalaridis et Neronis.

Body, soul, mind: the senses of the body, the impulses of the soul, the decrees of the mind. To be imprinted by the images of things seen, is also of beasts: to be moved by an internal impulse as if by strings, is also of wild animals and effeminate men and Phalaris and Nero.

Mentem ducem habere ad ea, quae convenire videntur, etiam eorum est, qui deos esse negant et patriam deserunt, qui faciunt, postquam forea clausere.

To have the mind as a guide to what seems fitting, is also of those who deny the existence of gods and desert their country, who do what they do, after they have closed the doors.

Si igitur cetera his, quae dixi, communia sunt, restat, quod proprium est viri boni, libenter amplecti ea, quae accidunt et a fato ei destinantur.

If therefore the other things are common to these, which I have said, it remains, that what is proper to a good man, is to willingly embrace those things, which happen and are destined to him by fate.

Genium vero intus in pectora habitantem nec polluere nec turba visorum perturbare, sed placidum servare et decenter Deo obsequentem, nihil a veritate alienum loquentem et nihil nisi iustum agentem.

But the genius that dwells within our breast, we must not pollute nor disturb with the crowd of visions, but keep it calm and obedient to God, speaking nothing contrary to the truth and doing nothing but what is iust.

Quod si nemo hominum fidem ei habet, eum simpliciter, modeste et tranquille vivere, neque horum cuiquam irascitur, neque declinat a via ea, quae fert ad vitae finem.

But the genius that dwells within our breast, we must not pollute nor disturb with the crowd of visions, but keep it calm and obedient to God, speaking nothing contrary to the truth and doing nothing but what is iust.

Ad quem par est accedere purum, quietum, ad decedendum promptum, et suapte sponte fato suo se accomodantem.

The Latin sentence you typed means: "To whom it is fitting to approach pure, calm, ready to depart, and of his own accord adapting himself to his fate.

LIBER IV

INTROSPECTIO ET DISCIPLINA

1. Quod intus dominatur, id, quando secundum naturam habet, ita stat adversus ea, quae accidunt, ut semper ad id, quod fieri potest et datum est, facile transeat:

What dominates within, when it is in accordance with nature, stands opposed to the things that happen in such a way that it always easily passes on to that which can happen and is given.

materiam enim appensam nullam amat, sed fertur ad praeposita cum exceptione: quod vero contra infertur, materiem sibi facit:

For it does not love attached material, but it is drawn to appointed things with exceptions; however, what is brought against it, it makes into its own matter.

quemadmodum ignis, ubi ea, quae insuper incidunt, superat, a quibus parva lucerna exstingueretur: splendidus autem ignis celerrime sibi vindicat ea, quae inferuntur, eaque consumit, et ex iis altius surgit.

Iust as fire, when it overcomes the things that fall upon it, from which even a small lamp would be extinguished: but a bright fire quickly claims for itself the things that are brought against it, consumes them, and rises higher from them.

2. Nulla actio temere aut aliter, quam secundum regulam, quae ad artem complendam spectat, efficiatur.

No action should be done rashly or otherwise than according to the rule that pertains to the fulfillment of the art.

34

3 ·

Secessus sibi quaerunt, casas rusticas, littora, montes: soles etiam tu eiusmodi loca maxime appetere.

They seek seclusion for themselves, country houses, shores, and mountains: even you, the sun, are most inclined to such places.

Sed totum hoc hominis est maxime rudis et imperiti, quum liceat, quacunque tibi visum fuerit hora, in te ipsum secedere.

But all of this is most unrefined and ignorant of a person when, at any hour you choose, it is permitted to withdraw into yourself.

Nullum enim in locum, ubi maior sit tranquillitas altiusve otium, homo secedit, quam in suum ipsius animum:

For into no place does a person withdraw more to find greater tranquility or deeper leisure than into their own mind.

potissimum, quicunque intus habet, in quae intuens statim in summa sit commoditate: commoditatem vero nihil aliud dico, nisi decentiam.

Especially whoever possesses within themselves that upon which they can immediately reflect with the greatest ease; but by "ease," I mean nothing other than propriety.

Continuo igitur hunc secessum tibi concede et refice te ipse.

Therefore, immediately grant yourself this seclusion and refresh yourself.

Brevia autem sunto et elementaria, quae, simul atque tibi occurrerint, sufficient ad eum *animum* totum occludendum, teque remittendum, nihil eorum moleste ferentem, ad quae reverteris.

Let them be short and elemental, which, as soon as they occur to you, will suffice to shut out your entire mind and bring yourself back, not resenting any of them to which you will return.

Quid enim moleste fers? hominumne pravitatem? Perpendens decretum illud, animalium ratione praeditorum alterum alterius causa natum esse, et tolerare partem esse iustitiae, et invitos peccare eos, et quam multi iam, qui infensissimo fuere animo, qui suspiciosi, qui odio incensi, post vehementissimas pugnas porrecti inque cinerem redacti sint, tandem aliquando desine indignari.

For what do you take to heart? The wickedness of people? Reflect on this decree: that beings endowed with reason are born for the sake of one another, and that to endure is part of justice, and that some act unwillingly, and how many now, who were once filled with the most bitter hostility, suspicious and inflamed with hatred, have been laid low after fierce battles and reduced to ashes. Finally, cease to be indignant.

Verum, ea, quae a rerum universitate tibi tributa sunt, iniquo animo fers? Revocans tibi in animum disiunctivum illud: aut providentia aut atomi, vel ea omnia, ex quibus demonstratum est, mundum esse instar civitatis.

Indeed, do you bear with an unfair mind the things that have been assigned to you by the universe? Recall to your mind that disiunctive proposition: either providence or atoms, or all those things from which it has been demonstrated that the world is like a city.

35

desine, ea iniquo animo ferre.

Verum tangent te etiam posthac quae corporis sunt? Considerans, spiritui sive leniter sive aspere moto non immisceri mentem, simul atque se ipsa abduxerit suamque cognorit potestatem, et reliqua omnia quae de dolore et voluptate audisti et consensu tuo comprobasti, desine tandem his tangi.

Verum gloriola te trahet in diversa? Respiciens celeritatem oblivionis, qua omnia sepeliuntur, quam vasta sit infinitas temporis in utramque partem, quam vanum, quod resonant, quam mutabiles iudicii expertes ii qui te laudare videntur, et quam angustus sit locus, quo circumscribitur eorum laus, desine tandem gloriola in diversa trahi.

Tota enim terra punctum, eiusque quantillus angulus haec habitatio, et hic quam pauci sunt et cuiusmodi homines, qui te celebrabunt.

Quod igitur reliquum est, memento secessus in illum, ipsius agellum, et ante omnia cave distraharis et nimium te intendas, sed liber esto et contemplare res ut homo, ut civis, ut animal mortale.

Inter ea, quae maxime in promptu sint, in quae intuearis, haec duo sunto: alterum.

Res externas non attingere animum, sed extra immotas stare, molestias autem ex sola interna opinione oriri: alterum omnia ea, quae vides, iamiam mutari neque amplius fore atque quam multarum rerum mutationi ipse interfueris fac cogites.

Cease to bear them with an unfair mind.

However, will you also touch henceforth the things that belong to the body? Considering that, when the spirit is moved either gently or roughly, it does not mix with the mind, as soon as it has drawn itself apart and recognized its own power, and all the remaining things that you have heard about pain and pleasure and have approved by your agreement, finally cease to be touched by these things.

But will petty glory also drag you into different directions? Looking at the speed of oblivion, in which all things are buried, how vast is the infinity of time in both directions, how empty is the echoing, how changeable are those who appear to praise you without experience of judgment, and how narrow is the space in which their praise is confined, finally cease to be drawn into different directions by petty glory.

For the entire earth is a point, and this dwelling place a tiny corner of it, and how few and what kind of people are here, who will praise you.

So, what is left, remember the retreat into that, your own little field, and above all, be cautious not to be pulled apart and overly stretched, but be free and contemplate things as a human, as a citizen, as a mortal being.

Among those things which are most readily available, into which you should direct your gaze, let these two be: the other.

Not to touch the external things with your mind, but to stand apart from them as if immovable, and to realize that troubles arise solely from your internal opinions; the other is to consider that all those things which you see will very soon be changed and will no longer exist, and you yourself are an integral part of this process of change.

Mundus, mutatio.

Vita, opinio.

4. Si intellectus nobis communis est, etiam ratio, qua rationales sumus, nobis communis.

si haec, etiam ea ratio, quae, quid faciendum sit, quid non, praecipit, communis.

si haec etiam lex communis.

si haec, cives sumus.

si cives, civitatis alicuius participes.

si hoc est, mundus instar civitatis est: cuius enim alius civitatis universum hominum genus particeps dixeris? Illinc autem, e communi hac civitate et ipsa intelligendi vis et rationalis et legis gnara nobis obvenit, aut unde? nam ut terrenum mihi e terra aliqua pro parte attributum est, et humidum ex alio elemento, et spirabile e fonte aliquo, et calidum igneumque e proprio quodam fonte - nihil enim ex nihilo oritur, quemadmodum etiam nihil in nihilum redigitur - ita utique etiam intellectus alicunde venit.

5. Mors tale quid est, quale ortus, naturae actio occulta, concretio ex elementis et dissolutio in eadem, omnino non cuius quemquam pudeat.

Neque enim ordini animalis intelligendi facultate praediti neque rationi constitutionis nostrae repugnat.

6. Natura ita comparatum est, ut haec non possint non ab huiusmodi hominibus sic fieri.

quod qui non vult, idem ficum vult succo carere.

World, change.

Life, opinion.

If understanding is common to us, also reason, by which we are rational, is common to us.

If these things, even that reason which directs what is to be done, what is not, is common.

If these things, even the law is common.

If these things, we are citizens.

If citizens, participants of a certain state.

If this is the case, the world is like a city: for where else will you find the entire human race participating in another city? Moreover, from this common city, the power of understanding itself, both rational and knowledgeable of the law, comes to us -- but from where? Iust as to me, something earthly is allotted from the earth to a certain extent, and something watery from another element, and something breathable from a certain source, and something warm and fiery from its own specific source – for nothing arises from nothing, iust as nothing is reduced to nothing – likewise, understanding also comes from somewhere.

Death is such a thing, like birth, a hidden action of nature, a concretion from elements and dissolution into the same; altogether, something of which no one should be ashamed.

For neither does it oppose the order of animals endowed with the faculty of understanding nor the reason of our constitution.

Nature is so arranged that these things cannot but happen in this manner to such humans.

One who does not wish for this also wants a fig to be without its sap.

Omnino illius memento, intra brevissimum tempus et te et istum morituros.

Always remember that both you and that person will die within a very short time.

paulo post ne nomina quidem vestra superfutura.

A little while later, not even your names will remain.

7. Tolle opinionem! sublatum est illud: "laesus sum".

Remove the notion! That thought has been removed: 'I have been harmed.'

tolle illud, "laesus sum!" sublatum est damnum.

Remove that, 'I have been harmed!' The loss has been taken away.

8. Quod hominum se ipso deteriorem non reddit, id vitam quoque eius non deteriorem reddit, neque damnum ei infert aut extrinsecus aut intrinsecus.

What does not make a person worse off in himself, also does not make his life worse off, nor does it bring any harm to him, either externally or internally.

9. Utilitatis natura non potest non hoc agere.

The nature of utility cannot fail to act in this way.

10. Quidquid accidit, iuste accidit, idque, si diligenter animadverteris, reperies: non tandum dico secundum id quod consequens est, sed secundum iustitiae rationem, quasi ab aliquo, qui secundum dignitatem distribuat.

Whatever happens, happens iustly, and if you observe carefully, you will find this to be the case. I do not mean only according to what follows, but according to the principle of iustice, as if it were distributed by someone who acts according to worth.

Animadverte igitur diligenter, ut coeperas, et quidquid agis, cum studio bonitatis age, idque eo sensu, quo quis proprie bonus dicitur.

Therefore, observe carefully, as you began, and whatever you do, do it with the pursuit of goodness, and in that sense by which one is properly called good.

Id in omni actione serva.

Maintain this in every action.

11. Noli talia ea opinari, qualia iniuriosus iudicat aut qualia te ea iudicare vult.

Do not think of things as iniurious iudges them, or as those who wish to iudge you think them.

sed vide ea, qualia revera sint.

But see things as they truly are.

12. Duplicem hanc promptitudinem, te habere oportet alteram, ut id tantum agas, quodcunque regiae ac legiferae facultatis ratio suggerit ad utilitatem hominum: alteram, ut sententiam mutes, si forte quis adest, qui eam corrigat et te ab opinione deducat:

You should have a twofold readiness: one, to do only what the reason of royal and legislative authority suggests for the benefit of people; the other, to change your opinion if perhaps someone is present who can correct it and lead you away from misconceptions.

oportet tamen hanc sententiae mutationem oriri a probabili quadam ratione, quasi ita iustum aut communioni utile sit: his similia tantum esse oportet, non quod gratum aut gloriosum videtur.

However, this change of opinion should arise from a reasonable basis, as if it is so just or beneficial for the community; only such things should be considered, not what appears pleasing or glorious.

13. Ratione praeditus es? - sum.

Are you endowed with reason? - I am.

Cur igitur ea non uteris? nam si haec facit, quod suum est, quid aliud desideras?

Why then do you not make use of it? For if it accomplishes what is its own, what else do you desire?

14. Substitisti ut pars.

You have taken your place as a part.

evanesces in eum, qui te generavit, seu potius recipieris in eius rationem seminalem per mutationem.

You will vanish into the one who generated you, or rather you will be received into his seminal reason through transformation.

15. Multae thuris glebulae in eandem aram, alia citius, alia tardius, decidunt: nihil autem interest.

Many grains of incense fall onto the same altar, some more quickly, others more slowly: however, there is no difference.

16. Intra decem dies Deus videberis iis, quibus nunc bestia ac simia, si ad decreta cultumque mentis redieris.

Within ten days, you will appear to those to whom you now appear as a beast and a monkey, if you return to the decrees and culture of the mind.

17. Ne ut qui millia annorum victurus sit.

Not as someone who will live for thousands of years.

fatum impendet.

Fate is approaching.

dum vivis, dum licet, fac bonus fias.

While you live, while it is allowed, become good.

18. Quantum negotii lucrabitur, qui non videt, quid alius dixerit, egerit, cogitarit, sed tantum, quid ipse agat, iustum sit ac pium, aut, ut Agathonis verbis utar, "noli nigros circumspicere mores, sed per lineam curre rectus nec vagus.

How much trouble he will save who does not see what another has said, done, or thought, but only what he himself does, what is just and righteous, or as I might use Agathon's words, "do not look around at the black deeds, but run straight along the line without straying.

19. Qui insana famae posthumae admiratione tenetur, non cogitat, unumquemque eorum, qui eius recordabuntur perbrevi et ipsum esse moriturum.

One who is held by the insane admiration of posthumous fame does not consider that every one of those who will remember him will also die very soon.

postea rursus etiam hunc, qui illum exceperit, donec omnis memoria per eos qui accenduntur et exstinguuntur, progrediens prorsus exstinguatur.

Afterwards, even he, who received that person, will be extinguished, until all memory, passing through those who are kindled and extinguished, is ultimately extinguished.

Fac autem, et illos, qui tui meminerint immortales fore, et immortalem tui memoriam, quid igitur hoc ad te? neque dico, quid ad mortuum, sed ad vivum quid laus, nisi forte dispensationis causa? Praetermittis enim nunc intempestive donum a natura datum, dum alicui rei adhaerescis quam rationi.

But make both those who will remember you immortal, and the immortal memory of yourself. So, what does this have to do with you? I'm not saying, what does it have to do with the dead, but what praise is there for the living, unless perhaps for the sake of distribution? For you are neglecting the gift given by nature, while you cling to something other than reason.

Reliquum.

The rest.

20. Quidquid quacunque tandem ratione pulcrum est, id per se pulcrum est, et in se terminatur nec partem sui habet laudem.

Whatever is beautiful by any reasoning, is beautiful in itself and is self-contained, having no part in need of praise.

Igitur certe neque deterius neque melius fit laudando.

Therefore, certainly, nothing becomes worse or better by being praised.

Atque hoc dico etiam de iis, quae vulgari usu pulcra dicuntur, ut de rebus corporeis et artificum operibus.

And I say this even about those things which are commonly considered beautiful, like physical objects and works of craftsmen.

Quod revera pulcrum, id scilicet laude indigeat? non magis quam lex.

Does what is truly beautiful, of course, need praise? No more than the law.

non magis, quam veritas.

No more than truth.

non magis, quam benevolentia aut verecundia.

No more than kindness or modesty.

Ecquid horum idcirco, quod laudatur, pulcrum est, aut eo, quod vituperatur.

Does any of these, just because it is praised, become beautiful, or that which is criticized is corrupted?

Corrumpitur? Smaragdus enim num se ipso deterior fit, si non laudatur? Quid vero aurum, ebur, purpura, lyra, gladiolus, flosculus, arbuscula?

Is it corrupted? Does an emerald become worse in itself if it is not praised? And what about gold, ivory, purple, a lyre, a little sword, a little flower, a little tree?

21. Si permanent animae, quo modo eas ab aeterno capit aer? - Quo modo vero terra capit corpora eorum, qui ab aevo tam immenso sepulti sunt? Quemadmodum enim hic corporum, postquam ad certum quoddam tempus permanserunt, mutatio et dissolutio aliis cadaveribus locum dat.

If souls endure, how does air capture them from eternity? - And how does the earth indeed capture the bodies of those who have been buried from such an immense time ago? Just as here, after bodies have persisted for a certain time, change and dissolution make room for other corpses.

sic animae, quae in aerem transferuntur, postquam aliquandiu diu perstiterunt, mutantur et funduntur et succenduntur in seminalem universitatis rationem receptae, eoque pacis iis, quae in easdem sedes recipiuntur, locum faciunt.

Similarly, souls, when they are transferred into the air, after having persisted for a while, are changed and dispersed and mingled into the seminal principle of the universe, and they make room for the harmonious order of those who are received into the same places.

Hoc igitur aliquis respondere possit posito hoc, animas permanere.

Therefore, someone might respond, assuming this, that souls endure.

Nequae vero solum reputanda est multitudo corporum sic sepultorum, sed etiam aliorum animalium, quae quotidie comeduntur et a nobis et ab aliis animantibus: quantus enim numerus consumitur et hoc modo quasi sepelitur in corporibus eorum, qui iis aluntur? et tamen ea regio illa recipit, dum partim in sanguinem, partim in aeriam igneamve materiam mutantur.

Yet, not only the multitude of bodies thus buried should be considered, but also the other animals which are consumed daily by us and by other living creatures: for what a number is consumed and in this way, as it were, buried in the bodies of those who feed on them? And yet, that region receives them, as they are partly transformed into blood, and partly into airy or fiery matter.

Quaenam hac in re veritatis explorandae ratio? Divisio in materiam et formam.

What method should be used to explore the truth in this matter? Division into matter and form.

22. Noli divagari, sed in omni agendi impetu id quod iustum est praesta, et in omni viso tene id quod comprehendi potest.

Do not wander, but in all your endeavors, present what is just, and in all your observations, hold onto what can be understood.

23. Quidquid tibi bene convenit, Munde, id mihi convenit: nihil mihi immaturum, nihil serum, quod tibi tempestivam.

Whatever suits you well, World, suits me well; nothing is untimely for me, nothing late, that is timely for you.

Quidquid tuae, Natura, ferunt Horae, mihi fructus.

Whatever the Seasons, Nature, bring forth, are fruits for me.

ex te omnia, in te omnia, ad te omnia.

From you all, in you all, to you all.

Ille ait: "O cara civitas Cecropis!" tune: "O cara civitas Iovis!" inquies?

He says: "Oh beloved city of Cecrops!" Then you might say: "Oh beloved city of Iupiter!"?

24. "Pauca age," inquit ille, "si vis tranquillo animo esse!" Nescio an melius sit "necessaria agere omniaque ea, quae ratio animalis socialis exigit eoque modo, quo exigit.

"Speak briefly," he says, "if you want to have a tranquil mind!" I don't know whether it is better to "deal with necessary things and all those things which the reasoning of a social being requires, and in the manner that it requires.

Hoc enim non solum animi tranquillitatem affert, quae a bene agendo gignitur, sed etiam eam, quae a pauca agendo oritur.

For this not only brings about the tranquility of the mind, which is produced by acting well, but also that which arises from doing few things.

Si quis enim plurima eorum, quae dicimus et facimus, utpote non necessaria, sustulerit, et otiosior erit et minus turbatus.

For if someone removes many of those things that we say and do, as they are unnecessary, they will be both more at leisure and less disturbed.

Quare oportet in singulis se ipsum commonefacere, numquid haec sint ex iis, quae non necessaria sunt.

Therefore, it is necessary for us to remind ourselves in each instance whether these things are among those that are not necessary.

Oportet nos autem non solum actiones non necessarias tollere, verum etiam visa: nam sic neque actiones supervacaneae subsequentur.

But it is necessary for us not only to remove unnecessary actions, but also unnecessary opinions: for in this way, unnecessary actions will not follow.

25. Fac periculum, quomodo tibi procedat vita boni hominis, eius, qui iis, quae ex universitate rerum ipsi attribuuntur, contentus est atque in iusta sua actione et benevola mentis affectione acquiescit.

Make an experiment with how the life of a good person proceeds for you, the person who is content with those things which are assigned to them by the totality of things, and who acquiesces in their proper action and benevolent mental disposition.

26. Vidisti illa? Vide etiam haec: te ipsum ne conturbes.

You have seen those things? Also see these things: do not disturb yourself.

simplicem te redde.

Make yourself simple.

Peccat aliquis? sibi ipsi peccat.

Does someone commit a fault? He does it to himself.

Accidit tibi aliquid? bene habet.

Did something happen to you? It's well.

ex rerum universitate tibi inde ab initio erat destinatum et quasi nendo connexum id quod accidit.

From the outset, that was destined for you from the universe of things and connected as if by a thread to what happened.

Summa eo redit: brevis vita.

The ultimate conclusion is this: life is short.

lucrandum quod instat tempus considerate et iuste agendo.

Work to gain what the present time requires, by acting thoughtfully and justly.

sobrius esto in animo remittendo.

Be sober in mind by relaxing.

27. Aut consilio dispositus mundus, aut cinnus, fortuito congestus, at mundus tamen.

Either the world is arranged by design, or it's a heap of chance, but still it's the world.

an vero fieri potest, ut in te mundus consistat, in universitate rerum autem mera confusio? praesertim omnibus sic discretis et diffusis et tamen consentientibus!

Can it really be that the world exists within you, while in the universe of things, it's mere confusion? Especially when everything is so distinct and diffused, yet still harmonious!

28. Nigri mores, effeminati mores, praefracti mores, belluini, pecuini, pueriles, stolidi, subdoli, scurriles, perfidi, tyrannici.

Ways of being dark, ways of being effeminate, ways of being stubborn, ways of being brutish, ways of being like cattle, ways of being childish, ways of being foolish, ways of being deceitful, ways of being vulgar, ways of being treacherous, ways of being tyrannical.

29. Si peregrinus mundi is est, qui ignorat ea, quae in mundo sunt, non minus peregrinus etiam is est, qui ignorat, quae fiunt: profugus, qui rationem civilem fugit.

If someone is a stranger to the world, who is ignorant of the things in the world, he is no less a stranger who is ignorant of what is happening: a fugitive who flees civil reasoning.

caecus, qui mentis oculos clausos habet: egenus, qui alius indiget neque in se habet, quibus ad vitam opus est: abscessus mundi, qui abscedit seseque a naturae communis ratione seiungit eo, quod iis, quae eveniunt, offenditur.

Blind, who has his mental eyes closed; needy, who needs something else and doesn't have it within himself, what is necessary for life; departed from the world, who separates himself from the common reasoning of nature and is offended by what happens.

illa enim hoc fert, quae te quoque tulit: avulsus a civitate, qui suam animam ab anima ratione praeditorum, utpote una, avellit.

For it brings forth what brought forth you too: one who is separated from the community, who tears his own soul away from the rational soul, as if it's one.

30. Hic sine tunica philosophatur, ille sine libro, iste tertius seminudus.

This one philosophizes without a tunic, that one without a book, the third almost naked.

"Pane careo," inquit, "et tamen in ratione persisto."

"I lack bread," he says, "and yet I persist in reason."

"Ego vero victum ex disciplinis non quaero et tamen persisto.

3 1 . Artem, quam didicisti, diligito et in ea acquiesceto: quod autem vitae super est, id ita exigito, ut qui Deo omnia ex toto animo commiseris, neque ullius hominis aut dominum aut servum te praebeto.

3 2 . Cogita, verbi gratia, tempora sub Vespasiani imperio acta, et videbis haec omnia: homines matrimonia ineun tes, liberos alentes, morbis laborantes, morientes, militantes, festa celebrantes, negotiantes, agros colentes, adulantes insolenter se gerentes, suspicantes, insidiantes, mortem quorundam exoptantes, murmurantes de praesenti rerum statu, amori indulgentes, thesauros colligentes, consulatum, imperium affectantes: nusquam profecto amplius eorum vita.

Rursus ad Traiani tempora transi: rursus eadem omnia.

haec quoque vita interiit.

Similiter et iam alios quasi titulos sepulcrales temporum totarumque gentium contemplare et vide, quam multi eorum, post summam virium contentionem, paulo post occiderint et in elementa dissoluti sint.

Potissimum autem ruminandi sunt ii, quos ipse novisti rebus vanis distractos id agere neglexisse, quod propriae eorum constitutioni conveniebat, huic firmiter adhaerescere, hoc contentos esse.

"But I, on the other hand, do not seek sustenance from teachings, and yet I persist."

Love the skill you have acquired and be content in it; however, for what remains of life, demand it in such a way that having entrusted everything to God with all your heart, you do not make yourself a slave or servant to any man or master.

Think, for example, about the times that passed under the rule of Vespasian, and you will see all these things: people entering marriages, raising children, suffering from illnesses, dying, fighting, celebrating festivals, doing business, cultivating fields, insolently carrying themselves with flattery, being suspicious, plotting, desiring the deaths of certain individuals, complaining about the present state of affairs, indulging in love, amassing wealth, aspiring to consulships and empires: nowhere does their life continue.

Again, move on to the times of Traian: once again, all the same things.

This life has also passed away.

Likewise, consider other, as it were, epitaphs of time and whole nations, and see how many of them, after the highest exertion of their strength, have died shortly after and dissolved into the elements.

However, above all, those should be contemplated who you yourself know to have been distracted by vain matters, neglecting to do what was suitable to their own nature, not firmly adhering to this, and being content with that.

Necesse autem est, hac a re illius memineris, diligentiam in singulis actionibus collocandam suam ac propriam habere dignitatem ac mensuram.

However, it is necessary that you remember this: you must allocate diligence in each action, having its own proper worth and measure.

Ita enim fiet, ut non omnem spem abiicias, quum non plus quam par est in rebus minoribus versatus fueris.

In this way, it will come about that you do not cast away all hope, when you have not been excessively engaged in minor matters.

Ita igitur nomina quoque eorum, qui olim longe clarissimi fuerunt nunc quodammodo glossemata sunt, Camillus, Caeso, Volesus, Leonnatus.

So, even the names of those who were once greatly renowned have now in a manner become glosses: Camillus, Caeso, Volesus, Leonnatus.

paulo post etiam Scipio et Cato: postea Augustus quoque.

Shortly thereafter, even Scipio and Cato: later on, Augustus as well.

postea etiam Hadrianus et Antoninus.

Afterwards, Hadrian and Antoninus as well.

Evanida enim omnia et cito in fabulas abeunt, cito plena oblivione obruuntur.

For all things fade away and quickly pass into myths, quickly buried under full oblivion.

Atque hoc dico de iis, qui admirabiliter quodammodo splenduerunt.

And I say this about those who in a certain way shone admirably.

Reliqui enim, simul at exspirarant, "ignoti nec fando auditi.

For the rest, as soon as they had breathed their last, "unknown and never heard of."

"Quid autem est aeterna memoria? nil nisi vanitas.

But what is eternal memory? Nothing but vanity.

Quid igitur est, in quo studium collocari oportet? Hoc unum, mens iusta et actiones communioni accommodatae et sermo mendacii ex et animi adfectio prompta ad amplectendum quidquid contingit ut necessarium, ut familiare, ut ab eiusmodi principio et fonte promanans.

So, what is it in which effort should be invested? One thing: a just mind, actions suited to the common good, and speech free from deception, with a disposition of the soul ready to embrace whatever happens as necessary, as familiar, as flowing from such a principle and source.

34. Parcae sponte te praebe, permittens, ut te quibuscumque tandem libuerit rebus innendo nectat.

The Fates willingly offer you, allowing you to be woven into whatever circumstances it pleases.

35. Unius diei et quod commemorat et quod commemoratur.

Of a single day, both what it recalls and what is recalled.

36. Continuo contemplare, omnia mutatione fieri, adsuesce intelligere, nihil neque diligere universitatis naturam atque ea, quae sunt, mutare et nova similia efficere: semen enim quodammodo quidquid est eius, quod ex eo oriturum est: tu vero ea tantum semina opinaris, quae in terram aut uterum sparguntur.

Continuously contemplate that everything undergoes change; accustom yourself to understand that nothing of the nature of the universe remains constant, and that it transforms and creates new things that are similar. For in a sense, everything is like the seed of whatever will arise from it. Yet you believe only those things to be seeds which are sown into the earth or the womb.

id autem est hominis admodum rudis et imperiti.

However, this is a very naive and unskilled way of thinking.

37. Iamiam morieris, et nondum firmus nec imperturbatus es nec liber suspicione, extrinsecus damnum tibi adferri posse, nec propitius omnibus neque is, qui prudentiam non nisi in iuste agendo positam existimes.

Very soon you will die, and yet you are not yet firm, not untroubled, nor free from the suspicion that harm can be brought to you from external sources, nor are you benevolent to all, nor do you believe that wisdom exists only in acting justly.

38. Mentes eorum intuere, adeoque prudentissimos, qualia fugiant, qualia sectentur.

Observe the minds of others, and even the most wise among them— what they avoid and what they pursue.

39. In alterius mente malum tuum non situm est, neque vero in quodam motu aut mutatione eius, quod te ambit.

The harm to you is not situated in another person's mind, nor is it truly in some movement or change of theirs that surrounds you.

Ubi igitur? ubi tibi id est quod de malis opinatur: id igitur ne opinetur, et omnia bene habent: etiamsi, quod huic proximum est, corpusculum secetur, uratur, suppuretur.

So where is it? Where you think that evil resides. Therefore, let it not think so, and all things are well. Even if, which is closest to this, your body is cut, burned, or oozes pus, putrefies— yet whatever opinion you have about these things, let that opinion rest.

putrescat, id tamen, quod de istis opinatur, quiescat, hoc est, iudicet nec malum esse nec bonum, quod similiter viro bono et malo accidere potest: quod enim ei, qui contra naturam, et ei, qui secundum naturam vivit, similiter contingit, id neque secundum naturam neque contra naturam est.

Even if it putrefies, yet let that which it thinks about these things remain at rest. That is, let it judge that it is neither evil nor good, which can similarly happen to both a good and a bad person. For what occurs in a similar way to someone who lives against nature and someone who lives according to nature is neither against nature nor according to nature.

40. Ut unum animal uno corpore et una anima praeditum continuo contemplari mundum: et quomodo in unum huiusce sensum omnia digerantur.

To continuously contemplate the world as one living being with one body and one soul, and how all things are arranged within the senses of this single being.

et quomodo uno impetu omnia agat.

And how all things act with a single impulse.

et quomodo omnia cum omnibus, quae fiunt, ut partes causarum cohaereant, et qualis quidem hic sit connexus et contextus.

And how all things, along with everything that happens, cohere as parts of causes, and what kind of connection and context this is.

41. Animula es, cadaver gestans, ut Epictetus dicebat.

You are a small soul, carrying a body, as Epictetus used to say.

42. Nil mali est rebus mutationem subeuntibus.

There is no harm in things undergoing change.

ut neque boni quidquam iis, quae per mutationem existunt.

Neither is there any good in things that arise through change.

43. Fluvius quidem eorum, quae fiunt, et rapidus torrens est aevum.

The river of things that happen is like a swift torrent of time.

simul atque quidquam comparuit, etiam abreptum est, et aliud abripitur et illud inferetur.

As soon as something appears, it is also swept away. and another is swept away, and that which is coming is carried along.

44. Quidquid accidit, tam consuetum est et familiare, quam rosa vere et fructus tempore messis.

Whatever happens is as customary and familiar as the true rose and the fruit of the harvest season.

Eiusdem enim generis est morbus, et mors, et infamia, et insidiae, et omnia, quae stultos hilares aùt tristes reddunt.

For of the same kind are disease, death, disgrace, deceit, and everything that makes fools cheerful or sad.

45. Subsquentia semper antecedentibus familiari quadam ratione succedunt: non enim est quasi computatio disiunctim et id tantum quod numerando coactum est continens, sed connexio rationi consentanea: et quemadmodum ea, quae sunt, convenienter sunt ordinata, sic ea, quae fiunt, non nudam successionem, sed admirabilem quandam familiaritatem prae se ferunt.

The things that follow always follow the things that go before in a certain familiar manner. It is not like a computation composed of distinct parts, only containing what has been counted, but a connection consistent with reason. And iust as the things that exist are appropriately ordered, the things that happen bear before them not mere succession, but an admirable kind of familiarity.

46. Semper Heraclitei meminisse: terrae mortem fieri aquam, aquae mortem fieri aerem, aeris ignem, et retro.

Meminisse vero etiam illius, qui, qua ducat via, obliviscitur et qua potissimum perpetuo familiariter utantur ratione rerum universitatem administrante, cum ea eos dissidere, et, in quae quotidie incidant ea ipsis videri peregrina: porro, non oportere nos instar dormientium agere et loqui, nam etiam tum nobis videmur agere et loqui, - neque instar liberorum parentibus obnoxiorum, quorum est illud: "simpliciter, prout accepimus.

Always remember Heraclitus: that earth becomes water, water becomes air, and air becomes fire, and vice versa.

But also remember that person who, forgetting which path to take, fails to use the universal reason perpetually at hand, causing them to be at odds with it, and things they encounter every day to seem foreign to them. We must not act and speak as if we were asleep, for even then we appear to ourselves to be acting and speaking—nor should we be like children who are dependent on their parents, saying, "Simply as we have been taught."

47. Quemadmodum si quis Deus tibi diceret cras aut ad summum perendie te moriturum, non amplius magni faceres, perendie potius, quam cras, obire, nisi abiectissimi esses animi: quantulum enim est intervallum? sic quoque certo aliquo anno e multis potius, quam crastino die, mori magnum esse noli existimare.

Just as if some god were to tell you that you will die tomorrow or at the latest the day after, you wouldn't be much more concerned about the day after than about tomorrow, unless you were of very base character. For what is the difference? In the same way, think it no great thing to die many years hence rather than tomorrow.

48. Perpetuo reputare: quam multi medici occubuerunt, qui saepe super aegrotis supercilia contraxerant, quot mathematici, qui aliorum mortem ut rem magnam praedixerant! quot philosopi, qui de morte et immortalitate acerrime et copiosissime disseruerant! quot bellatores, qui multos peremerant! quot tyranni, qui vitae necisque potestate horribili cum fastu tanquam immortales usi erant! quot urbes ut ita dicam, emortuae sunt, Helice et Pompeii et Herculanum et aliae innumerabiles! Adde quos ipse novisti, qui alium post alium, postquam hic illius exsequias curavit: et ipse elatus est, alius alium, atque haec omnia brevi tempore.

To continually reflect: how many physicians have died, who had furrowed their brows over the sick; how many astrologers, who had foretold the deaths of others as a great event; how many philosophers, who had argued most keenly and extensively about death and immortality; how many warriors, who had killed many; how many tyrants, who had used with dreadful pride the power of life and death as if they were immortal; how many cities, so to speak, have died – Helice, Pompeii, Herculaneum, and countless others! Add to this those whom you know yourself, who each after performing another's funeral, were laid out for their own, and in their turn were mourned; and all these things happened in a short space of time.

Summa est: semper humana spectari oportere ut in unum diem durantia et vilia, fieri mucum, oras salsuram aut favillam: hoc quod puncti instar obtinet tempus naturae convenienter transigere et aequo animo hinc discedere, perinde atque oliva maturitatem adepta decideret, genitricem [terram] collaudans arborique gignenti gratias agens.

In summary: it is necessary to consider human affairs always as fleeting and insignificant, like the foam, the salty froth, or the ashes; this moment, which occupies the space of a mere point, passes in harmony with nature and departing from it with a tranquil mind, just as a ripe olive falls when it has reached maturity, praising the tree that bore it and giving thanks to the mother earth from which it sprang.

49. Promontorii instar esse, ad quod fluctus perpetuo alliduntur: illud autem consistit et circa se maris aestum compescit.

To be like a promontory to which the waves are constantly crashing; however, it stands firm and contains the surges of the sea around itself.

"O me infelicem, cui hoc acciderit!" Minime vero, sed "O me beatum, qui, quum hoc mihi acciderit, sine dolore vivam, neque a praesente ictu vulneratus, neque futuri metuens!" Nam tale quid accidere poterat cuivis sed non quivis, si hoc ei accidisset, dolore vacuus mansisset.

"Oh, unfortunate me, to whom this has happened!" Not at all, but "Oh, fortunate me, who, when this happens to me, will live without pain, neither wounded by the present blow nor fearing the future!" For such a thing could happen to anyone, but not to everyone; if it had happened to someone, they would have remained free from pain.

Quare igitur illud infortunium potius, quam hoc felicitas! Num omnino id infortunium vocas, quo hominis fortuna non frustratur? hominis ne natura frustrari tibi videtur eo, quod non contra voluntatem naturae eius fit?

Why then call that misfortune rather than this happiness? Do you consider it misfortune when a person's fortune is not frustrated? Doesn't it seem to you that a person's nature is not frustrated when something is not done against the will of that nature?

Quid igitur? Voluntatem nosti: num igitur id quod tibi accidit, te impediet, quominus iustus sis, magnanimus, temperans, prudens, ab assentiendi temeritate alienus, erroris immunis verecundus, liber ceterisque virtutibus onatus, quae quando adsunt, natura hominis habet sibi propria?

What then? You know your own will. Will what has happened to you prevent you from being just, magnanimous, temperate, prudent, free from rash assent, immune to error, modest, and possessed of the other virtues that are truly proper to human nature when they are present?

Quod reliquum est, memento in omni re, quae ad dolorem te impellit illius decreti, id non esse infortunium, sed generose id ferre esse felicitatem.

As for the rest, remember in every situation that prompts you to feel pain, that it is not misfortune but rather a mark of true happiness to bear it nobly, in accordance with your own principles.

50. Plebeium quidem, efficax tamen est adiumentum ad mortem contemnendam, memoria recolere eos qui vitae pertinaciter inhaesere.

Quid igitur plus est iis, quam immature defunctis? Omnino alicubi iacent Caecidianus, Fabius, Iulianus, Lepidus aut si quis alius eius generis est, quum multos extulissent, et ipsi elati sunt! Omnino parvum alicubi est intervallum, idque per quot casus et cum quibus hominibus et quali in corpusculo exantlatum.

Ne igitur quasi magnum aliquid.

Considera enim praeteriti aevi immensitatem, futuri itidem alium immensitatem! in hoc vero quid differt, qui triduum vixit, ab eo, qui per tria hominum saecula vitam extraxit?

51. Ad compendiariam semper fac curras: compendiaria autem, quae secundum naturam est, ita ut ad sanissimam rationem quidquid loquaris et facias.

Tale enim propositum te molestiis liberabit et militia et omni dissimulatione et vafritie.

Indeed, it might be considered common, yet it is still an effective aid in despising death to recall those who have clung tenaciously to life.

So, what more do they have than those who died prematurely? Somewhere, Caecidianus, Fabius, Iulianus, Lepidus, or someone similar, lie buried, having carried many others, yet they themselves were carried away! Altogether, there is a small gap somewhere, extended through various occurrences, with different people, and in what kind of body.

So, not something great then.

For consider the vastness of past ages, and similarly the vastness of future ages! In this, what difference is there between someone who lived for three days and someone who lived through three human centuries?

Always aim for a concise path: and let that path be in accordance with nature, so that in all your words and actions, you adhere to the soundest reasoning.

Indeed, such a purpose will free you from troubles, warfare, pretense, and all forms of cunning.

LIBER V

HARMONIA UNIVERSI

I .

Mane, quum gravatim expergisceris, promptum sit hoc: ad hominis opus expergiscor: quid igitur moleste fero, quod pergo ad ea agenda, quorum causa natus sum, quorum causa in mundum veni? an vero ad hoc natus sum, ut in stragulis decumbens me foveam.

In the morning, when you wake up with a heavy heart, let this be ready: I wake up for a human task. Why then do I take offense? I continue towards the tasks for which I was born, for the sake of which I came into the world. Or was I born for this, to lie in bed and indulge myself?

At hoc magis delectat.

But this is more enjoyable.

Ad delectationem igitur natus es, non ad agendum seu opus faciendum?

Are you born then for pleasure, not for action or for work?

Videsne arbusculas, passerculos, formicas, araneas, apes, quum quod sui officii est, faciant, suum exornantes mundum?

Do you not see the little trees, sparrows, ants, spiders, bees, as they do what is their duty, adorning their part of the world?

itane tu ea, quae hominum sunt, Facere recusas? non properas ad id, quod secundum tuam naturam est?

So, do you refuse to do what is human? Do you not hasten to do what is according to your nature?

Verum etiam quiete opus est. Est. dedit tamen etiam huius mensuram natura.

But there is also a need for rest. Yes, there is. However, nature has also given a measure for this.

Dedit item mensuram edendi ac bibendi et tu tamen ultra mensuram, ultra ea, quae sufficiunt, progrederis.

And also, nature gave a measure for eating and drinking, and yet you still go beyond the measure, beyond what is sufficient.

in agendo autem non ulterius, sed intra id, quod fieri potest: nam te ipsum non diligis.

But in your actions, not beyond, but within what is possible: for you do not love yourself.

alioquin etiam naturam tuam eiusque voluntatem diligeres.

Otherwise, you would also love your own nature and its will.

Atque ii quidem, qui artes suas diligunt, earum operibus intabescunt, illoti et impransi.

And indeed, those who love their skills waste away on their works, unkempt and unfed.

tu naturam tuam minoris facis , quam tornator tornariam , quam saltator saltardi artem, quam avarus argentum, quam ambitiosus gloriolam.

You diminish your own nature more than a woodworker his lathe, a dancer his dance, a miser his money, an ambitious person his little glory.

Etiam hi, ubi his addicti sunt, neque cibum nec somnum magis capere expetunt, quam ea amplificare, quae ipsos delectant.

Even those who are devoted to these pursuits do not seek food or sleep more eagerly than they seek to amplify the things that delight them.

tibi autem actiones ad societatem perinentes viliores esse videntur et minore studio dignae?

Do actions related to social interaction seem less valuable to you and deserving of less effort?

2 . Quam facile, amoliri et abstergere visum quodvis vel molestiam excitans vel societati repugnans, et statim in summa tranquillitate esse.

How easy it is to dispel and wipe away any appearance that arouses annoyance or conflicts with society, and immediately be in the highest tranquility.

3 . Dignum te habeto quovis sermone et opere naturae conveniente, neque te avertat quae sequatur quorundam vituperatio aut sermo, si factu dictuve pulcrum est, noli te eo indignum iudicare: illi enim sua utuntur mente suoque ducuntur impetu.

Consider yourself worthy in every discourse and action that is in harmony with nature, and let neither the criticism nor the words of certain individuals turn you away. If something is beautiful in deed or in speech, do not judge yourself unworthy of it. They are guided by their own thoughts and driven by their own impulses.

haec tu noli circumspicere, sed recta perge, naturae et propriae et communi obsequens: una et eadem utriusque via.

Do not dwell on these things, but proceed straight ahead, obedient to your own nature as well as to the universal nature; for both paths lead to the same destination.

4 .

Proficiscor per ea, quae secundum naturam sunt, donec occumbens requiescam, in id animam exspirans, inde quotidie spiritum haurio et in id cadena, unde pater semen collegit, sanguinem mater, nutrix lac.

I journey through things in accordance with nature, until I rest by falling asleep, breathing out my last breath into that element, and each day I draw in the breath of life and am sustained by that source from which my father gathered the seed, my mother the blood, and my nurse the milk.

unde ex tot annis pascor et potor, quod me fert calcantem eoque ad tot res abutentem.

From which I have been nourished and sustained for so many years, and to which I am carried as I walk and on which I rely for so many things.

5 .

Ingenii tui acumen non est, quod admirentur.

The sharpness of your intellect is not something to be admired.

Sit ita.

So be it.

Verum multa alla sunt, ad quae te natura aptum esse negare non possis: haec igitur praesta, quae tota in tua sunt potestate, sinceritatem, gravitatem, laborum tolerantiam, voluptatibus abstinere, de sorte non queri, paucis indigere, benevolum esse, liberum, a luxuria, nugis et magnificentia alienum.

Certainly, there are many other things to which you cannot deny being suited by nature. Therefore, provide those qualities which are entirely in your power: sincerity, seriousness, endurance of hardships, abstinence from pleasures, not complaining about fate, needing little, being kind, free from excess, trivialities, and extravagance.

Sentisne, ad quam multa praestanda viribus pollens, ita ut, quin habilis aptusque sis, nihil sit, quod causeris, tamen adhuc infra ea sponte consistas? Num etiam murmurare et tenacem esse et adulari et corpusculum incusare et assentari et te ostentare et tot res animo volutare per naturalem ingenii hebetitudinem cogeris? Non, per Deos.

Do you feel how much there is to achieve, being capable of so much, that even though you are skillful and suitable, there's nothing to complain about, yet you still willingly remain below those standards? Are you compelled to grumble, be stubborn, flatter, blame your own body, agree with everything, show off, and constantly ponder so many things due to the dullness of your natural abilities? No, by the gods.

non.

No.

Sed his omnibus iampridem liber esse potuisti, et tantum, si modo, propter ingenii tarditatem et hebetudinem notari.

But you could have been free from all these things a long time ago, and only, if at all, been criticized for the slowness and dullness of your abilities.

Verum etiam in hoc te exerce, nec tarditatem illam negligens neque in ea tibi placens.

Indeed, also practice this, not neglecting that slowness and not finding pleasure in it either.

6. Alius simul atque gratum alicui aliquid fecit, promptus est ad beneficium illi in accepta referendum.

Another, as soon as they have done something pleasing to someone, is ready to expect a favor in return for the favor they have given.

Alius ad id non promptus est, ceterum tamen apud se ut de debitore cogitat et novit, quod fecit: alius quodammodo ne novit quidem, quod fecit, sed similis est viti, quae uvam protulit et nihil praeterea appetit, postquam semel fructum suum genuit.

Another is not quick to expect anything in return, but still keeps in mind and knows within themselves what they have done. Yet another almost doesn't even realize what they have done, but is like a grapevine that produces its grapes and desires nothing more once it has borne its fruit.

Ut equus, qui cucurrit.

Like a horse that has run its course.

Ut canis, qui feras investigavit.

Like a dog that has tracked down its prey.

Ut apis, quae mel confecit, ita homo qui bene fecit, uon clamore rem extollit, sed ad aliud transit, ut vitis ad uvam iterum, suo tempore gignendam.

Like a bee that has made honey, so too does a person who has done well not boast with loud praise, but moves on to another task, like a vine returning to its grape to bring forth fruit in its proper time.

Inter hos igitur esse oportet, qui quod agunt, ipsi nesciunt?

Indeed, among these must be those who do what they do without even knowing it themselves?

Oportet.

- It is necessary.

At hoc ipsum intelligere fas est: nam proprium est (inquit) illius, qui ad communionem natus est, ut sentiat, se quemadmodum societatis amantem decet agere, immo etiam velit, socius id sentiat.

But it is indeed permissible to understand this itself: for it is the nature of one who is born for social interaction to feel that they ought to act as befits a lover of society, and even more so, to desire that their fellow beings perceive them as such.

Verum quidem est, quod dicis, sed hoc dictum non recte accipis.

What you say is true indeed, but you are not understanding this statement correctly.

Hinc unus eris ex iis, quorum antea mentionem feci: nam hi quoque rationali quadam probabilitate ducuntur.

From this, you will be one of those whom I mentioned earlier, for they too are led by a certain rational probability.

Quod si intelligere volueris, quid tandem hoc dictum sibi velit, uoli timere, ne hac de causa quidquam, quod societati prodest, praetermittas.

And if you wish to understand what this statement means, be careful not to neglect anything that benefits society for fear of this.

7. Votum Atheniensium: "Pluviam, pluviam da, care Iupiter, arvis et pratis Atheniensium!" aut non oportet precari, aut sic, simpliciter et ingenue.

The Athenians' prayer: "Rain, rain, dear Iupiter, on the fields and meadows of the Athenians!" Either one should not pray, or do so in this way: sincerely and straightforwardly.

8. Cuiusmodi id est, quod vulgo dicunt, "Aesculapium huic vel illi, ut equitet aut frigida lavetur aut nudis pedibus incedat, constituisse.

It is of the sort that people commonly say, "Asklepios has prescribed for this person or that, to ride a horse or take a cold bath or walk barefoot."

"eiusmodi est etiam hoc, "naturam huic vel illi, ut aegrotet, ut membris mutiletur, ut suos amittat aut aliud eius generis constituisse.

"Likewise, it is of this nature: 'Nature has prescribed for this person or that, to fall ill, to have limbs amputated, to lose loved ones, or to experience other such things.'"

"nam et illic "constituisse" huiusmodi aliquid significat, "statuisse" huic illud [Aesculapium] ut sanitati conveniens, et hic quod cuique contingit, illi aliquo modo statuum esse, ut fato consentaneum.

Indeed, there 'constituting' signifies something of this kind: 'designating' for this person the fitting state of health, and here that whatever befalls each individual is in some manner ordained, as befitting their fate.

ita enim haec quoque nobis "contingere" dicimus, ut lapides quadratos in muris aut pyramidibus "contingere" dicunt artifices, quum sibi inter se quadam positione coaptantur.

For we also say that these things 'happen' to us in such a way that craftsmen, for example, call squared stones in walls or pyramids 'to happen,' when they are fitted together in a certain arrangement.

Omnino concentus est unus.

Indeed, there is one harmony.

et quemadmodum cunctis corporibus hic mundus, quo eiusmodi corpus sit, perficitur, ita ex universis Causis, ut huiusmodi causa sit, fatum perficitur.

And just as the world is constituted from all bodies, in a manner befitting its nature, so fate is constituted from all causes as a cause of this kind.

Intelligunt hoc, quod dico, etiam imperitissimi quique.

Even the most ignorant understand what I'm saying.

dicunt enim, "tulit hoc illi.

For they say, "This happened to him.

"Hoc igitur illi" ferebatur " et hoc "illi constituebatur.

So this was happening to him" and "this was being arranged for him.

"Accipiamus igitur haec ut ea quae Aesculapius "constituit".

So let us accept these as things that Aesculapius 'arranged'.

Multa enim etiam in his aspera sunt, quae tamen sanitatis spe amplectimur.

For many things even in these [difficulties] are rough, yet we embrace them with hope for health.

Eiusmodi igitur aliquid tibi videatur perfectio et absolutio eorum, quae naturae communi visa sunt, cuiusmodi est bona tua valetudo.

Therefore, something of this kind may appear to you as the completion and fulfillment of those things which have been deemed common to nature, such as your good health.

Et ita quidquid evenit, etiamsi asperum videatur, amplectere, quoniam eo tendit, ad mundi sanitatem et Iovis prosperitatem et felicitatem: non enim id cuiquam ferret, nisi ad universi bonum conferret: neque enim natura ubique obvia quidquam fert, quod rei a se administratae non consentaneum est.

And thus, whatever happens, even if it appears harsh, embrace it, for it tends toward the health of the world, the prosperity of Jupiter, and happiness. For it would not befall anyone if it did not contribute to the good of the whole, for nature does not provide anything everywhere that is not consistent with its own administration.

Duae igitur sunt rationes, cur singulari quodam amoris adfectu quidquid evenerit id amplecti te oporteat: altera, quod tibi factum est, tibi constitutum erat, certa quadam ratione ad te se habebat, inde a principio ex causis antiquissimis tibi contextum:

Therefore, there are two reasons why you should embrace with a particular affection of love whatever has happened: the first is that what has occurred to you was destined for you, had a certain connection to you in a definite manner, and was interwoven with you from the very beginning through the most ancient causes.

Altera, quod etiam id, quod singulis quibusque privatim contingit, naturae universitatem administranti in causa est prosperitatis et perfectionis et utique ipsius conservationis: mutilatur enim integrum ipsum, si vel minimum, ut partium, ita et rerum efficientium abscindas abscindis autem, quantum in te est, quando moleste fers aliquid et quodammodo tollis.

The other reason is that even what befalls individuals privately contributes to the overall management of nature, being a cause of prosperity, perfection, and certainly of its own preservation. For the whole is marred if, even in the slightest degree, you cut off—just as from parts—so from efficient causes; yet, as much as lies in your power, you cut off when you bear something with resentment and in a manner remove it.

9 .

Noli fastidire aut animum despondere aut desperare, si tibi secundum recta decreta singula agere cupienti non perinde semper res successerit.

Do not disdain, deiect your spirit, or despair if things do not always turn out as planned when you are striving to act according to right decisions.

Sed deturbatus iterum regredere et contentus esto, si plura homine digniora edideris et id, ad quod reversus es, fac diligas.

But if you are disheartened, return again and be content, if you have achieved more things worthy of a human being, and love what you have returned to do.

Neque tanquam ad paedagogum redi ad philosophiam, sed, ut qui oculis laborant ad penicillum et ovum, ut alius ad emplastrum, alius ad perfusionem: sic nihil * te mordebit obsequium rationi praestandum, sed in eo acquiesces.

And do not return to philosophy as to a schoolmaster, but as one who has sore eyes to a sponge and egg, as another to a plaster, and another to a fomentation: in this way, no servitude to reason will bite you, but you will acquiesce in it.

Illud autem memento, philosophiam ea sola postulare, quae natura tua postulet: tu autem aliud volebas non convenienter naturae.

Remember this, however: demand only those things from philosophy which your nature requires; but you wanted something else not in harmony with your nature.

Quid horum blandius est?

Which of these is more alluring? -

Nonne enim eapropter fallit voluptas?

Does not pleasure deceive for this reason? -

At vide, gratiorne sit magnanimitas, libertas, simplicitas, animi aequitas, sanctitas.

But look, is not magnanimity, freedom, simplicity, fairness of mind, and sanctity more pleasant?

Ipsa vero prudentia quid iucundius est? si eam cogitaveris eius facultatis, in qua intelligentia et scientia inest, praestantiam, quae in nulla re labitur et in omni re prospere fertur.

Truly, what is more delightful than wisdom itself? If you consider the excellence of that faculty in which intelligence and knowledge reside, it does not falter in any situation and is successful in all things.

10. Res quidem ipsae in tantis quodammodo involutae sunt tenebris, ut philosophis haud paucis nec vulgaribus omnino non comprehensibiles esse viderentur: praeterea ipsis adeo Stoicis perceptu difficiles videntur: etiam omnis noster assensus mutabilis.

Indeed, the things themselves are so wrapped in such great obscurities that they might seem to be incomprehensible even to not a few philosophers, and certainly not to the common people. Moreover, they seem difficult even to the Stoics themselves, and our own assent is always subject to change.

ubi enim est homo, qui sententiam non mutet? Proinde transi ad res subiectas quam caducae, quam viles et quae etiam a cinaedo aut scorto aut latrone possideri possint.

For where is the person who does not change their opinion? Therefore, move on to the things that are subject to decay, how trivial and cheap they are, and how they could even be possessed by a pimp, a prostitute, or a thief.

Tum porco accede ad mores eorum, quibuscum vivitur, quos sustinere vix festivissimi est, ue dicam, se ipsum quoque vix quemquam sustinere.

Then approach the habits of those with whom you live, which are scarcely endurable even for the most cheerful people, or shall I say, which even one's own self can hardly endure in anyone.

Tali igitur in caligine et sordibus et in tanto et materiae et temporis et motus et rerum motarum fluxu quid tandem magna aestimatione aut omnino studio dignum sit, non intelligo.

Therefore, in such darkness and filth, and in such vastness of matter and time and motion, and in the constant flux of things moved, I do not understand what could be worth great esteem or any earnest pursuit.

Contra fas est me ipsum consolari et exspectare naturalem dissolutionem, neque moram inique ferre, sed his tantum duobus acquiescere: primo, nihil mihi posse accidere, quod universitatis naturae non conveniat:

On the other hand, it is right for me to console myself and await natural dissolution, not to endure delay unfairly, but to be content with only these two things: first, that nothing can happen to me that is not in accordance with the nature of the universe;

Altero in mea situm esse potestate, ut nihil contra dei mei atque genii voluntatem agam: nemo enim est, qui hanc trans gredi cogat.

Second, that it is within my power to do nothing contrary to the will of my own divine spirit; for no one compels me to cross this boundary.

11. Quam tandem ad rem igitur nunc animo meo utor? In singulis hoc me ipsum interrogare me identidem oporet eti explorare, quid mihi nunc versetur ea in parte, quam animi principatum vocant.

So, to what purpose, then, shall I now direct my mind? In every matter, I must repeatedly ask myself this and examine what is occupying my thoughts at this moment in the domain they call the ruling center of the mind.

Cuius nunc gero animam? num gnid pueruli? adolescentuli? mulierculae? tyranni? iumenti? bellum?

Whose soul am I carrying now? Is it the soul of a child, an adolescent, a woman, a tyrant, a beast, or a soldier?

12. Qualia sint, qua.

What kinds of things they are, and in what manner.

Vulgo bona videntur, etiam hinc intelligas licet: nam si quis cogitaverit quaedam ut vera bona, velut prudentiam, temperantiam, iustitiam, fortitudinem, non poterit, his animo praeconceptis, amplius audire hoc: " Prae."

Indeed, you can understand even from this that certain things are commonly seen as good. For if someone considers certain things as true goods, like wisdom, self-control, iustice, courage, they will not be able, with these preconceived notions in mind, to hear this any longer: "Pre..."

Nam cum bono dissonabit.

Because it clashes with what is truly good.

Atqui ea, quae vulgo bona videntur, si animo praeconceperit, exaudiet et facile admittet ut apposite adiectum illud Comici dictum.

Certainly, if one preconceives in their mind what is commonly considered good, they will easily accept and be receptive to that well-placed saying of the Comic poet.

Sic etiam vulgus animo sibi fingit hoc discrimen.

In the same way, the common people also imagine this distinction in their minds.

Non enim illic offenderet et improbaretur, idemque de divitiis atque iis fortunae commodis, quae ad luxum et gloriam pertinent, acciperemus ut scite et urbane dictum.

For in that case, it would not offend or be disapproved of, and the same could be said about wealth and those advantages of fortune that pertain to luxury and glory, which we could accept as clever and refined expressions.

Igitur et percontare, num aestimanda et pro bonis babenda sint talia, quibus mente praeconceptis apte inferri possit illud, hominem iis instructum prae affluentia rerum non habere, quo ventris onus deponat.

Therefore, inquire also whether such things should be valued and regarded as good, considering that it can be aptly inferred that a person equipped with them does not have the burden of excess in material possessions.

I 3 . Forma et materia consto: harum neutra in nihilum interibit, quemadmodum neque ex nihilo exstitit.

Form and matter coexist: neither of these will perish into nothingness, just as neither emerged from nothing.

Itaque omnis mei pars per mutationem in aliquam mundi partern transferetur.

Therefore, every part of me will be transferred through change into some part of the world.

et liaec rursus in aliam mundi partem mutabitur, et sic porro in infinitum.

And this, in turn, will be changed into another part of the world, and so on, infinitely.

Secundum talem mutationem etiam ego ortus sum et ii, qui me genuerunt, et sic retro in aliud infinitum: nihil enim ita nos loqui vetat, etiamsi secundum periodos certis finibus terminatas mundus administretur.

According to such a change, I too have come into being, and those who gave birth to me, and so on in reverse to another infinite. Nothing, in fact, prevents us from speaking this way, even if the world is governed by cycles bounded by definite limits.

I 4 . Ratio et ars rationales sunt facultates sese ipsis suisque operibus contentae.

Reason and rational art are faculties content with themselves and their own works.

Cientur igitur a suo ac proprio principio et pergunt ad suum finem propositum: quapropter recte facta appellantur eiusmodi actiones, ipso nomine rectam viam significantes.

Therefore, they are directed from their own and proper beginning and proceed towards their intended end. For this reason, actions done rightly are called such, signifying by their very name the right path.

I 5 . Nihil horum liominis dicendum est, quae ad hominem, quoad homo est, non pertinent: non requiruntur ab homine, neque promittuntur a natura hominis, neque ad naturam hominis perficiendam faciunt:

Nothing of these things should be said about a human being that does not pertain to the human aspect. They are not required from a human, nor promised by the nature of a human, nor do they contribute to the fulfillment of human nature.

proinde neque furis homini propositus in iis consistit, neque id, quod ad hunc finem conticiendum facit, bonum.

Therefore, the purpose of a human being does not consist in those things, nor is what contributes to achieving this purpose inherently good.

Porro, si quid horum ad hominem pertineret, ea contemnere iisque se opponere non pertineret ad hominem, neque laude dignus esset, qui se his non indigentem praebet, neque qui aliquid ex iis sibi detrahit, bonus esset, si hac essent bona.

Furthermore, if any of these things were relevant to a human being, it would not be appropriate for a human being to despise them or oppose them, nor would it be praiseworthy for someone to present themselves as not in need of these things, nor would someone be considered good for depriving themselves of anything from these, if these were considered good.

Iam vero ut quisque maxime his et eius generis aliis sese ipse privat, aut etiam illis se privari sustinet, ita optimus est.

Indeed, the best person is the one who most completely and willingly deprives themselves of these things and others of the same kind.

16. Qualia sunt, quae saepe cogitaveris, talis tibi erit mens tua.

The kind of thoughts you frequently contemplate will shape your mind accordingly.

imbuitur enim cogitationibus animus.

Indeed, the mind is influenced by thoughts.

Itaque eum perpetuo imbue huiuscemodi cogitationibus, ut: ubi vivere licet, ibi etiam bene vivere licet.

Therefore, immerse your mind continuously in such thoughts: where it is possible to live, it is also possible to live well.

in aula autem vivere licet.

Indeed, it is possible to live in the court as well.

Ergo licet etiam bene vivere in aula.

Therefore, it is also possible to live well in the court.

Iterum, cuius rei causa aliquid comparatum est, * ad hanc (accommodate) comparatum est.

Again, for the sake of which thing something is obtained, it is obtained for this (appropriately).

ad quam rem comparatum est, ad hanc fertur.

It is carried towards the thing to which it has been compared.

ad quod fertur, in eo finis ipsius est.

Its end is in that to which it is directed.

ubi finis, ibi etiam bonum et utilitas cuiusvis: bonum igitur animalis rationalis in colenda societate: nam ad societatem nos esse genitos, dudum est demonstratum.

Where the end is, there also is the good and utility of anything: therefore, the good of a rational being is in cultivating society: for it has been shown that we are born for society.

An vero non liquet, deteriora praestantiorum, et ex his alterum alterius causa natum esse? inanimatis autem animata praestantiora, animatis autem ea, quae ratione praedita sunt.

Is it not clear that the worse is born for the sake of the better, and from the latter, the former? Among inanimate things, the animate are better; and among animate things, those endowed with reason are superior.

17. Ea, quae fieri nequeunt, sectari, insania mentis est.

To pursue things that cannot happen is the folly of a deranged mind.

fieri autem non potest, quin mali talia faciant.

However, it is impossible for such things not to be done by evil people.

18. Nihil cuiquam accidit, ad quod ferendum natura non sit comparatus.

Nothing happens to anyone that nature has not equipped them to bear.

Alii eadem accidunt, et aut ignorans, sibi ea accidisse, aut magnanimitatem ostentans, tranquillus manet et illaesus.

Some experience the same things, and either unaware that these things have happened to them, or displaying magnanimity, remain calm and untouched.

Indignum igitur, ignorantiam et obsequium plus posse, quam prudentiam.

It is unworthy, therefore, to believe that ignorance and subservience have greater power than wisdom.

19. Res ipsae ne minime quidem animum tangunt, neque ullum aditum habent ad animum, neque vertere nec movere possunt animum: se ipse solus vertit ac movet et qualibus se ipse dignum reddit iudiciis, talia sibi reddit ea, quae extrinsecus ipsi afferuntur.

Indeed, the things themselves do not touch the mind in the least, nor do they have any access to the mind, nor can they turn or move the mind. The mind alone turns and moves itself, and by the judgments it passes on itself, it renders to itself the things that are brought to it from outside.

20. Altera quidem ratione nobis res coniunctissima homo, quatenus iis bene facere eosque ferre nos oportet: quatenus autem quidam nos impediunt in operibus propriis, una e rebus mediis mihi fit homo, non minus quam sol, quam ventus, quam bellua.

By another reason, indeed, man is closely related to us, inasmuch as it is right for us to do well by them and to endure them. However, insofar as certain individuals hinder us in our own actions, man is no less a part of the intermediate class than the sun, the wind, or an animal.

Ab his autem effectus quidem impediri potest.

But from these, the effects can indeed be hindered.

Conatus autem et adfectionis nulla existunt impedimenta propter exceptionem et circumversionem.

However, efforts and intentions do not encounter hindrances due to exceptions and circumvention.

Convertit enim mens ac transfert unumquodque effectus impedimentum ad id, quod praepositum est: atque operi conducit id, quod hoc opus impedit, et ad viam confert id, quod in hac via obstat.

For the mind converts and transfers each hindrance of an effect to its purpose: it serves the work by using what obstructs that work, and it brings onto the path that which obstructs on that path.

21. Eorum, quae in mundo sunt, praestantissimum colito: id autem hoc est, quod omnibus utitur omniaque administrat.

Cherish the most excellent among the things in the world: and this is, that uses all and administers all.

Similiter eorum, quae in te sunt, praestantissimum colito.

Similarly, cherish the most excellent among the things within yourself.

Hoc autem id est, quod illi cognatum est nam etiam in te id, quod ceteris utitur, hoc est, atque vita tua ab hoc regitur.

However, this is what is related to them, for even within yourself, what others use, that is, your life, is governed by this.

Quod civitati non nocet, neque civi nocet.

What doesn't harm the community, doesn't harm the individual citizen either.

Ubicunque cogitatio de damno tibi incidit, hanc adhibe regulam si civitas ea re damnum non facit, neque ego damnum feci.

Whenever the thought of harm befalls you, apply this rule: if the community isn't harmed by it, then I haven't been harmed either.

Sin civitati nocetur, non irascendum est ei, qui civitati damnum infert, * sed ostendendum, quid sit, quod negligitur.

But if harm is done to the community, one should not be angry with those who cause harm to the community, but rather show what is being neglected.

23 Saepe animo reputa celeritatem, qua omnia, quae sunt et fiunt, abripiuntur et occultis subducuntur.

Often reflect on the swiftness with which all things that exist and happen are carried away and hidden from sight.

Nam et materia fluminis instar in perpetuo est fluxu, et effectus in perpetuis mutationibus, et causae efficientes in innumeris conversionibus.

For the material world is like a river in constant flow, effects are in perpetual changes, and efficient causes are in countless transformations.

Atque propemodum nihil est, quod perstat.

and there is almost nothing that persists.

item adiacentem hanc praeteriti et futuri temporis immensitatem, in qua omnia evanescunt.

likewise, consider the vastness of the past and future time that surrounds us, in which everything vanishes.

Quidni igitur stultus, qui his rebus inflatur aut angitur aut lamentatur quasi diutius vel minimam molestiam creantibus?

Why, then, should anyone be foolish enough to become inflated, distressed, or lamentful over these things as if they were creating even the slightest enduring discomfort?

24. Memento et universae materiae, cuius minimam obtines partem, et totius aevi, cuius brevissimum et puncti instar obtinens spatium tibi assignatum est, et fati, cuius quantilla pars es!

Remember also the whole of matter, of which you possess the smallest part, and the entire span of time, for which you have been allotted a brief space resembling a point, and fate, of which you are but a small portion!

25. Peccat aliquis.

Someone has sinned.

Quid ad me? ipse viderit: suam habet affectionem, suam agendi rationem.

What does that have to do with me? He should figure it out himself: he has his own feelings and way of acting.

Ego nunc habeo, quod me habere vult natura communis, et ago, quod me vult agere natura mea.

I now have what the common nature wants me to have, and I do what my own nature wants me to do.

26. Quae animae pars principatum et dominium obtinet ea immota maneat ad levem aspernmve carnis motum, neque ei se immisceat, sed se ipsa circumscribat et illas adfectiones intra limites particularum coerceat:

That part of the soul which holds the rule and dominion should remain unmoved by light or harsh movements of the flesh, neither should it become entangled with them, but it should enclose itself and confine those emotions within the bounds of its own nature:

quando autem per alterum consensum usque ad mentem perveniunt, ut in corpore unito, tum contra sensum quidem, quippe naturalem, non luctandum.

But when they attain agreement through the consent of the other part, as in a united body, then indeed they must not struggle against the sense, for it is the natural order.

 sed opinionem, quasi bonum aut malum sit animi principatus ne a se adiiciat.

but they should not engage in contention over opinions, as if the dominion of the mind should not add to itself either good or bad.

27. Cum diis vivere.

To live in accordance with the gods.

Cum diis autem vivit, qui perpetuo exhibet animum suum contentum iis, quae ipsi sunt assignata, et efficientem ea, quae iubet genius, quem vitae moderatorem ac rectorem cuique Iupiter tribuit, particulam a se delibatam.

But one lives with the gods who constantly presents his soul content with the things assigned to him and performs the actions commanded by his guiding spirit, which Jupiter has assigned to each person as the director and ruler of their life, a portion derived from himself.

hic autem genius cuiusque mens est ac ratio.

Here, however, the guiding spirit is the mind and reason of each individual.

28. Numquid ei, qui hircum olet, succenses? numquid ei, cui os foetet? Quid te faciat? eiusmodi os, eiusmodi alas habet , ut necesse sit eiusmodi inde exhalari.

Does one ridicule someone who smells of a goat? Does one avoid someone whose breath is foul? What difference does it make to you? Such a person has such a nature, such characteristics, that it is necessary for such an odor to emanate from them.

At homo, inquiet, ratione praeditus est atque, modo animum advertat, intelligere potest, quid delinquat.

But a person, endowed with reason and if they pay attention, can understand what they have done wrong, even if they are agitated.

Quod bene tibi vertat! Proinde etiam tu ratione praeditus es.

May it turn out well for you! Therefore, you too are endowed with reason.

rationali animi affectione move rationalem affectionem.

A rational affection of the soul moves a rational affection.

edoce, commonefac! nam si audiverit, eum sanabis, neque opus erit ira.

Teach, remind! For if he hears, you will heal him, and there will be no need for anger.

Neque tragoedus neque scortum.

Neither a tragedian nor a harlot.

29. Quemadmodum hinc egressus vivere in animum induxisti, ita etiam hic vivere licet.

Iust as you have made up your mind to live when you leave here, so too you can live here.

quod si tibi non concesserint, etiam e vita exi, ita tamen, ut qui nihil mali passus sis.

And if they do not grant you this, exit life also, but in such a way that it appears you have suffered no harm.

Fumus est, et abeo.

It is smoke, and I am leaving.

Cur id rem magnam putas? quamdiu autem nihil eiusmodi me hinc educit, liber maneo, nec quisquam me impediet, quominus faciam, quae volo: volo autem ea, quae cum natura animalis ratione praediti et ad societatem nati conveniunt.

Why do you consider it a significant matter? As long as nothing of that sort forces me away from here, I remain free, and no one will prevent me from doing what I wish. I wish, however, for those things that are in harmony with the nature of a rational being and born for society.

30. Universi mens communionis et societatis amans.

The mind of the universe, loving community and society.

hinc deteriora praestantiorum causa fecit et praestantiorum alterrum alteri conciliavit.

Hence, it has caused the better things for the sake of the worse, and reconciled one of the better things to the other.

Vides, quomodo subiecerit, congesserit, pro dignitate suum cuique tribuerit et praestantissima quaeque mutuo inter se consensu devinxerit.

You see how it has subiected, gathered, assigned to each according to its worth, and bound together the most excellent things by mutual agreement.

31. Quo modo te usque ad hoc tempus gessisti erga deos, parentes, fratres, uxorem, liberos, praeceptores, educatores, amicos, familiares, famalos? valetne ad hoc usque tempus erga omnes illud, "nil iniusti erga quemquam fecisse aut dixisse?"

In what manner have you conducted yourself up to this point toward the gods, parents, siblings, wife, children, teachers, educators, friends, relatives, servants? Is it possible for you up to this point to say that you have done or said nothing uniust to anyone?

Memento autem etiam illius, per qualia pertransieris, et qualibus perferendis par fueris: item, plenam tibi iam esse vitae contemplationem et absolutum eius ministerium.

However, remember also the circumstances through which you have passed and the challenges you have been capable of enduring. Likewise, consider that your life's journey is now complete and its service fulfilled.

quot pulcra visui oblata sint, quot voluptates ac labores contempseris, quot res gloriosas neglexeris, erga quot iniquos aequum te praebueris.

How many beautiful things have been presented to your sight, how many pleasures and hardships you have disregarded, how many glorious pursuits you have neglected, how iustly you have behaved toward the uniust.

32. Qui fit, ut ingenia artium rudia et imperita confundant artium gnara et perita?

How does it happen that inexperienced and unskilled individuals confuse themselves with those knowledgeable and skilled in the arts?

Quid igitur est ingenium artis peritum eaque instructum?

What then is skilled artistry and how is it accomplished?

Quod principium et finem novit rationemque per omnem materiam permeantem et per omne aevum certis quibusdam et definitis temporum cursibus universum administrantem.

It is the knowledge of the principles and the end, the understanding that permeates through all matter and governs the entire universe with certain and defined cycles of time.

33. Iamiam cinis eris aut nuda ossa, et aut nomen aut ne nomen quidem.

Soon you will be ashes or bare bones, and either a name or not even a name.

nomen autem nil nisi strepitus et resonantia.

A name, however, is nothing but noise and echoing.

quae in vita magni aestimantur, vana et putida et exilia, caniculae mordentes, pueruli contentiosi, modo ridentes, modo plorantes.

Things that are highly valued in life are vain, trivial, and fleeting, like biting midges, quarrelsome children who alternate between laughing and crying.

Fides autem et iustitia et verecundia et veritas "ad Olympum a terra spatiosa.

Faith, iustice, modesty, and truth "ascend from the spacious earth to Olympus."

Quid igitur amplius est quod hic te retineat?

"What then is there more to keep you here?"

si quidem res, quae sub sensus cadunt, mutationibus obnoxiae sunt nec persistunt, ipsi sensus obscuri et hebetes , qui facile falsas rerum species admittunt, ipsa animula exhalatio sanguinis, inter tales gloria florere vanitas.

since indeed the things that fall under the senses are subiect to change and do not endure, the senses themselves are dull and obtuse, easily admitting false appearances of things, the very soul is a breath of blood, amid such things vanity flourishes in glory.

Quid igitur? Aequo animo exspectas vel exstinctionem vel translationem.

What then? Are you waiting with equanimity for either extinction or translation?

Huius vera tempus donec advenit, quid sufficit? Quid aliud, nisi ut deos colas celebresque, hominibus bene facias, eos sustineas et ab iis te abstineas, quaecunque autem extra fines carunculae et animulae sita sunt, ea memineris nec tua esse neque in potestate tua sita.

Until the true time of this arrives, what is sufficient? What else but to worship the gods and honor them, to do good to fellow humans, to support them and refrain from them, and to remember that whatever lies beyond the confines of the flesh and soul is neither yours nor within your control.

34. Potes semper prosperum vitae cursum tenere, si quidem et certum iter tenere, si quidem via ac ratione et cogitare et agere potes.

You can always maintain a prosperous course of life, provided that you can both follow a certain path and proceed with reason and thought.

Haec duo et dei et hominis et cuiusvis animalis ratione praediti animo communia, non ab alio impediri et in animi affectione iustitiae studiosa habere bonam et hic terminare appetitionem.

These two things, common to both gods and humans and any rational creature, are not hindered by others and to have a good disposition in the pursuit of iustice in the mind's affection, and to set this as the end goal.

35. Si neque vitiositas haec mea est, neque meae vitiositatis effectus, neque respublica laeditur, cur propter hoc differor? Quid autem est damnum civitatis communis?

If neither is this my fault, nor the outcome of my fault, nor is the state harmed, why am I delayed because of this? But what is the harm to the commonwealth?

36. Noli ulla ex parte sinere te abripi visis, sed auxiliare pro viribus et dignitate etiam, quando in mediis illis rebus aliquid damni faciunt, quod tamen cave pro damno habeas malus enim, hic mos est.

Do not let yourself be carried away in any way by appearances, but assist to the best of your abilities and even with your dignity, when in the midst of those situations they cause some harm, which, however, you should not consider as a true loss. For this is a bad habit.

Sed quemadmodum senex abiens petebat, pueruli turbinem, memor, turbinem esse, sic igitur etiam hic agendum.

But iust as the old man who was departing asked for a whirlwind, remembering that it was a whirlwind, so in this case also it must be done.

Atqui in ius vocas pro rostris, Oblitusue es, homo, qualia haec sint?

But you call them to court, O man, forgetting what these things are like?

Nequaquam , sed illis videntur studio dignissima.

- By no means, but they seem most worthy of pursuit to those people.

Eapropter tu quoque stultus fias? Fui olim.

- So should you also become foolish? I was foolish once.

Ubicunque derelictus, bene fortunatus homo: "bene fortunatus," qui bonam fortunam sibi comparavit.

- Wherever abandoned, a person is fortunate: "fortunate indeed" is the one who has acquired good fortune for themselves.

bona autem fortuna, boni animi motus, bona agendi ratio, bonae actiones.

Good fortune, good movements of the soul, a good course of action, and good deeds.

LIBER VI

SECUNDUM NATURAM VIVENS

1. Universi materia obsequens est et fingenti bene, parata:

The matter of the universe is obedient and ready to be shaped by the one who acts wisely.

ratio eam administrans nullam in se habet male faciendi causam.

Reason, which governs it, has no cause for acting wrongly within itself.

malitiam enim neque habet nec male faciet cuiquam, neque ab ea quidquam laeditur. Omnia vero secundum hanc fiunt ac perficiuntur.

For it has no malice, and it will neither do harm to anyone nor is it harmed by it. Indeed, all things are accomplished and perfected according to it.

2. Nihil tua referat, utrum rigens an calore fotus id, quod te decet, facias, neque utrum dormituriens an somni satur, male audiens an fama florens, moriens an aliquid diversum faciens. Etenim ex huius vitae officiis hoc est etiam quod morimur.

It matters not whether you do what becomes you when you are shivering with cold or warmed by heat, whether you act while drowsy with sleep or satisfied with dreams, whether you are poorly heard or well-spoken of, dying or doing something else. For these are also part of the duties of this life, and even in them, death is found.

sufficit igitur et in hoc, quod prae manibus est recte disponere.

Therefore, it is enough to arrange things rightly that are before you.

3. Acriter intuere.

Look at them keenly.

neque propria ullius rei natura nec dignitas te fugiat!

Let neither the nature nor the dignity of any particular thing escape you!

4. Omnia, quae sunt, celerrime mutantur et aut in exhalationem abibunt, si unita est materia, aut dissipabuntur.

All things that exist are swiftly changing and will either evaporate into vapor if they consist of matter, or they will disperse.

5. Ratio universi gubernatrix novit certo modo se habens, quod agit et in qua materia versatur.

The governing principle of the universe is guided by reason, and it has a definite nature in which it acts and within which matter operates.

6. Optima ratio ulciscendi, non similem malis fieri.

The best way of seeking revenge is not to become like the wrongdoers.

7. Delectet te tibique satisfaciat ab una actione, quae societati prodest, transire ad aliam eiusdem generis, memorem dei.

May it bring you delight and satisfaction to transition from one beneficial action for society to another of the same kind, mindful of the divine.

8. Principalis animi pars ea est, quae se ipsa suscitat et vertit et talem se ipsa facit, qualis demum sit et esse velit, quaeque facit, ut quidquid contingit tale videatur, quale ipsa vult.

The principal part of the mind is the one that stirs and directs itself, making itself into the kind of being it desires to be. It shapes itself so that whatever happens appears to be as it wants it to be.

9. Secundum universi naturam singula perficiuntur.

According to the nature of the universe, individual things are perfected.

neque enim secundum aliam ullam vel extrinsecus ambientem vel intus inclusam vel foris suspensam.

For indeed, they are perfected neither according to any other nature that surrounds them from the outside, nor according to any nature enclosed within, nor according to any suspended outside.

10. Aut confusio et mutuus complexus et dissipatio, aut unitas et ordo et providentia:

Either confusion and mutual entanglement and dispersion, or unity and order and providence:

si priora, quid est, cur huic mixturae fortuitae et colluviei immorari cupiam? quid aliud mihi curae est, quam quomodo "terra fiam?" Cur etiam perturbor? Veniet enim ad me dissipatio, quidquid faciam Si altera sunt, veneror et tranquillo sum animo et confido rectori.

If the former is true, why should I desire to linger in this haphazard mixture and jumble? What else do I care about other than how I will become part of the earth? Why do I even get upset? For dissolution will come to me, no matter what I do. If the latter is true, I worship and am at peace of mind and trust the Director.

11. Quando a rebus, quae circumstant, quasi perturbari coactus es, cito ad te redi, neque ultra, quam necesse est a tenore dimovearis:

When you are compelled to be disturbed by external things, quickly return to yourself and do not stray from your normal behavior any longer than necessary.

eo enim facilius concentum tueberis, quo saepius ad eum redieris.

For the more frequently you return to it, the more easily you will maintain harmony with it.

12. Si novercam simul et matrem haberes, illam quidem coleres, ad matrem tamen te frequentissime reciperes. Harum instar nunc tibi aula est, et philosophia:

If you had both a stepmother and a biological mother, you would indeed honor the stepmother, but you would most often return to your biological mother. In a similar way, now the court and philosophy are like this for you:

ad hanc saepe revertere et in ea acquiesce, per quam etiam quae illic sunt tibi tolerabilia videntur, et tu ipse in illis tolerabilis.

Return to this frequently and find contentment in it. Through it, even what is tolerable there will seem so to you, and you yourself will become tolerable in those circumstances.

13. Quemadmodum iam de obsoniis atque eiusmodi eduliis imaginem animo concipimus, ut, hoc piscis cadaver esse, illud cadaver avis aut porci, item, Falernum esse succulum uvulae, praetextam oviculae pilos, conchae cruore infectos.

Just as we now form a mental image of delicacies and such edibles, such as imagining that this is the carcass of a fish, that is the carcass of a bird or pig; likewise, we consider Falernian to be the juice of grapes, mullet to be a kind of lettuce, and oysters to be seasoned with blood.

De coitu, esse intestini frictionem et excretionem muci cum convuisione quadam - quales utique sunt rerum imagines, quae res ipsas assequuntur easque penetrant, ut, quaenam tandem eae sint videre liceat - sic etiam per totam vitam nos facere oportet ac res, ubi vel maxime fide dignae videantur, denudare et vilitatem earum spectare et externam speciem, qua superbiunt, tollere.

Just as when we think about sexual intercourse, we imagine it as friction of the intestines and the excretion of mucus with a certain convulsion—imagery that truly reflects the actual processes and penetrates them, allowing us to see what they truly are—so too, throughout our lives, we must approach things and events, especially those that appear most worthy of belief, by exposing them and considering their triviality, lifting the external appearance by which they appear impressive.

Nam gravis impostor est fastus, et quando maxime putas, te res serias agere, tum maxime in fraudem inducit. Vide saltem, Crates quid de ipso Xenocrate dixerit.

Indeed, pride is a heavy deceiver, and when you think you are engaging in serious matters, it leads you most into deceit. Consider at least what Crates said about Xenocrates himself.

14. Pleraque, quae vulgus hominum admiratur, ad generalia rerum capita referuntur:

Most of what the common people admire is related to the general principles of things.

Alia quae vi copulante aut natura continentur, lapides, arbores, ficus, vites, oleae alia, quae paulo moderatiores admirantur, inter ea, quae anima continentur, ut greges, armenta.

Other things that are held together by force or nature are stones, trees, fig trees, vines, olive trees, and others that are slightly more restrained, such as flocks and herds among the things that are contained by the soul.

Alia, quibus urbaniores capiuntur, inter ea quae anima rationali praedita sunt, non tamen universali, sed quatenus artium perita aut alia quadam sollertia excellit autsimpliciter rationalis est, ut servitiorum turbam possidere.

Others that captivate the more urban individuals among those endowed with a rational soul, although not in a universal sense, but rather insofar as they excel in the arts or in some other skill, or are simply rational, include having a retinue of servants.

Qui autem animam rationalem universalem et societatis amantem veneratur, nihil amplius cetera curat, ante omnia vero animum suum ita affectum et se moventem, ut rationi et civitati convenit, conservat et cognatum suum, ut idem consequatur, adiuvat.

However, the one who venerates the universal rational soul and loves society, cares about nothing more than this. Above all, they maintain and keep their own mind in such a state and movement that is in harmony with reason and the community. They nurture and uphold what is connected to them, and in doing so, they achieve the same outcome as they assist in furthering the common good.

15. Haec properant fieri, illa properant fuisse, quin etiam eius quod fit, iam aliquid evanuit:

These things hasten to come into being, while those things hasten to have already been, to the point that even what is currently happening has already begun to disappear:

Fluxus et mutationes mundum perpetuo renovant, quemadmodum immensum illud aevum continuus temporis lapsus novum semper praestat. In hoc igitur flumine ecquis horum, quae praeterlabuntur, quidquam in pretio habeat?

The flow and changes renew the world perpetually, just as the continuous passage of time presents an ever-new immense age. In this river of existence, then, does anyone attach any value to those things that pass by?

Perinde ac si quis praetervolantium passerculorum aliquem diligere coepisset, is vero iam e conspectu abisset.

Just as if someone were to start loving a flock of passing sparrows, yet they would soon have vanished from sight.

Eiusmodi sane est vita cuiusque, cuiusmodi est exhalatio sanguinis aut spiritus ab aere attractio.

Indeed, the life of each individual is like that, just as the exhalation of blood or the drawing of breath from the air.

Quale enim est, semel animam attrahere et efflare, quod quidem singulis temporis momentis facimus, tale etiam est, omnem illam respirandi facultatem, quam heri aut nudiustertius in ortu accepisti, eo reddere, unde eam primo hausisti.

For iust as it is, to draw in and exhale the breath once, which we do at every moment of time, so it is the same, to restore all that breathing faculty which you received yesterday or the day before in birth, to the place from which you first drew it.

16. Neque quod perspiramur, ut stirpes, aestimatione dignum est, neque quod respiramus, ut pecudes et belluae, neque quod species rerum per visa nobis imprimuntur, neque quod agendi impetu huc illuc rapimur, neque quod congregamur et nutrimur:

Neither is it worthy of consideration that we perspire like plants, nor that we breathe like animals and beasts, nor that the impressions of things are imprinted on us through our senses, nor that we are carried hither and thither by the impulse of action, nor that we gather and nourish ourselves.

Hoc enim perinde est atque alimenti quod supertluum est excernere.

For this is the same as excreting the excess of nourishment.

Quid igitur est, quod aestimatione dignum sit?

What, then, is worthy of esteem?

Num plausu excipi? Nequaquam. Itaque nec linguarum plausu excipi:

Certainly not by applause. Therefore, it is not to be received by the applause of tongues either.

Multitudinis enim laus quid aliud est, nisi linguarum strepitus? Sustulisti igitur gloriolam quoque.

For the praise of the multitude is nothing more than the noise of tongues. Therefore, you have also removed the applause of vainglory.

Quid restat, quod aestimatione dignum sit?

What remains that is worthy of consideration?

Hoc opinor, secundum propriam constitutionem et moveri et motum sistere, quo etiam et studia et artes ducunt.

I believe that what remains worthy of consideration is the ability to move and be moved according to one's own nature, which also guides both pursuits and arts.

Nam etiam omnis ars id spectat, ut id, quod paratur aptum sit ad opus, ad quod paratur:

Indeed, every art aims to ensure that what is prepared is suitable for the purpose for which it is prepared:

Et vinitor, qui vites colit, et qui equos domat et qui canes huic studet operi. Puerorum educatio et disciplina aliquem finem consequi student.

And iust as the vintner tends to the vines, the one who tames horses, and the one who trains dogs all work toward their respective goals. Similarly, the education and discipline of children aim to achieve a certain end.

Ibi igitur id, quod aestimatione dignum est.

So, there lies what is worthy of esteem.

Quod si bene habuerit, nihil ceterorum tibi comparare studebis.

And if you possess that well, you will strive for nothing else in comparison.

Non desines multa alia aestimare? Itaque nec liber eris, nec tibi sufficiens, neque animi perturbationibus vacuus.

You won't cease to value many other things? Thus, you won't be free, nor self-sufficient, nor free from disturbances of the mind.

Non enim fieri potest, quin invideas aemuleris eosque suspectos habeas, qui illis te privare sint, et insidias struas iis, qui id, quod a te tanti aestimatur, possident.

For it is impossible not to envy and emulate those and to be suspicious of those who seem to deprive you of those things, and to plot against those who possess what you value so highly.

Omnino necesse est te perturbari, si qua illarum rerum indigeas, praeterea saepe de diis conqueri.

Certainly, it is necessary for you to be disturbed if you are in need of any of those things, and furthermore, often to complain about the gods.

Sed propriae mentis verecundia et honor et te tibi gratum reddet et sociis commodum et diis consentientem, hoc est, quaecunque attribuunt et constituunt, laudibus celebrantem.

But the genuine modesty and honor of your own mind will make you pleasing to yourself, and your conduct will benefit your associates and be in harmony with the gods, that is, praising whatever they attribute and establish.

17. Sursum, deorsum, in orbem feruntur elementa.

Upward, downward, in a circle, the elements are carried.

Virtutis autem motus nulla barum viarum fertur, sed divinior quaedam res et via difficili comprehensu incedens feliciter progreditur.

The movement of virtue, however, is not carried along any of these paths, but it proceeds through a more divine manner, a path difficult to comprehend, and it progresses successfully.

18. Quale est, quod faciunt! homines eiusdem aetatis et qui cum ipsis vivunt, eos laudare nolunt, ipsi vero a posteris, quos nec viderunt neque unquam videbunt, celebrari plurimi faciunt.

Such is the case! People of the same age and those who live alongside them are reluctant to praise them, but they themselves, from posterity, who neither saw them nor will ever see them, make them highly celebrated.

Hoc propemodum idem est, ac si doleres, quod prisci illi te non celebrarunt laudibus.

This is almost the same as if you were to feel pain because those of the past did not praise you with accolades.

19. Noli, si quid tibi effectu difficile, opinari, hominem id non posse praestare, sed si quid ab homine effici potest eique est familiare, id te quoque assequi posse persuasum habe.

Do not believe that something is impossible for a human to achieve just because it is difficult for you. If something can be accomplished by a human and is within your capabilities, be convinced that you can achieve it as well.

20. In palaestra vel unguibus nos laceravit aliquis vel illiso capite vulnus nobis inflixit.

In the gym or during wrestling, someone may have wounded us with scratches or inflicted a wound on our head with a blow.

Verum neque notamus, neque offendimur, neque in posterum, ut insidiatorem suspectum habemus, quarrrquam cavemus, nec tamen tanquam ab hoste, neque cum suspicione, sed benevola cum declinatione. Idem etiam in ceteris vitae partibus fiat:

However, we neither take offense, nor do we hold a grudge, nor do we treat the person as a potential attacker, nor do we constantly guard against them in the future. We should do the same in other aspects of life:

Ad multa eorum, quae faciunt, qui nobiscum quasi in certamine:

in many of their actions, just as those who are competing with us:

Committuntur, animum non advertamus. Licet enim, ut dixi, declinare, et nec suspiciosum esse, neque odio illos habere.

They are engaged, but let's not pay attention to them. For it is permissible, as I said, to avoid and not to be suspicious, nor to hold them in hatred.

21. Si quis me convincere mihique ostendere potest, me me non recte sentire aut agere, laeto animo ad meliorem frugem redibo:

If anyone can convince me and show me that I do not think or act correctly, I will return to a better course with a joyful mind.

Veritatem enim sector, a qua nemo unquam laesus est, laeditur autem, qui in errore suo et ignorantia persistit.

For I seek the truth, from which no one has ever been harmed; on the other hand, one is harmed who persists in their error and ignorance.

22. Ego, quod meum est officium, facio:

I am doing what is my duty.

Cetera me non distrahunt.

Other things do not distract me.

Aut enim anima aut ratione carent, aut aberrarunt et viam ignorant.

For either they lack soul or reason, or they have gone astray and do not know the way.

23. Animantibus ratione carentibus omninoque rebus et conditionibus tu, ut ratione praeditus, ratione carentibus, magno ac libero animo fac utaris.

For beings devoid of reason, and in all circumstances and conditions, use your rationality, as one endowed with reason, with a great and free mind.

Hominibus ut ratione praeditis ita utere, ut communionis ratio postulat.

For humans endowed with reason, use it in a way that corresponds to the demands of social harmony.

In omnibus deorum auxilium implora nec tua intersit, quam longo tempore haec facturus sis:

In all things, invoke the assistance of the gods and don't concern yourself with how long it will take you to accomplish them.

Nam sufficient tres horae sic exactae.

For three hours have been spent in this way.

24. Alexander Macedo eiusque mulio post mortem in idem redacti sunt:

Alexander the Great and his mule-driver have been reduced to the same state after death.

Nam aut in easdem mundi rationes seminales redacti sunt, aut pariter in atomos dispersi.

For either they have been reduced to the same seminal principles of the world, or they have been equally scattered into atoms.

25. Considera, quam multa. uno eodemque temporis puncto in uniuscuiusque nostrum et animo et corpore fiunt atque ita non miraberis, si multo plura, imo vero omnia, in uno hoc atque universo, quod mundum vocamus, simul exsistunt.

Consider how many things are happening at the same moment in the mind and body of each one of us, and do not be surprised if many more, or indeed all things, exist simultaneously in this single and universal entity which we call the world.

26. Si quis te interrogaverit, Antonini nomen quo pacto scribatur, num magna vocis contentione singulas edes literas?

If someone were to ask you how the name "Antoninus" is spelled, would you, with a great effort of your voice, pronounce each letter separately?

Quid igitur? si tibi irascuntur, numquid tu vicissim iis irasceris? nonne illi placide omnes ac singulas enumerabis literas?

What then? If they were to get angry with you, would you in turn become angry with them? Would you not calmly enumerate each and every letter to them?

Sic igitur etiam istic memento, omne officium quibusdam numeris absolvi, quos te oportet servare, et nec perturbatum, neque aliis indignantibus vicissim indignantem recta pergere ad id, quod propositum est.

So, in the same way, remember that every duty is completed through certain steps, which you must observe, and proceed directly to what you have set out to do without becoming upset or reciprocating indignation when others are indignant.

27. Quam durum est, non ea permittere hominibus quae ad se pertinere sibique conducere opinantur! attamen quodammodo non permittis, ut hoc faciant, quum aegre fers, illos peccare.

How difficult it is not to allow people to do what they believe pertains to themselves and is beneficial for them! Yet, in a way, you also do not allow them to do so when you bear it with difficulty, as you find it distressing that they are in error.

Feruntur enim omnino ad ea, quae ad se pertinere sibique conducere ipsis videntur. - Verum res non ita habet.

For they are entirely inclined towards those things which they believe pertain to themselves and are beneficial for them. - True, but the reality doesn't always align with their perception.

Tu igitur id doce et ostende sine indignatione.

Therefore, teach and show them without indignation.

28. Mors, quies a sensuum repercussione, ab impulsu affectuum animi quasi fidiculis trahentium, a discursibus mentis et a carnis ministerio.

Death is brought about by the cessation of sensory perception, by the cessation of the impulses of the emotions as if they were the strings of a lyre being plucked, by the cessation of the movements of the mind, and by the cessation of the body's functions.

29. Turpe est, in qua vita corpus non succumbit, in ea prius succumbere animam.

It is disgraceful, for the soul to yield first in that life in which the body does not succumb.

30. Cave, ne in mores Caesareos degeneres, ne inficiaris:

Beware lest you degenerate into un-Caesar-like habits, lest you disavow:

Solet enim fieri. Serva te igitur simplicem, bonum, integrum, gravem, ab elegantiae studio alienum, iustitiae studiosum, pium in deos, benevolum, tuorum amantem et ad officia praestanda strenuum.

For it is wont to happen. Keep yourself therefore simple, good, upright, serious, detached from the pursuit of elegance, a lover of justice, pious towards the gods, kindly, affectionate towards your own people and energetic in carrying out your duties.

Adnitere, ut talis permaneas, qualem te facere voluit philosophia:

Endeavor to remain such as philosophy wished to make you:

Venerare deos.

worship the gods.

prospice saluti hominum. Brevis vita est et unus fructus vitae terrestris, sancta animi affectio et actiones societati utiles. Omnia nt Antonini discipulus:

Consider the welfare of mankind. Life is short, and the only fruit of earthly existence is sacred affection of mind and actions beneficial to society. Do all things as a disciple of Antoninus:

Constantem illius firmitatem in iis, quae naturae convenienter aguntur, et aequabilitatem in omnibus rebus et sanctitatem et vultus serenitatem et comitatem et gloriae inanis contemptum

His constant firmness in those things which are done agreeably to nature, and his equability in all things, and his sanctity, and serenity of countenance, and kindliness, and contempt of vain glory,

et diligens in rebus percipiendis studium et quem admodum ille omnino nihil praetermisit priusquam sedulo id consideraverat et accurate intellexerat.

and diligence in the things which he undertook to learn, and how he spared no pains to understand accurately everything which occurred.

Quemadmodum ille tulit eos, qui immerito eum reprehendebant neque eos vicissim reprehendebat.

In the manner in which he bore with those who uniustly blamed him, and did not himself in turn blame them.

Quemadmodum ad nihil festinabat.

In the manner in which he was never in a hurry for anything.

Ut non delationes admisit.

In the manner in which he was never in a hurry for anything.

Ut accuratus ille erat morum actionumque explorator.

He was indeed a careful observer of morals and actions.

Neque calumniator, nec meticulosus, nec suspiciosus, nec sophista.

He was neither a slanderer, nor overly cautious, nor suspicious, nor a sophist.

et quam paucis erat. contentus, velut domo, strato, veste, victu, famulitio.

And how frugal he was! Content with a simple home, bed, clothing, food, and servants.

Ut laboris tolerans et leni animo. Poterat idem propter victus tenuitatem in eodem usque ad vesperam versari nec nisi consueta hora excernere ei necesse erat:

Enduring labor with a gentle spirit. He could maintain the same disposition throughout the day due to his frugal diet, and he wasn't bound to specific times for excretion.

Constantiam eius et aequabilitatem in amicitiis colendis, facile ferre eos, qui sententias eius libere impugnabant, atqde gaudere, si quis melius aliquid proferret.

His steadfastness and consistency in cultivating friendships, his easy tolerance of those who openly challenged his opinions, and his ioy in hearing someone present a better argument.

Et quam pius in deos sine super stitione - ut tibi bene factorum conscio, sicut illi, obveniat hora novissima.

And how devout he was towards the gods, without excessive superstition – may the hour of your departure, iust as his, find you conscious of your good deeds.

31. Redii ad sobrietatem et revoca te. Somno iterum excusso quum intellexeris, somnia fuisse, quae te perturbabant, vigilans denuo haec intuere, quemadmodum illa intuitus es.

I return to sobriety and remind you to do the same. When you wake up again after having dispelled sleep, realizing that the dreams which disturbed you were indeed dreams, look at these things again while awake, iust as you examined them while dreaming.

32.

Ex corpusculo consto et anima. Corpusculo indifferentia sunt omnia:

non enim possunt eius differre.

Menti autem indifferentia sunt, quaecunque non sunt ipsius actiones.

Quaecunque autem sunt eius actiones, in potestate eius sitae sunt omnes. Ex his tamen eae tantum ei curae sunt, quae circa id, quod praesens est, versantur:

Quae enim futurae sunt eius actiones aut praeteritae, et ipsae ei nunc indifferentes.

33.

Neque manui labor est neque pedi contra naturam, quamdiu pes facit, quod pedis est, et manus, quod manus est.

Sic igitur neque homini ut homini, labor est contra naturam, quamdiu facit, quod hominis est.

Quod si contra naturam eius non est, nec malum ei est.

34.

Quantis voluptatibus delectati sunt latrones, cinaedi, parricidae, tyranni?

35.

Videsne, ut qni illiberales profitentur artes, aliquatenus quidem ad imperitos se accommodent, nihilominus tamen artis rationem retineant neque ab ea discedere sustineant?

Nonne turpe est, architectum ac medicum artis suae rationem magis vereri, quam hominem suam ipsius rationem, quae ei cum diis communis est?

36.

Asia, Europa, anguli mundi:

I consist of a little body and a soul. In the case of the little body, everything is indifferent: .

for none of these things can differ from it

But in the case of the mind, those things are indifferent which are not its own actions.

However, whatever its actions are, they are all within its power. Yet, it only concerns itself with those which pertain to the present;

For actions which are either future or past are themselves indifferent to it at the moment.

Neither is it laborious for a hand to do what a hand naturally does, nor for a foot to do what a foot naturally does, as long as the foot does what is characteristic of a foot, and the hand what is characteristic of a hand.

So, by the same token, it is not laborious for a human being to do what is characteristic of a human being, as long as they do what is characteristic of a human being.

And if it's not contrary to their nature, it's not harmful to them either.

With what great pleasures have robbers, effeminates, parricides, and tyrants been delighted?

Do you see how those who profess unbecoming arts somehow adapt themselves to the unskilled, yet nevertheless retain the method of their art and do not depart from it?

Isn't it shameful that architects and doctors are more afraid of straying from the principles of their art than people are of straying from their own principles, which they share with the gods?

Asia, Europe, corners of the world:

omne mare, guttula mundi:

Athos, glebula mundi:

Omne quod instat tempus, punctum aevi:

Omnia parva, caduca, evanida:

Omnia inde veniunt, a communi illo principatu profecta, vel per consequentiam.

Itaque etiam leonis rictus et venennm mortiferum et noxium quidvis, ut spina, ut lutum, honestarum illarum et pulcrarum rerum appendices agnatae sunt.

Noli igitur ea ab eo, quem colis, aliena opinari, verum omnium fontem tecum perpende.

37. Qui praesentia cernit, omnia vidit, quae ab aeterno fuerunt et in infinitum usque erunt:

Omnia enim eiusdem generis eiusdemque formae sunt.

38. Saepe tecum perpende rerum omnium, quae in mundo sunt, connexum et mutuam rationem:

Quodammodo enim omnia inter se sunt implicita et eatenus inter se amica:

Nam alii consequens est hoc per tendentem connexum, et conspirationem et unitatem materiae.

39. Quibus sorte addictus es rebus, iis te accommoda, et quibuscum forte coniunctus es hominibus, eos amore, eoque vero, prosequere.

Every sea, a droplet of the world:

Mount Athos, a speck of the world:

All that approaches in time, a point of eternity:

All things small, fleeting, transient:

All things come from there, proceeding from that common principle, or through consequence.

Thus, even the lion's roar and deadly poison, anything harmful, like a thorn or mud, are recognized as the companions of those honorable and beautiful things.

Therefore, do not consider them foreign to the one you worship, but reflect on the source of all things within yourself.

One who perceives the present sees everything that has existed from eternity and will continue to exist to infinity:

For all things are of the same kind and of the same form.

Often contemplate the interconnectedness and mutual relationship of all things in the world:

In a way, everything is intertwined with each other and to that extent, friendly to each other:

For one thing follows this by tending toward connection, and there is a harmony and unity of matter.

To those things to which you are assigned by fate, adapt yourself, and to those people with whom you happen to be associated, show love and kindness.

40. Organum, instrumentum, vas quodlibet, si ad qui fabricatum est, id facit, bene habet, quamquam ibi, qui condidit, opifex abiit:

An instrument, tool, or any vessel, when it serves the purpose for which it was made, is functioning well, even though the craftsman who created it has departed;

in iis vero, quae a natura continentur, intus est et permanet quae condidit vis.

But in those things which are contained by nature, the force that created them is within and remains.

Proinde vel magis eam vereri te oportet atque existimare, si secundum eam te habeas et degas, omnia tibi ex animi sententia habere:

Therefore, you should revere and esteem her even more if you conduct yourself and live according to her, having everything in accordance with your own judgment.

sic etiam universo omnia ex sui animi sententia se habent.

Thus, all things also in the universe exist in accordance with their own conviction.

41. Si quid eorum, quae arbitrii tui non sunt, bonum malumve esse in animurn induxeris.

If you have considered as good or evil anything that is not within your control.

non poterit non fieri, quin, si istiusmodi vel in malum incideris vel bono excideris, de diis queraris, homines autem oderis, ut qui, auctorea sint aut ex suspicione tua futuri sint ut altero excidas, in alterum incidas.

It will unavoidably happen that if you happen to fall into such a situation, whether it turns out badly or well, you will complain about the gods, and you will dislike people as if they were responsible or were going to become your adversaries out of suspicion, so that you either blame one or fall into the other.

Et utique multa iniuste facimus idcirco, quod illarum rerum nostra interest.

And certainly, we often do many uniust things precisely because our interests are involved in those matters.

Quod si ea sola, quae in nostra sunt potestate, bona malaque censeamus, nulla iam restat causa, cur deum accusemus aut contra homines inimici partes geramus.

But if we consider only those things which are within our control as good or bad, then there is no longer any reason to accuse God or engage in hostile interactions with other people.

42. Omnes ad unum eundemque effectum operam conferimus, alii scientes et intelligentes, alii quod faciunt nescientes.

We all contribute to the same end result, some knowingly and intelligently, while others do so unknowingly and without understanding.

Quemadmodum etiam dormientes Heraclitus, opinor, operarios esse dixit et conferre ad ea, quae in mundo fiant.

Similarly, Heraclitus also said that even those who are sleeping are laborers and contribute to the things that happen in the world.

Alius vero alio modo operarn confert, ex abundanti vero etiam is, qui queritatur et iis, quae fiunt, reniti conatur eaque tollere.

Nam tali quoque homine mundo opus erat. Igitur quod reliquum est tu cogita, quorum in numerum te referas:

Ille enim, qui rerum universitatem administrat, omnino bene te utetur atque te in partem operariorum eorumque, quae opus adiuvant, recipiet:

Tu autem cave, ne talis pars fueris, qualis in fabula vilis ac ridiculus versus, cuius meminit Chrysippus.

43. Numquid sol quae pluviae sunt facere cupit? numquid Aesculapius quae Frugiferae sunt? Quid siderum quodvis? nonne, quamquam diversa, idem opus adiuvant?

44. Si quidem dii de me iisque quae mihi evenire oportet, consuluerunt, bene consuluerunt.

Etenim consilii expertem esse deum ne ad cogitandum quidem facile est.

Ut autem mihi malefaciendi consilium caperent, quaenam eos causa impulisset?

Quid enim ipsis aut communitati, cuius maximam curam gerunt, inde accederet?

Sin de me privatim nihil, de rebus universi certe consuluerunt, ex quibus quum ea quoque, qum mihi eveniunt, necessario consequantur, amplecti haec debeo atque diligere.

Indeed, each person contributes to the work in their own way. Moreover, even the one who questions and tries to resist and remove those things that are happening contributes in an excessive manner.

For such a person was also needed in the world. Therefore, consider what remains for you to contribute, and how you align yourself with them in purpose:

For he who governs the universe will indeed make good use of you and include you among the workers and contributors to those things which support the task:

But be careful not to be such a part as in the fable, a cheap and ridiculous verse, as Chrysippus recalls.

Does the sun desire what belongs to rain? Does Aesculapius desire what belongs to fertility? What about the stars in the heavens? Don't they all, though diverse, contribute to the same purpose?

Indeed, if the gods have taken care of me and those things which ought to happen to me, they have taken care of me well.

For indeed, it is not easy for a god to be free from the need of deliberation or even from thinking.

But if they have not concerned themselves with me individually, they have certainly taken care of the universe, from which, when those things also happen to me, they necessarily follow. I should therefore embrace and cherish these things.

Sin vero de nulla prorsus re consuluerunt - credere tamen non fas est aut neque sacra faciamus neque preces fundamus, neque per eos iuremus neque alia faciamus, quae quidem singula facimus tanquam diis nobis praeaentibus et nobiscum viventibus - sin vero, inquam, de nulla mearum rermn consaluere, mihi quidem licet de me ipso consilium capere.

But if, indeed, they have not concerned themselves with any matter at all, it is not permissible to believe, nor should we perform sacred rites or offer prayers, nor swear by them, nor do any other things which we do individually as if the gods were present and living with us. But if, I say, they have not concerned themselves with any of my matters, then it is certainly permitted for me to take counsel for myself.

Mea autem deliberatio ad id quod utile est, spectat:

But my deliberation is aimed at what is useful.

Utile vero cuivis est, quod constitutioni ipsius ac naturae convenit:

Indeed, what is useful to anyone is what is in accordance with their own constitution and nature.

Natura autem mea rationalis est et societatis amans:

But my nature is rational and fond of social connections.

Civitas et patria mihi, ut Antonino, Roma, ut homini, mundus.

The city and country are for me, as for Antoninus, Rome; for a human being, the world.

Bis igitur civitatibus qum utilia sunt, ea mihi sola sunt bona.

Therefore, what is beneficial to the cities is beneficial to me twice over; those things alone are good for me.

45. Quaecunque singulis eveniunt, ea universo prosunt hoc suffecerit. Verum praeterea illud, quod, si animum adverteris, ubique videbis, quaecunque homini etiam aliis hominibus prodesse.

Whatever benefits each individual also benefits the whole; this will be sufficient. But furthermore, you will notice if you pay attention, that whatever benefits a person also benefits other people.

Vocabulum "utilis" nunc vulgari sensu de rebus mediis accipias.

Now take the term "useful" in the common sense, referring to ordinary things.

46. Quemadmodum te taedio afficiunt, quae in amphitheatro et eiusmodi locis spectantur, quippe quae quum eadem semper eiusdemque generis sint, quae spectantur, spectandi satietatem afferant, idem te in tota vita pati necesse est.

Just as you become bored with things that are watched in the amphitheater and similar places, precisely because they are always the same and of the same kind, and watching them brings about satiety, the same will be necessary for you to endure throughout your whole life.

Cuncta enim sursum deorsum eadem et ex iisdem. Quousque igitur?

For all things are from the same source and return to the same source. Therefore, where to?

47. Considera perpetuo, omnis generis omniumque et studiorum et gentium homines mortuos, ita ut ad Philistionem, Phoebum, Origanionem descendas. Transi nunc ad alia genera.

Constantly contemplate that people of all kinds, pursuits, and nations are dead – just as you would descend to Philistion, Phoebus, Origanion. Now transition to other types.

Eodemnos concedere oportet, quo tot oratores diserti, tot philosophi venerabiles, Aeraclitus, Pythgoras, Socrates, tot prisci heroes, tot postea imperatores, tyranni, post hos Eudoxus, Hipparchus, Archimede, alii porro acutis praediti ingeniis, magnanimi, laboriosi, versuti arrogantes, ipsi denique vitae hominum caducae et in diem durantis subsannatores, ut Menippus et omnes huius generis. Hos omnes cogita iamdudum iacere:

We must yield to the same fate as so many eloquent orators, revered philosophers, Heraclitus, Pythagoras, Socrates, ancient heroes, later emperors, tyrants, and after them Eudoxus, Hipparchus, Archimedes, others still endowed with sharp intellects, magnanimous, industrious, cunning, arrogant, and ultimately those mocking the fleeting life of humans day by day, like Menippus and all of this sort. Consider that all of these have long since been lying down:

Quid igitur iis inde mali? quid vero iis, qui ne nominantur quidem? Unum hic magni aestimandum, ut ipse veritatem et iustitiam colens erga mendaces et iniustos benevolum te praebeas.

What then is the harm to them from there? And what about those who are not even mentioned? One thing here is to be highly valued: that you, valuing truth and justice yourself, maintain a benevolent attitude towards liars and unjust people.

48. Si quando te exhilarare tibi libet, in mentem tibi revoca virtutes eorum, qui tecum vivunt, ut huius alacritatem in negotiis obeundis, illius verecundiam, huius munificentiam, illius aliam aliquam.

If ever you desire to cheer yourself up, call to mind the virtues of those who live with you, like the enthusiasm for undertaking tasks of one, the modesty of another, the generosity of this person, or some other trait of that person.

nihil enim ita animum oblectat, quam imagines virtutum in moribus eorum, quibuscum, vivitur, expressae et quam frequentissime visui sese offerentes. Quamobrem ad manum eas fac habeas.

For nothing delights the mind so much as the images of virtues embodied in the characters of those with whom you live, presented to the eye and frequently offering themselves to view. Therefore, keep these images at hand.

49. Numquid aegre fers, te tot pondo nec trecentorum esse? Sic vero etiam, quod tot annos neque ulterius victurus es.

Do you find it difficult to accept that you are not even worth as much as three hundred pounds? Likewise, do you also struggle with the fact that you will not live for many more years?

quemadmodum enim, quantum materiae tibi assignatum est, tanto es contentus, sic etiam quod attinet ad tempus.

Just as you are content with the amount of material assigned to you, so too should you be content with the time allotted to you.

50. Conemur iis persuadere. Verum etiam iis invitis age, quum iustitiae ratio sic exigit:

Let us try to persuade them. However, even if they resist, act in accordance with the dictates of justice.

si quis tamen vi tibi resistit, ad lenitatem et tranquillitatem te transfer et utere impedimento ad aliam virtutem exercendam.

If someone, however, resists you forcefully, shift yourself to leniency and tranquility, and use the obstacle as an opportunity to exercise another virtue.

ac memento, te cum exceptione rem aggredi, neque ea te voluisse, quae fieri nequeant. Quid igitur? ut talem agendi conatum habeas.

And remember, approach the matter with the reservation that you did not desire things that cannot be achieved. So, what then? Have the intention to act in such a way.

atque hunc assequeris:

and in this way, you attain it.

ad quae impulsi sumus, ea fiunt.

We do what we are driven to do.

51. Gloriae cupidus in aliena actione bonum suum situm esse opinatur.

The one eager for glory believes that their own good is situated in the actions of others.

voluptati deditus in sua ipsius affectione.

Devoted to pleasure in its own affection.

ratione utens in sua ipsius actione.

Using reason in its own action.

52. Licet de hac re nihil opinari, neque animo perturbari.

It is allowed to have no opinion on this matter and not be disturbed in mind.

res enim ipsae non ea sunt natura, ut iudicia nostra cogant.

For the things themselves are not of such nature that they compel our judgments.

53. Adsuesce iis, quae ab alio dicuntur, animum sedulo adhibere, et, quantum fieri potest, in dicentis animo esse.

Get accustomed to diligently paying attention to what is being said by others, and, as much as possible, being present in the speaker's mind.

54. Quod examini non prodest, neque api prodest.

What does not benefit the examination, nor benefits the bee.

55. Si vectores gubernatori, aegroti medico maledicerent, num ad aliud aliquid animum adverterent, quam ut ipse navigantibus salutem, aegrotantibus sanitatem pararet?

If sailors cursed the helmsman and sick people cursed the doctor, would they be paying attention to anything other than ensuring the helmsman's success in navigating for the sailors and the doctor's efforts in providing health for the sick?

56. Quam multi, quibuscum mundum intravi, iam excesserunt!

How many people I met when I entered the world have already passed away!

57. Aurigine affectis mel amarum videtur, et iis.

To those afflicted by iaundice, honey seems bitter, and to them...

Qui a cane rabido morsi sunt, aqua formidini est, et pueris pila res pulcra.

Those who have been bitten by a rabid dog fear water, and a ball is a beautiful thing for children.

Quid igitur irascor? an vero minus valere putas falsam opinionem, quam apud lymphaticum bilem, apud arquatum virus?

So why should I get angry? Do you really think a false opinion is of less value than lymphatic bile or bile from the gall bladder?

58. Quominus secundum tuae naturae rationem agas, nemo te impediet:

No one will hinder you from acting in accordance with your own nature's reason:

contra communis naturae rationem nihil tibi accidet.

Nothing contrary to the reason of universal nature will happen to you.

59. Quales sunt, quibus placere student et qualia ob emolumenta et qualibus actionibus! Quam cito aevum omnia abscondet et quam multa iam abscondidit!

What kinds of people are those who strive to please others, and for what rewards and actions! How quickly time will cover everything, and how much it has already covered!

LIBER VII

PAX INTERNA INTER CAOS

1. Quid est malitia? Id est, quod saepe vidisti.

What is wickedness? That is, what you have often seen.

Quidquid accidat, hoc tibi in promptu sit, esse id, quod saepe videris.

Whatever may happen, let this be readily available to you: to be what you have often seen.

Omnino sursum deorsum eadem deprehendes, quibus refertae sunt historiae priscae, mediae, recentes, quibus nunc refertae urbes et domus.

By all means, you will detect the same things up and down, with which ancient, middle, and recent stories are filled, with which cities and houses are now filled.

Nihil novi, omnia et usitata et brevi tempore durantia.

Nothing new, everything is both customary and enduring for a short time.

2. Placita qua alia ratione aboleri possunt, quam visis quae iis respondent, exstinctis? quae ut * non suscites continenter.

Opinions can be extinguished in no other way than by counteracting them with evidence that contradicts them, which you should consistently avoid arousing.

in tua potestate situm est.

It is within your power.

Possum, quod oportet, hac de re existimare.

I can assess what is necessary regarding this matter.

si possum, quid animo perturbor? quae extra mentem sunt, omnino nihil ad mentem meam.

If I can, why should I be disturbed in mind? Things that are outside the mind have absolutely no impact on my mind.

Sic affectus sis, et rectus es.

Thus, may you be in such a state, and you are upright.

reviviscere tibi licet.

You are allowed to come to life again.

intuere rursas res, ut eas intuitus es:

Look again at things, as you observed them:

in eo enim situm est reviviscere.

for it lies in that to come back to life.

3 · Inane pompae studium, fabulae scenicae, greges, armenta, velilationes, ossiculum canibus proiectum, offula in piscinas iniecta, formicarum aerumnae et baiulationes, musculorum perterritorum discursas, sigillaria verticillis commota.

The emptiness of the pursuit of pomp, the spectacle of plays, herds, flocks, cockfights, a bone thrown to dogs, bait thrown into fishponds, the troubles of ants and their flatteries, the scurrying of frightened mice, toy chariots moved by whirligigs.

Oportet igitur in his benevolo animo et sine ferocia consistere, animadvertere tamen, tanti quemvis esse, quanti sint ea, in quibus studium ponat.

Therefore, it's necessary to remain in these things with a benevolent and non-ferocious mind, to notice, however, that anyone's value is as much as the things on which they place their pursuit.

4 · In sermone iis, quae dicuntur, animum advertere te oportet, agendi impetu iis, quae fiunt, atque hic videre, ad quem finem referantur, illic observare, quid sit, quod significetur.

In conversation, it is necessary for you to pay attention to what is said, in actions to what is done, and to consider here what purpose they are aimed at, and there to observe what it is that is signified.

5 · Sufficitne mens mea ad hanc rem, necne? Si sufficit, ea utor ad rem efficiendam ut instrumento ab universi natura mihi dato:

Is my mind sufficient for this matter or not? If it's sufficient, I use it to accomplish this task as a tool given to me by the nature of the universe:

sin minus, aut hoc opus illi concedo, qui me melius id exsequi potest, si modo id me deceat, aut ipse pro viribus perago, adsumpto mihi auxiliario, qui mentis meae opera adiutus id efficere possit, quod societati hoc ipso tempore tempestivum et utile est.

but if not, either I yield this work to someone who can execute it better, if it is fitting for me to do so, or I myself undertake it to the best of my abilities, with the help of an assistant who, supported by my mental efforts, can achieve what is timely and useful for society at this very moment.

quidquid enim vel per me vel per alium facio, eo spectare debet, ut communi societati utile et consentaneum sit.

For whatever I do, either on my own or through someone else, it should aim to be useful and appropriate to the common society.

6. Quam multi, qui clarissimi fuerunt, iam oblivioni traditi sunt! quam multi, qui eos celebrarunt, e medio sublati!

How many, who were once renowned, have now fallen into oblivion! How many, who celebrated them, have been taken from our midst!

7. Auxilii ne te pudeat tibi enim propositum est, id quod tuum est facere, ut militi in moenium oppugnatione.

Do not be ashamed of seeking help, for it is your purpose to do what is yours, just as a soldier is in the assault on the walls.

Quid igitur, si claudicans ad propugnaculum solus adscendere nequeas, cum alio autem id fieri possit?

So what if you, limping, cannot ascend alone to the battlements, while it can be done with someone else?

8. Futura ne te perturbent.

Do not let future events disturb you.

venies enim ad ea, si opus erit, eadem ratione instructus, qua nunc ad praesentia uteris.

For you will approach them, if necessary, with the same strategy that you currently use for present matters.

9. Omnia inter se implexa sunt, et sanctum vinculum et nihil fere alterum ab altero alienum.

Everything is intertwined with each other, a sacred bond, and almost nothing is foreign to another.

nam inter se ordine composita sunt et simul eundem mundum exornant.

For they are arranged in an order with each other, and together they adorn the same world.

Nam et unus mundus ex omnibus, et unus Deus in omnibus, et una lex, ratio omnibus animalibus ratione praeditis communis, et una veritas, si quidem etiam una est perfectio animalium eiusdem generis et eiusdem rationis participum.

For there is one world out of all things, and one God in all things, and one law, a common reason for all creatures endowed with reason, and one truth, for indeed there is one perfection of animals of the same kind and participants of the same reason.

10. Quidquid materia constat, id celerrime in universi materiam evanescit, et quidquid causam continet, in omnium rerum rationem celerrime recipitur, et cuiusvis rei memoria celerrime in aevo sepelitur.

Whatever consists of matter quickly dissolves into the matter of the universe, and whatever contains a cause is quickly integrated into the understanding of all things, and the memory of any thing is quickly buried in the passage of time.

11. Animali ratione praedito eadem actio et secundum naturam et secundum rationem est.

For an animal endowed with reason, the same action is both according to nature and according to reason.

12. Rectus aut erectus.

Upright or erect.

13.

Quam rationem in unitis membra corporis habent, eandem in dissitis obtinent ea, quae ratione sunt praedita ad unam quandam mutuam operam comparata.

Just as they have a certain organization in the united members of the body, they maintain the same order in the separated things that are endowed with reason, arranged for a certain mutual cooperation.

Magis autem huius rei cogitatio animum tuum tanget, si saepius tibi ipse dixeris:

But the thought of this matter will touch your mind more if you often say to yourself:

"membrum sum eius, quod ex ratione praeditis compositum est, corporis.

I am a member of that which is composed of things endowed with reason, a body.

" Sin vero "partem" illius te esse dicis, nondum ex animo diligis homines:

But if you say that you are a "part" of it, you do not yet love people from your heart:

nondum te simpliciter delectat bene facere.

You are not yet genuinely pleased by doing good.

adhuc tanquam quod fieri decet id duntaxat facis, non tanquam tibi ipsi bene faciens.

You still do what is proper only as if it's necessary, not as someone truly doing good for themselves.

14.

Quidquid velit, extrinsecus accidat iis, quae eiusmodi casu affici possunt.

Whatever happens externally to those things that can be affected by such events, let it be.

illa enim quae affecta sunt, conquerantur, si velint.

For those things that have been affected may complain if they wish.

ego vero, si id, quod accidit, malum non censeo, nondum laedor:

But as for me, if I do not consider what happens to be bad, I am not hurt:

licet autem mihi non opinari.

Though I may not be of the same opinion.

15.

Quidquid aliquis vel faciat vel dicat, me probum esse oportet, non aliter ac si aurum aut smaragdus aut purpura semper hoc diceret:

Whatever someone does or says, I must be virtuous, as if gold or emerald or purple were always saying this:

Quidquid vel faciat aliquis vel dicat, me smaragdum esse oportet et colorem meum retinere.

Whatever someone does or says, I must be an emerald and maintain my own color."

16.

Principalis animi pars se ipsa non perturbat, hoc volo, se ipsa non in terrorem * doloremve iniicit.

The principal part of the mind does not disturb itself, I desire this, it does not throw itself into fear or pain.

si autem quis alius eam terrere aut ei dolorem afferre potest, faciat.

But if someone else can terrify or cause pain to that part of you, let them do it.

nam se ipsa non talibus dabit motibus opinando:

For it will not give itself such impulses by thinking:

corpusculum ne quid patiatur, sibi curae habeat, si potest, et, si quid patitur, queratur:

"Let the little body suffer something, let it take care of itself, if it can, and if it suffers something, let it complain."

animula autem quae terretur et dolet et de his omnino opinatur, nihil patietur.

But the small soul that can be frightened and feel pain and has such thoughts about these things will suffer nothing.

nam eam non * trahes in tale iudicium.

For you won't drag it into such judgments.

Nullius rei, quantum ad ipsum attinet, indigens est animi principatus, nisi sibi ipse indigentiam faciat, eaque de causa etiam sine perturbatione est, neque impediri potest, nisi se ipse perturbet et impediat.

It doesn't need the control of the mind regarding anything, as far as it is concerned, unless it makes itself needy, and for this reason, it remains without disturbance, and it cannot be hindered unless it disturbs and hinders itself.

17. Felicitas est bonus genius seu bonum.

Happiness is a good spirit or good.

Quid igitur, hic facis, phantasia? Abi, per deos! ut accessisti:

So what, are you doing here, imagination? Go away, by the gods! Now that you've come:

nihil enim te opus habeo.

I have no need of you.

Accessisti, autem e prisca cousuetudine:

You came, however, from ancient habit:

non succenseo tibi.

I do not hold a grudge against you.

abi tantum!

Iust go away!

18. Mutationem quis metuit? Quid vero fieri potest sine mutatione? quid vero gratius aut fa miliarius universi naturae?

Who fears change? But what can happen without change? What is more pleasing or familiar to the nature of the universe?

tune ipse balneo uti potes, nisi lignis mutatis?

Can you take a bath yourself unless the wood is changed?

num ali, nisi cibis mutatis?

Can you eat anything else unless the foods are changed?

num quid aliud perfici potest sine mutatione?

Can anything else be accomplished without change?

Non igitur vides par esse tui mutationem et pariter necessariam universi naturae?

So don't you see that your own change is in harmony and equally necessary with the nature of the universe?

19. Per rerum omnium materiam, tanquam per torrentem, transeunt omnia corpora, universo cognata et cooperantia, ut nostrae inter se partes.

Through the material of all things, like through a stream, all bodies pass, related and cooperating with the whole, iust as the parts are among themselves.

Quot iam Chrysippos, quot Socrates, quot Epictetos aevum absorpsit!

How many Chrysippuses, how many Socrateses, how many Epictetuses has time swallowed up!

Idem vero et de quovis homine et de quavis re tibi succurrat!

Indeed, let the same thought come to you about any person or any thing!

20. Me hoc unum sollicitum tenet, ne quid ipse faciam, quod hominis conditio nolit aut sic nolit aut nunc nolit.

This one thing worries me, that I do nothing that the nature of a human being would not want or would not want in that way or at this moment.

Instat tempus, quo tu omnium oblitus eris:

The time is pressing when you will forget all things:

instat, quo omnes tui obliti erunt.

the time is pressing when all will forget you.

22. Homini proprium, etiam eos, qui offendunt, diligere hoc autem fit tum, quum tibi succurrit, et cognatos tibi esse, et inscios invitosque peccare, et paulo post utrumque vestrum esse moriturum, et ante omnia te ab ea non esse laesum.

It is natural for a person to love even those who offend him, but this happens when it occurs to you that they are related to you, and that they sin out of ignorance and against their will, and shortly thereafter both of you will die, and above all, that you have not been harmed by them.

non enim principatum animi tui deteriorem reddidit, quam antea erat.

For it has not made the dominion of your mind worse than it was before.

23. Universitatis natura ex universa materia, tanquam ex cera, nunc equuleum effinxit, nunc, hoc dissoluto, materia eius ad arborem gignendam usa est, tum ad homunculum, deinde ad aliud quidpiam:

The nature of the universe has fashioned from the entire material, iust as from wax, now a little horseman, now, with this dissolved, it has used its material to create a tree, then a little man, then something else:

horum autem quodlibet ad brevissimum temporis spatium subsistit.

But each of these lasts only for a very short period of time.

Iniquum autem nequaquam est arculae dissolvi, ut neque compingi.

However, it is by no means unjust for a little chest to be destroyed, just as it is not unjust for it to be put together.

24. Iratus vultus admodum contra naturam, quum saepe immoriatur decus et ad extremum ista exstinguatur, ut omnino suscitari nequeat:

An angry expression is quite contrary to nature when often beauty dies and in the end it is extinguished, so that it cannot be revived at all:

atque ex hoc ipso fac intelligas, etiam contra rationem esse.

And from this very fact, you should understand that it is even against reason.

Nam si etiam conscientia peccandi abibit, quaenam erit vivendi causa?

For if even the consciousness of sinning departs, what will be the reason for living?

25. Quaecunque vides, haec omnia iamiam natura, quae res omnes administrat, mutabit, aliaque ex eorum materia faciet, et ex horum rursus alia, ut mundus semper sit novus.

Whatever you see, all these things will soon be changed by nature, which governs all things, and it will make other things from their material, and then from those others again, so that the world is always new.

26. Si quando aliquis aliquid in te peccavit, statim considera, qua boni aut mali opinione ductus peccaverit, hoc enim intellecto, misereberis illius, neque aut miraberis aut succensebis.

If someone has done something wrong to you, immediately consider with what opinion of good or evil he was led to do wrong. With this understanding, you will have compassion for him, neither wondering nor being angry.

nam aut et ipse idem, quod ille, adhuc bonum opinaris aut aliud eiusdem generis oportet igitur illi ignoscas:

For either he himself still thinks the same thing that he did, good, or you must pardon him of the same kind:

si non amplius eiusmodi res bona aut mala esse opinaris, facile benignus eris visu laboranti.

If you do not think such things are good or bad anymore, you will easily be kind in your appearance to someone struggling.

27. Noli absentia cogitare ut iam praesentia, sed ex praesentibus optima quaeque elige, eorumque gratia tunc reputa, quanto studio requirerentur, si non adessent.

Do not think of absence as if it were present, but choose the best from what is present, and consider for their sake how much effort they would require if they were not present.

Simul tamen cave, ne idcirco, quod ea libenter accipis, animo suescas, tanti ea aestimare, ut, si quando defuerint, animo perturberis.

However, be cautious not to become accustomed to valuing things so highly just because you accept them willingly, that you are troubled in mind if they ever go missing.

28. In temet ipsum te contrahe:

Withdraw into yourself:

ea est natura mentis ratione praeditae, ut sibi sufficiat ipsa, quando iusta agit atque eo ipso tranquillitate fruitur.

Contract yourself into yourself:

29. Dele visum:

Delete the appearance:

compesce affectuum motum:

Restrain the movement of emotions:

circumscribe praesens tempus:

Narrow down the present moment:

cognosce id, quod accidit sive tibi sive alii:

Understand what happens, whether to you or others:

divide rem menti subiectam in materiam et formam cogita horam novissimam:

Divide the matter subiect to the mind into material and form, think of the final hour:

quod ab illo peccatum est, ibi relinque, ubi peccatum est.

Leave behind what was wrong there, where it was wrong.

30. Intendere animum in ea, quae dicuntur:

Direct your mind to things that are said:

mente penetrare in ea, quae fiunt, et ea, quae faciunt.

Penetrate with your mind into things that are done, and into those who do them.

31. Exhilara te ipsum simplicitate, verecundia et indifferentia adversus ea, quae medio inter virtutem et vitiositatem loco sunt.

Reioice in yourself with simplicity, modesty, and indifference towards things that lie in the space between virtue and vice.

Dilige genus humanum.

Love humanity.

Obsequere deo.

Obey the divine.

"Omnia," inquit ille, "legitiime.

"Everything," he said, "legitimately.

" Praeterea* aut dii aut elementa - sed sufficit illud, omnia ex lege fieri.

" Moreover, either gods or elements - but it is enough to say that all things happen according to law.

- Utique pauca.

- Certainly few things.

32. De morte:

Regarding death:

si dissipatio, aut atomi, aut exinanitio, aut exstinctio, aut translatio.

if dispersion, or atoms, or annihilation, or extinction, or transition.

33. De dolore:

Regarding pain:

si intolerabilis est, e vita educit.

si durat, tolerabilis est:

mens, dum in semet se recipit, suam tranquillitatem servat, nec deterior fit principalis animi pars:

membra vero, quae dolore afficiantur, si possunt, de eo statuant.

34. De gloria:

intuere mentes eorum, quales sint, qualia fugiant, qualia sectentur.

et, sicut arenarum cumuli alii super alios aggesti priores abscondant, ita etiam in vita priora a succedentibus celerrime abscondi.

35. Platonicum.

"Qui mente praeditus est sublimi et tempus omne omnemque rerum naturam contemplatus est, num is tibi videtur vitam humanam magni aestimare? Non potest fieri, inquit ille.

Igitur nec mortem ille terribilem existimabit.

Minime vero.

36. Antisthenicum.

Regium est, quum recte facias male audire.

37. Turpe est, vultum obsequentem esse atque ita se conformare et componere, ut mens iubet, ipsum autem animum ad suum ipsius arbitrium non conformari et componi.

38. Nam neutiquam homines rebus irasci decet:

nil quippe curant ipsa?.

if it is unbearable, it takes you out of life.

If it endures, it is tolerable:

The mind, while it withdraws into itself, maintains its tranquility and does not become worse, the principal part of the mind:

But the limbs that are affected by pain, if they can, should make decisions about it.

Regarding glory:

Observe the minds of those people, what they are like, what they avoid, what they pursue.

And just as heaps of sand, when piled one upon the other, conceal the earlier ones by the later ones, so also in life, the past is quickly concealed by what comes after.

Following the Style of Plato:

"Someone who possesses a lofty mind and has contemplated all time and the entire nature of things, does he seem to you to value human life greatly? It cannot be, he says.

Therefore, he will not consider death to be terrible.

Indeed not.

in the style of Antisthenes:

It's royal when you do right and hear it spoken of as wrong.

It's disgraceful to have a compliant face and to so conform and compose yourself as your mind dictates, yet not to conform and compose your own mind according to its own judgment.

Indeed, it is by no means fitting for people to be angry at things:

For do they care at all?

39.	Immortalibus et nobis tu gaudia dones!
	Grant us, both the immortal beings and ourselves, joys!
40.	Vitam metere ut aristam frugiferam,
	To measure life like a fruitful ear of grain,
	atque hunc esse.
	and to consider this to be it.
	illum non.
	But not that.
41.	Si me meosque liberos di negligant,
	If the gods neglect me and my children,
	huius quoque constat ratio.
	the same reasoning applies here too.
42.	Aequum et iustum a me est.
	It is fair and iust for me.
43.	Noli cum aliis lamentari aut exsultare.
	Do not mourn or reioice with others.
44.	[Platonicai.]
	Platonic.
	"Ego vero huic haud iniuria hoc responderim:
	"I have indeed responded to this argument without unfairness:
	Non bene statuis, homo, si putas, viro, qui vel minimi sit usus, consentaneum esse, vitae discrimen aut mortem respicere, ac non id unum potius considerare, quando agit, utrum iusta an iniusta agat, ea, quae probi, an ea, quae improbi viri sunt."
	You do not iudge well, man, if you think that it is fitting for a man, who is of little use, to contemplate the distinction between life and death, and not to consider this one thing above all, whether he acts iustly or uniustly, whether his actions are those of an honorable or a dishonorable man."
45.	"Profecto res se ita habet, Athenienses:
	"Indeed, Athenians, the matter stands thus:
	quo quisque loco te ipse constituerit, id ipsum sibi optimum ratus.
	each person esteems as best for himself the position in which he has placed himself.
	aut ab imperatore constitutus fuerit, in eo, ut mihi videtur, oportet eum manentem periclitari et nec mortem neque aliud quidquam magis formidare, quam turpitudinem."
	Or if he has been appointed by an emperor, in that case, as it seems to me, he must face danger while remaining in it, and not fear death or anything else more than dishonor."

46.
"Verum vide, o bone, ne aliud quid sit generosum et bonum, quam servare et servari, ne ei, qui vere sit vir, hoc, ut quam diutissime vivat, mittendum nec vitae adhaerescendum sit, sed his Deo permissis et fide habita mulierculis, fieri nou posse, ut fatum quisquam effugiat, deinde hoc ei sit perpendendum, qua ratione hoc ipso tempore, quo vita fungetur, quam optime vivat."

"But truly see, my good friend, that nothing else is noble and good but to preserve and be preserved, that a true man should not focus on living as long as possible and cling to life, but that when these things are entrusted to God and with faith in little women, it can happen that no one escapes fate, then it must be considered by him how he can live best during this very time in which he lives."

47.
Contemplare astrorum cursus quasi cum iis circumactus.

Contemplate the movements of the stars as if you were moving with them.

et elementorum alius in aliud mutationes continenter considera:

And continuously observe the transformations of the elements into each other:

harum enim rerum considerationes sordes vitae terrestris abstergunt.

For these considerations cleanse the filth of earthly life.

48.
Praeclarum est illud Platonis:

The saying of Plato is excellent:

Atque utique eum, qui de hominibus loquitur, oportet etiam terrestria e superiore aliquo loco intueri, singulos greges, exercitus, agricolationes, nuptias, reconciliationes.

And certainly, the person who speaks of human affairs must also look down on earthly matters from some higher place, considering the individual herds, armies, agricultural activities, marriages, reconciliations.

ortus, interitus, iudiciorum strepitus, loca deserta, varias barbarorum gentes, festa, lamentationes, nundinas, promiscuam colluviem et quod e contrariis adornatum est.

Births, deaths, the noise of judgments, deserted places, various barbarian tribes, festivals, lamentations, marketplaces, a mingled stream of various things and what is adorned with contrasts.

49.
Praeterita animo recolere oportet et tot imperiorum mutationes:

It is necessary to recall the past in the mind and the many changes of empires:

licet etiam futura prospicere.

It is even possible to foresee the future.

eiusdem enim omnino generis erunt neque fieri potest, ut extra numerum eorum, quae nunc fiunt, se moveant.

For they will be of the same kind altogether, and it is impossible for them to move beyond the number of those things that are happening now.

quamobrem perinde est, per quadraginta annos vitam humanam perlustrare atque per, decem millia annorum.

Therefore, it is just the same, to explore human life for forty years or for ten thousand years.

Quid enim plus videbis?

For what more will you see?

50. Retroque meant, quae terra dedit, iterum in terram:

And return again what the earth has given, back to the earth:

quod ab aetherio venerat ortu, coeleste poli repetit templum.

What came from the ethereal rising returns to the celestial temple of the heavens.

Aut hoc atomorum inter se adhaerentium dissolutio et talis aliqua dispersio elementorum sensu carentium.

Or the dissolution of adhering atoms among themselves and some kind of dispersion of elements devoid of sensation.

51. Et:

And:

Cibo potuque et magicis artibus.

Turning the course of fate, so that they do not die.

Fati cursum avertentes, ne moriantur.

Turning away the course of fate, so that they do not die.

Divinitus at spirantem auram

Breathing the divine air.

pati necesse est cum labore et lacrimis.

Someone might be more skilled in mourning.

52. Est aliquis luctu peritior.

There is someone more skilled in mourning.

verum non societatis amantior, non verecundior, non constantior in iis, quae accidunt nec lenior erga aliorum peccata.

But not more fond of society, not more modest, not more steadfast in things that happen, nor more lenient towards the mistakes of others.

53. Ubi effici potest ullum opus secundum rationem diis et hominibus communem, ibi nihil est, quod reformides.

Where any work can be accomplished in accordance with reason, shared by both gods and humans, there is nothing you should fear.

iam ubi utilitatem consequi potes per actionem prospere progredientem et secundum constitutionem tuam procecedentem, ibi ne suspicio quidem damni esse debet.

Now, when you can attain utility through an action that is progressing successfully and proceeding in accordance with your nature, there shouldn't even be a suspicion of harm.

54. Ubique ac semper penes te est, et in casu praesente pie acquiescere, et cum hominibus, qui nunc sunt ex iustitiae lege versari, et visum, quod nunc se offert, explorare, ne quid quod comprehendi nequit, subrepat.

It is always and everywhere within your power to acquiesce piously in the present circumstance, and to abide by the law of justice with the people who are currently present, and to examine the appearance that presents itself now, lest something that cannot be grasped escapes.

55. Noli aliorum mentes circumspicere, sed eo recta intuere, quo natura ducit, universi natura per ea, quae tibi accidunt, tua per ea, quae agere debes.

Do not inspect the minds of others, but look straight ahead where nature leads, the nature of the universe through what happens to you, your own nature through what you must do.

Id autem cuique agendum, quod constitutioni eius consentaneum est.

But each person must do what is suitable for their own constitution.

comparata autem cetera ratione praeditorum causa, ut in omnibus aliis deteriora meliorum gratia.

Yet, when compared by the standard of beings endowed with reason, they exist to make the better things worse in all other respects.

Praestantissimum vero in hominis natura est societatis studium.

But the most excellent quality in human nature is the pursuit of social life.

secundum, se non permittere corporeis affectionibus.

Second, not to allow oneself to be controlled by bodily emotions.

motui enim, qui a ratione et intellectu oritur, proprium est, se ipsum circumscribere, neque unquam sensuum aut impetus affectionibus succumbere:

For the motion that arises from reason and intellect is characteristic of itself, to circumscribe itself, and never to yield to the passions of the senses or impulses:

animalium enim utrique motus sunt.

For both of these are motions of animals.

sed qui ab intellectu oritur principatum sibi vindicat, neque ab illis se regi patitur:

But the one that arises from intellect claims dominion for itself and does not allow itself to be ruled by those:

idque iure.

And this is rightfully so.

natura enim ita est constitutus.

For nature is thus constituted.

ut omnibus illis utatur.

In order to make use of all those things.

Tertium in natura rationali est, a temeritate in assentiendo et errore alienum esse.

The third characteristic in rational nature is to be free from rash assent and the error of others.

Haec igitur firmiter tenens principatus animi recta procedat et habet quae sua sunt.

Holding firmly to these, let the governing part of the mind proceed rightly and possess what is its own.

56. Ut mortuum et qui ad hoc duntaxat tempus vixerit, quod reliquum estex abundanti vivere naturae convenienter.

To live in accordance with nature, iust like one who is dead and has lived only up to this point, which is the remaining time of abundant life.

57. Id solum diligere, quod ipsi accidit et fato connexunt est.

To love only what happens to you and is connected by fate.

Quid enim concinnius?

For what could be more harmonious?

58. In singulis, quae accidunt, eos ante oculos habere, quibus eadem obveniebant et qui deinde ea aegre ferebant, ut nova admirabantur, querebantur.

In each thing that happens, to have before your eyes those to whom the same things occurred and who afterwards bore them with difficulty, as they admired and complained about new things.

ubi iam sunt illi? nusquam.

Where are they now? Nowhere.

Cur igitur tu similiter agere vis ac non potius alienos illos motus iis relinquere, qui eos movent iisque moventur? ipse vero totus in eo esse, quomodo iis uteris? autem recte tibique materia erunt:

Why then do you want to act in the same way and not rather leave those motions to others who move them and are moved by them? But to be entirely absorbed in how you use them? And truly, they will be materials for you:

huc modo animum adverte et operam da, ut in omni actione bonum te praestes.

Now, turn your mind here and give effort, so that you show yourself to be good in every action.

Denique memento utriusque, nihil tua interesse quae eveniant, interesse autem tua, quae agas.

Finally, remember that it does not matter to you what happens, but it matters to you what you do.

59. Intus fode:

Delve into your inner self:

intus fons boni isque qui semper scaturiat, si quidem semper fodias.

dig inwardly to the source of good, and that which always springs forth, if indeed you dig continually.

60. Oportet vero etiam corpus fixum esse et neque in motu neque in gestu temere iactari.

Certainly, the body must also be steady and not be carelessly thrown into motion or gesture.

sicut enim in vultu mens se prodit, eumque et compositum et decorum servare studet, ita ut idem in toto corpore fiat, studendum est:

Iust as the mind reveals itself in the countenance, and strives to maintain composure and dignity, so it should be in the entire body:

haec autem omnia sine affectatione observanda.

All these things, however, should be observed without affectation.

61. Ars vivendi luctatoriae similior, quam saltatoriae, quatenus adversus ea, quae incidunt et improvisa sunt, parata et immota consistit.

The art of living is more like that of a wrestler than a dancer, insofar as it stands prepared and unmoved against things that happen unexpectedly.

62. Assiduo perpendere, quales sint, a quibus testimonium tibi exhiberi cupis et qualibus praediti sint mentibus.

Constantly reflect on the qualities of those from whom you desire to receive testimony and what kind of minds they possess.

Neque enim incusabis invite peccantes, neque testimonio indigebis, perspectis opinionum et consiliorum fontibus.

For you will neither reproach those who make mistakes unwillingly, nor will you require testimony, having considered the sources of opinions and advice.

63. "Quaevis anima," inquit "invita privatur veritate.

"Any soul," he says, "deprived of truth unwillingly."

"Itaque etiam iuatitia et temperantia et benevolentia et aliis eiusmodi virtutibus.

And so also with iustice, temperance, benevolence, and other such virtues.

Necesse autem est, huius continuo memineris.

However, you must constantly remember this.

eris enim erga omnes mitior.

For you will be gentler towards everyone.

64. In omni dolore hoc in promptu sit, eum nec turpem esse, nec mentem gubernatricem reddere deteriorem.

In every pain, let it be readily available that it is neither disgraceful nor does it make the governing mind worse.

neque enim eam, quatenus ratione praedita est.

For it does not corrupt it as long as it is endowed with reason.

neque, quatenus societatis amans, corrumpit.

Nor does it corrupt it as long as it loves society.

In plerisque tamen doloribus tibi adiumento sit illud Epicuri, neque intolerabilem esse dolorem, neque aeternum, si modo finium, quibus continetur, memor sis neque opinione quidquam adiicias.

However, in most pains, that saying of Epicurus should assist you: that pain is neither intolerable nor eternal, provided you remember the limits within which it is contained and do not add anything through opinion.

Id quoque recordare, multa, quae eandem cum labore naturam habent, clam molestiam creare, ut dormiturire, aestu affici, nausea laborare:

Also, remember this: many things that have a similar nature with pain cause annoyance secretly, like falling asleep, being affected by heat, suffering from nausea.

quando igitur horum aliquid moleste fers, dic tibi, te dolori succumbere.

Therefore, whenever you bear any of these things with difficulty, tell yourself that you are submitting to pain.

65. Cave unquam erga inhumanos sic adficiaris, ut homines erga homines.

Never let yourself be affected by inhumane treatment in such a way as humans treat other humans.

66. Unde nobis constat, an Telauges non praestantior Socrate fueriti? Neque enim satis est, quod Socrates gloriosiore morte occubuit et acutius cum sophistis disserebat et patientius in frigore pernoctabat, et Salaminium illum sistere iussus generosius resistere decrevit, et in viis fastum prae se ferebat, ad quod quis vel maxime animadverteret, si quidem verum esset.

Hence, is it clear to us whether Telauges was not superior to Socrates? For it is not enough that Socrates died a more glorious death and debated more shrewdly with sophists and endured the cold more patiently and, when ordered to stop the Salaminian fleet, decided to resist more nobly, and carried himself with arrogance on the streets, which anyone would notice most, if it were true,

sed hoc considerari oportet, quali animo fuerit Socrates, an potuerit contentus esse eo, quod se erga homines iustum et erga deos pium praeberet, nec temere malitiam cuiusquam indignaretur, neque ignorantiae serviliter assentaretur aut tanquam peregrinum quidquam exciperet ab universo ipsi assignatum aut tanquam intolerandum sustineret, neque carunculae affectionibus mentem afiici pateretur.

But this must be considered: with what kind of mindset was Socrates, whether he could be content with presenting himself as just toward humans and pious toward gods, whether he would not rashly be indignant at anyone's malice, whether he would not servilely assent to ignorance or accept anything assigned to him by the universe itself as if it were foreign, whether he would not endure anything as intolerable, whether he would not allow his mind to be affected by the affections of the flesh.

67. Non ita te natura huic mixtioni commisit, ut tibi non liceat te ipsum circumscribere, et, quae tui sunt muneris, tuae potestati subiicere.

Nature has not entrusted you to this mixture in such a way that you are not allowed to circumscribe yourself and subject to your own power what is your duty.

omnino enim fieri potest, ut divinus vir sis et a nemine agnoscaris.

For it is entirely possible for you to be a divine person and yet not be recognized by anyone.

Huius semper memento, simul etiam illius, in paucissimis vitam beatam esse positam, et quamvis desperes te logicorum aut physicorum peritum fore, noli tamen desperare, te liberum et verecundum et societatis amantem et deo obsequentem esse futurum.

Always keep this in mind, along with the fact that a happy life is based on very few things. And although you may despair of becoming skilled in logic or physics, do not despair of becoming a free, modest, sociable, and God-obeying person.

68. Tutum ab omni vi in summa animi tranquiliitate vivere, etiamsi omnes quaecunque velint adversus te vociferentur, etiamsi membra corporeae illius massae, quae te circumdat, a feris lanientur.

It is safe to live in the utmost tranquility of mind, untouched by any force, even if all those who wish could shout against you, even if the members of that body mass that surrounds you were torn by wild beasts.

Quid enim obstat, quominus inter haec omnia mens tranquillam se servet, de rebus, quae circumstant, vere iudicantem, iisque, quae prae manibus sunt, prout decet, utentem? ita ut iudicium rei, quae incidit.

For what prevents your mind from remaining calm among all these things, judging things truly as they are, and using those that are at hand as appropriate? Thus, let the iudgment of the matter that has arisen

dicat:

say:

"hoc es revera, quamquam ex opione alius generis videris," et usus rei, quae accidit:

"This is indeed what it is, even though you seem to be of a different kind according to opinion," and the use of the matter that has happened:

"te quaerebam.

"I was looking for you."

"Semper enim mihi quaelibet res praesens materia est virtutis rationi et societati consentaneae omninoque artis humanae aut divinae.

For always, to me, any present thing is the material of virtue, congruent with reason and society, and entirely within the realm of human or divine art.

Quidquid enim accidit, id vel deo vel homini familiare redditur, neque novum est, neque ad tractandum difficile, sed familiare et tractabile.

For whatever happens, it is rendered familiar either to God or to humanity, and it is neither new nor difficult to handle, but familiar and manageable.

69. Hoc praestat pertectio morum, ut omnem diem tanquam supremum agas nec palpites nec torpeas nec simules.

This is the practice of moral integrity, that you live each day as if it were your last, neither hesitating nor growing sluggish nor pretending.

70.

Dii, quum immortales sint, non aegre ferunt, quod in aevo tam diuturno eos omnino semper oportet tam multos tamque improbos perferre, immo vero etiam omni modo eorum curam gerunt.

The gods, being immortal, do not take offense, since in their everlasting existence, they must always endure so many and such wicked beings, and in fact they care for them in every way.

tu vero, qui iamiam moriturus es, defatigaris, idque quum ipse ex eorum numero sis?

But you, who are about to die very soon, do you grow weary, considering that you are one of them?

71.

Ridiculum est, tuam ipsius vitiositatem non fugere, quod fieri potest, aliorum autem fugere, quod fieri nequit.

It is ridiculous to avoid your own imperfections, which is possible, and yet try to avoid the imperfections of others, which is not possible.

72.

Quidquid vis rationalis et societatis amans neque rationi consentaneum neque societati utile reperit, id iure infra se positum iudicat.

Whatever a rational and sociable person does not find to be in accord with reason or useful for society, they judge rightly to be beneath them.

73.

Ubi tu alteri bene fecisti et hic a te beneficio affectus est, quid praeterea stultorum exemplo tertium quaeris, ut bene fecisse aliis videaris et gratiam recipias?

When you have done good to another and they are grateful to you for it, why, following the foolish example, do you look for a third party so that you appear to have done good to others and receive gratitude?

74.

Nemo defatigatur utilitatem accipiendo:

No one is worn out by receiving benefit:

utilitas autem est actio naturae consentanea.

benefit, indeed, is an action in accordance with nature.

Noli igitur defatigari tibi prodesse in eo, in quo alii prodes.

Therefore, do not grow weary of benefiting yourself in the same way that you benefit others.

75.

Universi natura mundi condendi consilium cepit:

The whole nature of the universe decided on the plan of creating the world:

iam vero aut, quidquid fit, per necessariam consequentiam fit, aut nulla ratione gubernautur ea quoque, quae principia lia sunt, ad quae gignenda singulari consilio utitur mundi principatus.

Indeed, either whatever happens, happens by necessary consequence, or those things are not governed by any reason, even the very principles to which the ruler of the world resorts in creating them, through a special plan.

In multis te tranquilliorem reddet hoc memoria servatum.

Preserving this in memory will make you more tranquil in many aspects.

LIBER VIII

PRAESENS MOMENTUM AMPLEXANS

I. Hoc quoque ad contemnendam vanam gloriam facit, quod non amplius totam vitam, eam saltem, quae a prima aetate peracta est, ut philosophum decet, peregisse potes sed et multis aliis et tibi ipsi visus es longissime a philosophia abesse.

This also contributes to the disregard of empty fame, for you have not spent your whole life, even that part which is already behind you, as a philosopher should. You have also appeared to others, and even to yourself, to be far from philosophy.

Perturbatus igitur es, ut philosophi nomen tueri non amplius tibi facile sit:

Thus, you are disturbed, so that it is no longer easy for you to maintain the name of philosopher;

adversatur autem vitae quoque institutum.

yet, it also conflicts with your way of life.

Siquidem igitur recte intellexisti, quo in loco res sit posita, missa existimatione tua, eo contentus sis, si quod reliquum est vitae, quantumcunque donum natura tibi dare velit bene transigis.

Therefore, if you have understood correctly where matters stand, let go of your reputation, and be content if whatever portion of life remains is spent well according to whatever gift nature may bestow upon you.

Disce, igitur, quid velit, neque aliud quidquam te distrahat:

So, learn what it desires, and let nothing else distract you:

expertus enim es, circa quot res vagatus beatam vitam nusquam inveneris, non in ratiocinationibus, non in divitiis, non in gloria.

For you have experienced how, wandering through so many things, you have not found a happy life anywhere— not in reasonings, not in wealth, not in glory, nowhere in pleasure,

non in oblectatione, nusquam.

Not in pleasure either, nowhere.

Ubi igitur sita est? In eo, ut facias, quae hominis natura exigit:

So where is it then? In doing what human nature demands:

haec vero quomodo facies? si decreta habes, ex quibus agendi conatus et actiones existunt.

But how will you do this? If you have principles from which efforts and actions arise.

Quaenam decreta? de bonis et malis nihil bonum esse homini, quod eum non iustum, temperantem, fortem, liberum reddat, nihil malum, quod non efficiat contraria iis, quae dixi.

What principles? That in matters of good and evil, there is nothing good for a person that does not make them iust, temperate, courageous, and free; nothing bad that does not lead to the opposite of these qualities that I mentioned.

2 . In singulis actionibus te ipse interroga:

In each action, ask yourself:

Quomodo haec mihi habet? num eius me poenitebit? breve est tempus, et mortuus sum et omnia evanuerunt.

How does this benefit me? Will I regret this? Time is short, I will die, and everything will fade away.

Quid est, quod amplius requiram, si id quod nunc facio est animalis ratione praediti, societatis studiosi, ex eadem, qua deus, lege agentis?

What more do I need, if what I am doing now is in accordance with the reason of a rational being, a lover of society, acting by the same law that governs the divine?

3 . Alexander et Gaius et Pompeius quid ad Diogenem et Heraclitum et Socratem?

What do Alexander, Gaius, and Pompeius have to do with Diogenes, Heraclitus, and Socrates?

Hi enim et res et earum causas ac materias perspectas habebant et eorum mentes erant semper eaedem.

For the latter had insight into both things and their causes and materials, and their minds were always the same.

In illis vero quot rerum erat cautio, quantarum rerum servitus!

In those people, how much was guarded against, how much servitude to things!

4 . Nihilominus eadem facient, etiamsi tu ruptus fueris.

Nonetheless, they will do the same, even if you are broken.

5 . Primum noli perturbari:

First, do not be disturbed:

omnia enim secundum universi naturam eveniunt, et intra breve tempus nullus usquam eris, ut neque Hadrianus neque Augustus:

For all things happen according to the nature of the universe, and in a short time, you will be nowhere, just as neither Hadrian nor Augustus will be.

dein in rem intentus eam considera, memor simul, te oportere esse virum bonum, et, quod hominis natura exigit, id fac simpliciter, et loquere, ut iustissimum tibi videtur, modo placide, verecunde et sine simulatione.

Then, focused on the matter at hand, consider that you ought to be a good person, and do what human nature requires of you in a straightforward manner. Speak as you believe to be most iust, but do so calmly, modestly, and without pretense.

6. Rerum omnium natura hoc agit, ut quae hic sunt, illuc transferat et mutet, hinc tollat et illic deponat:

The nature of all things works to transfer and change what is here to there, take away from here and deposit there.

omnia mutantur;

All things change;

hinc non est ut metuas, ne quid novi:

therefore, there is no need to fear anything new.

omnia usitata, sed etiam omnia aequaliter distribuuntur.

All things are familiar, and all things are distributed equally.

7. Omnis natura sese ipsa contenta est, quando prospere procedit:

Every nature is content with itself when it proceeds prosperously.

natura autem ratione praedita prospere procedit, ubi in oblatis rerum visis neque falso neque dubie assen titur;

However, nature endowed with reason proceeds prosperously when it neither accepts things presented falsely nor in doubt.

animi porro impetus ad solas actiones societati convenientes dirigit;

Furthermore, the impulses of the soul direct towards actions that are appropriate for society alone.

ea denique tantum appetit et aversatur, quae in nostra potestate sita sunt et quidquid a communi natura assignatum est amplectitur;

It seeks only what is within our power and embraces whatever is assigned by the common nature.

eius enim pars est, quemadmodum natura folii pars est naturae arboris, nisi quod folii natura pars est naturae sensu ac ratione carentis eiusdemque, quae impediri potest;

For it is a part of it, iust as the nature of a leaf is a part of the nature of a tree, except that the nature of the leaf is a part of the nature lacking in sense and reason, and of that which can be hindered.

hominis contra natura pars na turm, quae impediri non potest, rationalis et iustae, si quidem ex aequo pro cuiusque dignitate tempus, materiam, formam, facultatem, eventum singulis tribuit:

The part of a human being, on the other hand, is not contrary to nature; it cannot be hindered. It is rational and iust, indeed, as long as it impartially assigns to each person, in accordance with their dignity, the time, material, form, capacity, and outcome.

considera autem, non, an singula cum singulis comparando aequalia in omnibus reperias, sed, an universis alterius cum alterius confertim comparatis.

However, consider not whether you find equality in each particular compared with another, but whether when comparing the general tendencies of one with those of another, you find equality.

8. Legere non licet.

   Reading is not permitted.

   At contumeliam arcere licet;

   But you are permitted to ward off insult;

   at voluptates ac dolores contemnere licet;

   you are permitted to disregard pleasures and pains;

   at gloriola supe.

   you are permitted to be above petty glory;

   riorem esse licet;

   you are permitted to consider yourself richer;

   at stupidis et ingratis non irasci, adeoque eorum curam gerere licet.

   you are permitted not to get angry with the foolish and ungrateful, and therefore, you are permitted to care for them.

9. Nemo te posthac aut vitam aulicam aut tuam reprehendentem audiat.

   Henceforth, let no one hear you criticizing either court life or your own.

10. Poenitentia est reprehensio quaedam sui ipsius, quasi utile quid neglexerit;

    Regret is a kind of self-reproach, as if one has neglected something useful;

    bonum autem sit utile quid necesse est, et quod curae esse debeat viro bono et honesto;

    but what is good must necessarily be useful, and what should concern a good and honorable person;

    neminem vero bonum et honestum poeniteret, si voluptatem aliquam neglexisset neque igitur utile neque bonum est voluptas.

    and surely no honorable and good person would regret having passed up some pleasure. Therefore, neither pleasure nor good is useful.

11. Hoc quidnam per se est et ex propria eius constitutione? quaenam eius vera natura et materia et forma? Quid facit in mundo? quamdiu subsistit?

    What then is this thing by itself and from its own constitution? What is its true nature, matter, and form? What does it contribute to the world? How long does it endure?

12. Cum gravatim e somno expergisceris, reminiscere, et constitutioni tuae et naturae humanae esse consentaneum, ut actiones societati utiles edas, dormire autem tibi etiam cum brutis animantibus commune esse;

    When you rise reluctantly from sleep, remember that it is in accordance with your nature and the nature of humans to perform actions beneficial to society, and that sleep is shared even with the animals;

quod vero cuique secundum naturam est, id ei eat familiarius et aptius et vero iucundius.

But what is in accord with each person's nature is more familiar, suitable, and truly pleasant to them.

13. In omni viso, quantum potes, physicas et pathologicas et dialecticas rationes in usum perpetuo adhibe.

In every encounter, to the extent possible, apply physical, pathological, and dialectical reasoning for perpetual use.

14. Quemcunque conveneris, statim tu tecum loquere quaenam hic habet placita de bonis et malis? non si qua eiusmodi de voluptate et dolore iisque, quae utrumque efficiunt, de fama porro, ignominia, morte et vita habet placita, neque mirum neque novum mibi videbitur, si eiusmodi faciat;

Whomever you meet, immediately converse with yourself about what opinions they hold about good and bad? Not only if they hold such opinions about pleasure and pain, and about those things which result in both, and about reputation, ignominy, death, and life; nor will it seem strange or novel to me if they do so;

et memor ero, eum vi cogi, ut ita agat.

and I will remember that he is constrained by force to act in that way.

15. Memento, quemadmodum turpe sit, tanquam de re insueta mirari, quod ficus ficum ferat, ita quoque, si mundus ea, quorum ferax sit, ferat;

Remember how disgraceful it is to marvel as at something unfamiliar that a fig tree bears figs, likewise if the world produces those things of which it is productive;

et vero medico atque gubernatori turpe, obstupescere, si quis febri laboret aut ventus adversus existat.

and it is disgraceful for a physician and a captain to be astonished if someone has a fever or if a contrary wind arises.

16. Memento, sententiam mutare et recte monenti obsequi, pariter liberi hominis esse:

Remember to change your judgment and to heed sound advice, for it is equally the act of a free man;

tua enim est actio quae secundum tuum consilium atque iudicium et vero ex animi tui sententia perficitur.

for your action is accomplished according to your own plan, judgment, and true opinion of your mind.

17. Si tui est arbitrii, cur facis? sin alius, quid accusas? atomos, an deos? utrumque est insani.

If it is within your power, why do you do it? But if it is up to someone else, why do you blame them? Atoms or gods? Both are nonsensical.

Nihil reprehendendum.

Nothing deserves reproach.

Si enim potes, corrige peccantem;

For if you can, correct the wrongdoer;

si hoc nequis, rem ipsam;

if you cannot do this, correct the thing itself;

si ne hoc quidem potes, quid tibi amplius confert reprehendisse? nihil enim temere faciendum.

and if you cannot do this either, what does it avail you to have found fault? For nothing should be done recklessly.

18. Quod mortuum est, mundo non excidit.

What is dead does not vanish from the world.

Si hic manet, etiam mutatur hic, et dissolvitur in elementa sua, quae eadem et mundi sunt et tua:

If it remains here, it still undergoes changes here and is dissolved into its elements, which are the same for both the world and you:

haec quoque mutantur nec mussant.

These also change and do not complain.

19. Unumquodque alicuius rei causa natum est;

Everything exists for the sake of something;

quid miraris? Sol quoque dicet:

why are you amazed? The sun too will say:

alicuius rei causa factus sum idem reliqui dii.

I was made for the sake of something, I too am a god's handiwork.

Tu igitur cuius rei causa? num ut delecteris? vide, num intelligentia hoc ferat.

So what is your purpose? Is it to take pleasure? See if your rationality can endure this.

20. Natura cuiusque rei rationem habet, non minus, quod ad eius finem attinet, quam ad ortum eius et transitum, ad instar eius, qui pilam emittit.

The nature of each thing has a reason, as much as it pertains to its end as to its origin and transition, like one who throws a ball.

Quid igitur boni pilae sursum missae aut mali eidem descendenti aut adeo delapsae? quid boni, bullae consistenti, aut mali dissolutae? Eadem de lucerna valent.

So what good does it bring when the ball is thrown upwards or what evil when it descends or even falls down? What good does it bring when the bubble maintains its form, or what evil when it bursts? The same holds true for the lamp.

21. Inverte corpus et vide, quale sit, senio confectum quale fiat, morbo languidum, proclinatum.

Turn your body upside down and observe, how it appears, worn by old age, how it becomes weakened by illness, bent forward.

Brevis est vita et eius, qui laudat, et eius, qui laudatur, eius, qui mentionem facit, et eius, cuius mentio fit.

Life is short, whether of the one who praises, or of the one praised, of the one who makes mention, or of the one whose mention is made.

Praeterea hoc fit in angulo huius plagae, et ne ibi quidem omnes consentiunt, immo ne sibi ipse quisquam tota denique terra puncti instar.

Moreover, this happens in a corner of this region, and not even there do all agree, indeed not even to oneself does anyone, in the end, agree like a point on the entire earth.

22. Animum adverte ad rem subiectam aut decretum aut vim aut id, quod significatur.

Direct your attention to the subiect matter, decree, force, or whatever is signified.

Merito haec pateris:

You endure these things rightfully:

mavis enim cras bonus fieri, quam hodie bonus esse.

For you prefer to be good tomorrow rather than good today.

23. Facio aliquid? ita facio, ut ad hominum salutem id referam:

Am I doing something? I do it in a way that I refer it to the well-being of humanity.

accidit mihi aliquidi? ita accipio, ut id ad deos referam et fontem omnium rerum, a quo omnia, quae fiunt, inter se connexa proficiscuntur.

Does something happen to me? I accept it in a way that I refer it to the gods and to the source of all things, from which all things that happen are interconnected.

24. Quale tibi videtur lavari, oleum, sudor, sordes, aqua viscida, omnia putida; talis quaevis vitae pars est et quaevis res subiecta.

What does bathing seem to you? Oil, sweat, dirt, sticky water, all things putrid; every part of life is like this and every subiect matter.

25. Lucilla Verum, deinde Lucilla;

Lucilla first, then Lucilla;

Secunda Maximum, deinde Maximus;

Secondly, Maximus, then Maximus;

Epitynchanus Diotimum, deinde Epitynchanus;

Epitynchanus Diotimus, then Epitynchanus;

Faustinam Antoninus, deinde Antoninus.

Faustina Antoninus, then Antoninus.

Huiusmodi omnia:

All things of this kind:

Celer Hadrianum, deinde Celer;

Celer first, then Celer;

quin etiam acres illi et futurorum praescii et fastu elati ubi nunc sunt? ut ex acribus Charax, Demetrius Platonicus, Eudaemon et si quis alius eiusmodi.

Even those sharp-witted ones, knowledgeable about the future and puffed up with pride, where are they now? Like Charax the sharp-witted, Demetrius the Platonist, Eudaemon, and anyone else of that sort.

Omnia caduca et iam dudum emortua:

All things perishable and long ago dead:

aliorum ne minimum quidem tempus mansit memoria;

The memory of others has not even lasted a little time;

alii in fabulas abierunt;

Some have gone into stories;

alii iam adeo e fabulis evanuerunt.

Others have faded away completely from stories.

Horum igitur memento, aut dissipatum iri compagem tuam aut exstinctum iri spiritum aut migratarum esse et alibi constitutum iri.

Therefore, remember these things: either your framework will be dispersed, your breath will be extinguished, or you will migrate and be established elsewhere.

26. Laetatur homo, quum facit, quae homini propria sunt:

A person reioices when doing what is characteristic of a human:

proprium autem, est homini, benevolum esse erga contribules, motus sensuum contemnere, visa probabilia discernere, naturam universitatis et ea, quae secundum hanc fiunt, contemplari.

However, what is truly characteristic of a human is to be benevolent toward fellow humans, to disdain the movements of the senses, to distinguish probable perceptions, and to contemplate the nature of the universe and the things that occur according to it.

27. Tres rationes:

Three principles:

una ad vas circumdatum, altera ad causam divinam, a qua omnibus evenit quidquid evenit, tertia ad eos, quibuscum vivis.

one related to the vessel that encloses us, another related to the divine cause from which whatever happens, happens to all, and a third related to those with whom you live.

28. Dolor aut corpori malum:

Pain is either a physical ailment or an evil for the soul:

ergo hoc pronunciet! aut animo;

Therefore, pronounce this: either for the body or for the soul;

verum huic licet, serenitatem suam et tranquillitatem servare et non opinari, esse malum;

indeed, for the latter, it is permissible to maintain its serenity and tranquility and not to consider it an evil;

omne enim iudicium et impetus et appetitus et aversatio intus est, eoque nihil mali adscendit.

for all iudgment, impulse, desire, and aversion are within, and nothing evil ascends there.

29. Exstingue visa, saepe tecum loquens:

Extinct the perceptions, often speaking to yourself:

Nunc in potestate mea situm est, ut nulla in hoc animo improbitas insit, nulla cupiditas, nulla omnino perturbatio, sed ut, omnibus, qualia sint, perspectis, singulis pro dignitate utar.

Now it is in my power that no dishonesty resides in this soul, no craving, no disturbance whatsoever, but that, having perceived all things as they truly are, I will use each according to its worth.

Memor esto huius potestatis a natura tibi tributae.

Remember this power bestowed upon you by nature.

30. Loqui et in senatu et cum quolibet modeste nec voce nimis intenta:

Speak both in the senate and with anyone else with modesty, and not with an overly intense voice:

sano sermone uti.

Speak in a rational manner.

31. Aula Augusti, uxor, filia, nepotes, privigni, soror, Agrippa, cognati, familiares, amici, Areus, Maecenas, medici, sacrificuli:

The court of Augustus, his wife, daughter, grandchildren, stepchildren, sister, Agrippa, relatives, family, friends, Areus, Maecenas, doctors, priests:

totius aulae mors.

the death of the entire court.

Tum perge ad alia, quae non ad unius mortem pertinent, ut Pompeiorum, ad id, quod in monumentis inscribitur:

Then proceed to other matters that do not pertain to the death of a single person, like the Pompeys, to that which is inscribed on their monuments:

Ultimus centis suae, et reputa tecum, quanto studio maiores eorum in id incubuerint ut successorem relinquerent:

"The last of his line." Reflect within yourself how much effort their ancestors put into leaving a successor:

tum, necesse esse, ut aliquis ultimus sit:

then it must be necessary that someone be the last;

hic iterum totius gentis mortem.

here, again, the death of an entire family.

32. Componere te oportet vitam ex singulis actionibus atque si singulae, quantum fieri potest, praestant, quod suum est, in eo acquiescere;

You must assemble your life from individual actions, and if individual actions are, as much as possible, excellent and what is proper, then be content with that;

nemo autem prohibere potest, quin quaevis praestet, quod suum est.

but no one can prevent you from achieving excellence in individual actions.

- Verum extrinsecus aliquid obstabit.

- However, something external may stand in your way.

- Nihil certe, quo minus iuste, moderate et considerate agas.

- Certainly nothing that prevents you from acting justly, moderately, and thoughtfully.

At alius fortasse effectus impedietur.

But perhaps another outcome will be impeded.

Verum hoc ipsum impedimentum placide ferendo et aequo animo ad id, quod conceditur, te transferendo alia statim succedit actio, quae cum illa, quam dixi, vitae compositione conveniet.

However, by bearing this very obstacle with equanimity and transferring yourself with a calm mind to that which is granted, another action immediately follows that will be in harmony with the composition of life that I mentioned earlier.

33. Sine fastu accipere, aequo animo dimittere.

Receive without arrogance, let go with an even mind.

34. Si quando manum vidisti abscissam aut pedem aut caput [amputatum], seorsim alicubi a reliquo corpore, iacens, scito talem se facere, quantum penes ipsum est, eum, qui id, quod contingit, non vult, aut aliquid facit quod societatis saluti obest.

If ever you see a hand, foot, or head cut off and lying separately from the rest of the body, know that it behaves in this way as far as it can, the one who does not desire what has happened or does something harmful to the well-being of society.

Abiectus iaces alicubi revulsus ab ea, quae secundum naturam est, unione:

You lie abandoned somewhere, torn away from what is in accordance with nature, in separation:

pars enim natura fuisti, nunc autem te avulsisti.

for you were once a part of nature, but now you have torn yourself away.

Verum hic scitum est illud, quod tibi licet, te rursus unire.

But here is the wise saying: what is allowed to you is to unite yourself again.

Hoc nulli alii parti deus concessit, ut revulsa et praecisa denuo coalesceret.

To no other part has God granted this, that when torn and cut off, it might reunite and come together again.

Verum considera benignitatem, quae homini tantum honoris tribuit:

But consider the benevolence which bestows such an honor upon humans:

nam in hominis potestate posuit, ut ab initio ne avelleretur a toto, et ut avulsus redire et coalescere et partis locum recuperare possit.

For in the power of man, it has been placed that from the beginning he may not be separated from the whole, and that when torn away, he may return, reunite, and regain his place as a part.

35. Sicut reliquas facultates unicuique eorum, qui ratione praediti sunt, * ac propemodum quantum habet ipsa attribuit rationalis universi natura*, sic hanc quoque ab ea accepimus.

Just as the rational nature of the universe assigns to each of those endowed with reason their other faculties, and almost as much as it itself possesses, so we have received this ability also from it.

Quemadmodum enim illa quidquid obstat et resisiit, circumvertit et in necessaria rerum serie collocat et sui partem facit, ita etiam animal ratione praeditum omne impedimentum suam ipsius materiam facere potest eoque uti ad consilium suum consequendum, qualecunque hoc fuerit.

Just as the rational nature of the universe arranges and adapts whatever opposes and resists it, placing it in the necessary sequence of events and incorporating it as a part of itself, in the same way, an animal endowed with reason can transform every impediment into its own material and use it to achieve its purpose, whatever that may be.

36.
Ne te confundat totius vitae cogitatio, neque animo simul complectere, quot et quantas molestias tibi superventuras esse vero simile est, sed in singulis, quae adsunt, te ipse interroga, quid hac in re sit, quod ferri et sustineri nequeat;

May the contemplation of your entire life not confuse you, nor should you embrace in your mind how many and how great troubles might come upon you, for it is akin to something false. But instead, in each present circumstance, interrogate yourself, question what this matter truly is, which cannot be borne and endured;

erubesces enim, id confiteri.

for you will feel ashamed to admit it.

Tum in memoriam tibi revoca, neque futurum nec praeteritum tibi molestiam allaturum esse, sed semper id tantum, quod praesens est.

Then remind yourself that neither the future nor the past will bring you distress, but only what is present at any given moment.

Hoc autem minuitur, si suis id limitibus terminas et mentem tuam redarguis, quod ne huic quidem soli ferendo par est.

However, this is diminished if you set limits to it and admonish your own mind, for it is not even fitting to endure this alone.

37.
Numquid nunc domini tumulo assidet Panthea et Pergamus? num Hadriani Chabrias aut Diotimus ridiculum.

Is Panthea now sitting by her master's tomb, or Pergamus? Are Chabrias or Diotimus now ridiculing Hadrian?

Quid vero si assiderent, sentirentne illi?

But what if they were to sit there, would they feel it?

quid si sentirent, num voluptatem inde caperent? quid, si hanc caperent, num hi immortales essent?

But what if they were to feel it? Would they derive pleasure from it? And if they were to derive pleasure, would they become immortal?

Nonne etiam his fato constitutum erat, ut senes ac vetulae fierent, deinde morerentur?, quid igitur postea illi facerent, his mortuis? Foetor est hoc omne et sanies in sacco.

Wasn't it also destined for them to become old and feeble, and then die? So, what would they do afterward, once they are dead? All of this is decay and decayed matter in a bag.

38.
Si potes acute videre, vide, inquit, ut quam sapientissime iudices.

If you can see keenly," he says, "see how most wisely you iudge.

39.
Quae iustitiae opponatur virtutem nullam video in natura animalis ratione praediti;

As for what opposes iustice, I see no virtue in the nature of a rational being;

at voluptati quae opponatur, video temperantiam.

but I see temperance opposing pleasure.

40.
Si opinionem ab eo, quod tibi dolorem efferre videtur, seiungis, ipse in tutissimo es collocatus.

If you separate the opinion from that which seems to cause you pain, you are placed in the safest position by yourself.

- Quis ipse?

— Who is it?

- Ratio.

— Reason.

- Verum non sum ratio.

— But I am not reason.

- Esto.

— So be it.

Igitur ne ratio se tristitia affciat;

Therefore, let not reason be affected by sadness;

si quid aliud male habet, id ipsum de se ipso opinetur.

If it has any other malady, let it consider that malady as coming from itself.

41. Impedimentum sensus est malum naturae animantis;

An impediment to sensation is a detriment to the nature of a sentient being.

impedimentum motus pariter naturae animantis malum:

An obstacle to movement is also a harmful thing for the nature of a living being with sensation.

est vero etiam aliud, quod pariter vegetabilem naturam impediat eiusque malum sit:

And indeed, there is something else that equally hinders the nature of a plant and is its harm.

ita porro impedimentum mentis malum naturae ratione praeditae.

In the same way, there is an impediment to the mind, which is a harm to the nature endowed with reason.

Iam vero haec omnia ad te transfer.

But now, transfer all these considerations to yourself.

Dolor aut voluptas tangit te? Viderit sensus.

Does pain or pleasure affect you? Let the senses decide.

Consilio obstitit aliquid? si quidem sine exceptione hoc moliebaris, iam malum est tuum ut animalis ratione praediti;

Did something hinder your plan? If, indeed, you were pursuing this without any reservation, then it is already your fault as a being endowed with reason.

sin commune et universum intelligis, nec laesus es, neque impeditus:

But if you understand the common and universal, then you are neither harmed nor hindered.

mentis sane quae propria sunt, nemo solet impedire;

Indeed, no one usually hinders the things that belong to the mind itself.

hanc enim neque ignis nec ferrum nec tyrannus neque criminatio neque aliud quidquam tangit.

For these things, neither fire, nor iron, nor tyrant, nor accusation, nor anything else can touch.

Quum sphaera facta est, teres ac rotunda manet.

When a sphere is made, it remains smooth and round.

42. Indignum est, me mihi dolorem afferre, qui neminem unquam alium meapte sponte laeserim.

It is unworthy of me to bring suffering upon myself, as I have never willingly harmed anyone else.

43. Alia alios oblectant:

Others find pleasure in the following:

me, si animi principatum habeo sanum neque hominem neque quidquam quod homini accidit aversantem, sed quidquid evenit benignis oculis adspicientem et excipientem et singulis pro dignitate utentem.

For myself, if I maintain a healthy dominance over my emotions and do not turn away from any person or situation that befalls a human being, but rather look upon whatever happens with kind eyes, accept it, and use it according to its worth.

44. Hoc, quod est, tempus fac tibi impertias.

This, which is present, make time for yourself to enjoy.

Qui studiosius famam posthumam sectantur, non cogitant, alios quosdam eiusmodi fore illos, cuiusmodi hi sunt, quos gravatim ferunt:

Those who zealously pursue posthumous reputation do not consider that some others of their kind will be as they are, burdened by the same concerns:

etiam illi mortales.

even those mortals.

Quid vero omnino tua interest, si talibus vocibus illi strepant aut sic de te opinentur?

But what does it truly matter to you if they clamor with such voices or hold such opinions about you?

45. Tolle me et proiice, quocunque vis.

Take me and cast me away wherever you wish.

Nam ibi genio meo utar propitio, hoc est, contento, si se habet et agit naturae meae convenienter.

For there I will use my favorable nature, that is, my contentment, if it is present and acts in accordance with my essence.

Num hoc tanti est, ut animus meus eius causa male se habeat et se ipso deterior sit, depressus, cupiditate extensus, in semet compressus, consternatus?

Is this of such importance that my soul should fare poorly for its sake and become worse by its influence, weighed down, stretched by desire, compressed upon itself, dismayed?

Atque quid reperies, quod tanti sit?

And what will you discover that is of such great worth?

46. Nulli homini aliquid evenire potest, quod non sit casus humanus, neque bovi, quod bovis non sit, neque viti, quod non sit vitis, neque lapidi, quod lapidis non sit.

Nothing can happen to any person that is not a human occurrence, nor to an ox that is not ox-like, nor to a vine that is not vine-like, nor to a stone that is not stone-like.

Si igitur singulis accidit, quod et consuetum et a natura advectum est, quid est, quod aegre feras?

nihil enim tibi ferebat natura communis, quod ferri non possit.

47. Si quam ob rem externam te, dolore affectum sentis, non res ipsa, sed tuum de ea iudicium dolore te afficit id autem delere in tua est potestate.

Si in tua dispositione inest, quod te dolore afficit, quis te prohibet, quominus decretum corrigas?

Ita quoque si doles idcirco, quod non id facis quod sanum videtur, cur non potius hoc facis, quam doles?

Verum obstat aliquid potentius.

- Noli igitur dolere:

non enim penes te est causa, quod nihil agitur.

- Verum nullius pretii est vita, si hoc non agitur.

- Decede igitur e vita aequo animo, * ut is quoque qui agit moritur, atque propitius obstantibus.

48. Memento, partem tui principalem fieri inexpugnabilem, quum, in, se collecta, contenta sit se ipsa nihil, quod nolit, faciente, etiamsi sine ratione obstet.

Quid igitur, ubi ratione in consilium adhibita de re aliqua iudicat?

Hinc arx quaedam est mens perturbationibus libera:

So if what happens to each individual is both customary and brought about by nature, what is it that you bear with difficulty?

For nature, in common, does not bring upon you anything that cannot be borne.

If, for any external reason, you feel affected by pain, it is not the thing itself, but your iudgment about it that afflicts you. However, the power to erase this iudgment is within your control.

If within your disposition there exists something that troubles you with pain, what prevents you from correcting your iudgment?

Similarly, if you feel pain because you are not doing what seems reasonable, why not do this instead of feeling the pain?

But something more powerful is obstructing you.

- Therefore, do not grieve.

For the cause is not within your control, as nothing is being done.

- Indeed, life is of no value if this is not pursued.

- Therefore, depart from life with a calm spirit, just as even the one who accomplishes something dies, and be gracious to those who obstruct.

Remember, let the principal part of yourself become invulnerable when, gathered within itself, it is content with nothing that it does not will, even if something irrational stands in the way.

So, what then, when reason is applied to deliberate about something?

From this arises a certain fortress of the mind, free from disturbances:

nihil enim munitius habet homo, quo quum confugerit, in posterum expugnari nom possit.

For nothing has a person in his defense that is more secure, to which, when he retreats, he cannot be attacked in the future.

Hoc igitur qui non videt, imperitus est;

Therefore, whoever does not perceive this is unskilled;

qui videt nec tamen eo se recipit, infelix.

whoever perceives it but does not retreat into it is unfortunate.

49. Noli quidquam ultra tecum addere iis, quae visa praeeuntia renunciant.

Do not add anything beyond to the things which are perceived as preceding appearances.

Nunciatum est, illum tibi male dicere? nunciatum est hoc, neque vero etiam illud, te laesum esse.

Has it been reported that someone spoke ill of you? It has been reported, but neither has it been reported that you have been harmed.

Video, puerulum aegrotare:

I see a little child sick:

video;

I see it;

eum autem in vitae discrimen adduci, non video.

but I do not see that he is at death's door.

Sic semper in primis visis consiste neu quidquam intrinsecus iis adiice, et nihil tibi accidit;

Thus, always stand firm on first appearances and do not add anything intrinsically to them, and nothing happens to you;

aut potius adiice, sed ut qui omnia, quae in mundo eveniunt, perspecta habeas.

or rather, do add, but as someone who has a clear view of all the things that happen in the world.

50. Cucumis amarus:

A bitter cucumber:

mitte! Vepres in via:

discard it! Thorns in your path:

declina! sufficit.

turn aside! It is enough.

Noli haec verba addere:

Do not add these words:

"Quare quaeso haec quoque in mundo sunt?" ludibrio enim fores homini rerum naturalium perito, perinde atque fabro et sutori ludibrio esses, si ei exprobrares, quod eorum, quae conficiuntur, ramenta et segmenta in officina eius vides.

"Why, pray, are these things also in the world?" For you would be mocking a person skilled in natural things, just as you would be mocking a carpenter or cobbler if you were to reproach them because you see shavings and scraps in their workshop.

Quamquam ii quidem, quo talia proiiciant, habent;

Although the former do indeed have a place to cast such things;

rerum natura autem nihil extra se habet:

however, nature has nothing outside of itself:

sed quod potissimum in hac arte admireris, hoc est, quod, quum se certis finibus circumscripserit, quidquid intra se corrumpi, senescere et inutile fieri videtur, id in se ipsam mutat rursusque ex his alia nova efficit, ita ut neque materia extrinsecus opus habeat, neque, quo putrefacta proiiciat, desideret:

But what is most admirable in this art is that when it has circumscribed itself within certain limits, whatever appears to be corrupt, aging, and becoming useless within itself, it transforms into itself again and from these things produces new things, so that it neither requires external material nor desires a place to discard what has rotted:

itaque manet contenta, suo loco, et sua materia, et arte sibi propria.

thus, it remains content in its own place, with its own material, and its own skill.

51. Neque in actionibus negligentem esse, neque in sermonibus turbidum, neque in visis vagari, neque animo omnino contrabi aut exsilire, neque in vita negotiis districtum esse.

Neither be careless in actions, nor confused in words, nor wander in your visions, nor let your mind shrink or leap away, nor be absorbed in worldly tasks.

Occidunt, mactant, diris devovent.

They kill, sacrifice, and devote with curses.

Quid igitur haec obstant, quominus mens pura maneat, prudens, moderata, iusta? Perinde ac si quis fonti limpido ac dulci adsistens eum vituperaret, at ille nihilominus non cessaret aqua potui apta scatere;

What then obstructs these things from the mind remaining pure, wise, temperate, and iust? Iust as if someone were to insult a clear and sweet spring, it would not cease to provide water fit to drink;

quin etiam si quis lutum iniecerit aut stercus, cito haec disperget et eluet, neque ullo modo inquinabitur.

indeed, even if mud or filth were thrown into it, it would quickly disperse and cleanse itself, never becoming polluted.

Quomodo igitur fontem habebis perennem, [non puteum]? * Vindica te quavis hora in libertatem cum benevolentia, simplicitate et verecundia.

How then will you have an enduring spring [not a well]? Free yourself at any moment with goodwill, simplicity, and modesty.

52. Qui, quid mundus sit, ignorat, is etiam, ubi sit, ignorat.

He who is ignorant of what the world is also does not know where it is.

Qui vero, ad quid natus sit, ignorat, non, quis ipse sit, novit, neque, quid mundus sit:

But whoever is ignorant of why they were born, does not know who they themselves are, nor what the world is:

qui in horum alterutro deficit, neque, ad quid natus sit, dixerit.

Whoever lacks either of these, neither speaks of why they were born.

Quis igitur tibi videturis, qui eorum hominum plausum [fugit aut] captat, qui neque ubi sint, neque quinam sint ipsi, norunt?

So, in your opinion, who do you think is seeking the applause of those people who do not know where they are or who they themselves are?

53. Laudari cupis ab homine, qui intra unius horae spatium se ipse ter exsecratur? placere cupis ei, qui sibi ipse non placet? Num vero sibi placet, quem omnium fere, quae ipse facit, poenitet?

Do you desire to be praised by a person who curses themselves three times within the span of an hour? Do you want to please someone who does not please themselves? But does someone who regrets almost everything they do please themselves?

54. In posterum non tantum cum aere ambiente conspirare te oportet, verum etiam cum mente, quae omnia continet, consentire.

In the future, you must not only harmonize with the surrounding air but also with the mind that encompasses everything.

Non minus enim vis intelligendi ubique funditur et permeat per ea, quae eam attrahere possunt, quam aerea per ea, quae respirare possunt.

For the power of understanding is poured out and permeates everywhere just as much as air does through things that can breathe.

55. Omnino vitiositas non nocet mundo, singulatim non nocet alteri.

Indeed, corruption does not harm the world at all, nor does it harm any individual in particular.

Ei tantum damnum affert, cui concessum est, ea liberari, quam primum ipse voluerit.

It only causes harm to the one to whom it has been granted to be liberated from it as soon as they themselves wish.

56. Arbitrio meo pariter indifferens est alterius arbitrium, atque animula eius et caruncula.

To my choice, another person's choice is equally indifferent, just as their little soul and flesh are.

Etenim si vel maxime alter alterius causa nati sumus, tamen mentium nostrarum cuivis propria sua constat potestas:

For even if we were born largely for the sake of one another, nonetheless each person's own power over their mind remains to them:

alioquin profecto alterius vitiositas meum malum foret:

otherwise, surely someone else's faults would be my downfall;

quod deo non visum est, ne in alterius esset potestate, me miserum reddere.

which God did not see fit to be in another's power, to make me miserable.

57. Sol diffundi videtur et ubique funditur, non effunditur tamen.

The sun appears to spread out and is poured out everywhere, yet it is not depleted.

Fusio enim hasc tensio est.

For this diffusion is a kind of tension.

Quapropter radii eius aktines dicuntur ab *ekteinesthai, extendi.

Therefore, its rays are called "aktines" from the Greek word "ekteinesthai," meaning to extend.

Qualis autem res sit radius, intellexeris, si per angustum, foramen in domum tenebricosam lumen a sole profectum videris immissum:

But what a ray is, you will understand if you see light from the sun entering through a narrow hole into a darkened room:

recta enim tenditur et quasi illiditur sane ad solidum, quodcunque el obstiterit, aerem arcens;

for it extends straight and, as it were, strikes against any solid object that it encounters, excluding the air;

ibi, autem consistit et nec delabitur nec decidit.

there, it remains and neither slides nor falls.

Eiusmodi igitur fusionem et diffusionem mentis habere te oportet, minime effusionem, sed tensionem, atque adversus impedimenta ei obiecta nec violento nec rapido illisu ferri, neque vero decidere, sed consistere et illustrare id quod eam recipit.

Therefore, you should have such fusion and diffusion of the mind, not an outpouring but a tension, and against obstacles presented to it, it should not be carried with violence or rapid collision, nor should it fall, but remain and illuminate what receives it.

Ipsum enim se splendore privabit, quod eam praetermittit.

For it will deprive itself of its brilliance by passing beyond it.

58. Qui mortem timet, aut sensuum exstinctionem timet, aut diversam sensuum affectionem.

He who fears death fears either the extinction of his senses or a different state of sensory experience.

Verum sive nullum amplius habebis sensum, neque mali quid senties, sive diversum alignem sensum habebis, aliud animal eris nec vivere desines.

But whether you will no longer have any sensation and will not feel any evil, or whether you will have a different and foreign sensation, you will still be a different being and will not cease to live.

59. Homines, alter alterius causa nati sunt.

Humans are born for the sake of each other.

Eos igitur doce aut fer.

Therefore, instruct them or bear with them.

60. Aliter sagttta, aliter mens fertur;

Arrows behave differently, and so does the mind;

mens utique etiam, quum cavet et quam in considerando versatur, non minus recta fertur et ad propositum.

and the mind, indeed, even when it is watchful and focused on something, moves straight and toward its purpose no less.

61. Intrare in mentem cuiusvis, sed etiam alteri concedere, ut in suam ipsius mentem intret.

Entering into anyone's mind, but also granting entrance to another, so that they may enter into their own mind.

LIBER IX

VIRTUS VERA MENSURA

I .

Qui iniuste agit, impie agit. Quum enim natura universitatis animalia ratione praedita, alterum alterius causa, condiderit, ut sibi pro cuiusque dignitate mutuo prosint, minime vero noceant, is, qui huius voluntatem transgreditur, manifesto impius est in antiquissimam deorum.

Porro qui mentitur, impie agit adversus eandem deam:

nam universi natura est natura eorum, quae sunt;

ea autem, quae sunt, ad ea, quae exsistunt, familiari ratione se habent;

praeterea et veritas ipsa appellatur et omnium, quae vera sunt, prima est causa.

Qui igitur volens mentitur, impie agit, quatenus eo, quod decipit, impie agit:

Who acts unjustly, acts impiously. For when nature, endowed with reason, has established animals of the universe for the sake of one another, so that they may mutually benefit according to the dignity of each, and certainly not harm, he who goes against this intention is clearly impious towards the most ancient gods.

Furthermore, one who lies acts impiously against the same goddess:

For the nature of the universe is the nature of those things which exist;

and those things which exist are related to those things which come into being in a familiar manner;

moreover, truth itself is both named and is the primary cause of all things that are true.

Therefore, one who lies willingly acts impiously, inasmuch as through deceiving, they act impiously;

qui nolens, quatenus cum universi natura dissentit et quatenus mundi ordinem turbat, contra naturam eius pugnans;

contra hanc enim pugnat, qui suapte sponte ad ea fertur quae veris contraria sunt:

praesidia enim veritatis a natura acceperat, quibus neglectis iam falsa a veris discernere nequit.

At vero etiam is, qui voluptates ut bona sectatur et dolores ut mala fugit, impie agit.

Nam necesse est, ut ita adfectus saepe de communi natura conqueratur, quasi nulla dignitatis ratione habita improbis ac probis aliquid tribuat, quoniam improbi saepe voluptatibus fruuntur, eaque possident, quibus voluptates parari possunt, probi contra in dolorem incidunt et in ea, quibus dolores creantur.

Praeterea qui dolorem timet, is etiam interdum aliquid eorum timebit, quae in mundo futura sunt;

atque hoc iam impium est.

Et vero qui voluptates sectatur, ab iniuste agendo non abstinebit;

id autem aperte impium.

Oportet vero ad quae communis natura ex aequo se habet (non enim utrumque fecisset, si ad utrumque se non ex aequo habuisset), ad ea quoque ex aequo affectos esse eos, qui naturam, quippe cum ea consentientes, tanquam ducem sequi velint.

one who lies unwillingly, inasmuch as they disagree with the nature of the universe and disrupt the order of the world, thereby going against its nature;

for he battles against this nature, who of his own accord inclines towards things that are contrary to the truth.

For they had received safeguards of truth from nature, which, when neglected, now renders them unable to distinguish falsehoods from truths.

But indeed, even one who pursues pleasures as goods and avoids pains as evils acts impiously.

For it is necessary that in such cases, often he laments about common nature, as if no consideration of virtue is given, attributing something to the wicked and the righteous, since the wicked often indulge in pleasures, and they possess those things by which pleasures can be obtained. On the other hand, the righteous encounter pain and those things by which pains are created.

Furthermore, one who fears pain will also at times fear some of those things which are to come in the world;

and this is now impious.

And indeed, one who pursues pleasures will not abstain from acting unjustly;

and this is clearly impious.

But it is necessary that toward those things which the common nature relates to equally (for it would not have made both, if it had not related to both equally), those who follow nature, since they are in agreement with it, should also be equally affected by them, as if they desire to follow it as their guide.

Qui igitur ad dolorem et voluptatem mortem et vitam, ad gloriam et infamiam, quibus ex aequo utitur universi natura, non ipse ex aequo affectus est, eum manifestum est impium esse.

Dico autem, his ex aequo uti communem naturam, pro, haec pariter accide iis, quae per necessariam rerum seriem fiunt et deinceps nascuntur antiquo quodam consilio Providentiae, ex quo a principio quodam accessit ad hunc mundi ordinem condendum, conceptis quibusdam rerum futurarum ratitionibus et electis viribus genitalibus eorum, quae sic subsistunt, mutantur, succedunt.

2. Elegantioris quidem foret hominis, expertem mendacii et omnis simulationis et luxus et fastus hac vita defungi;

horum autem satietate affectum e vita migrare, secunda navigatio.

An vero malis assidere improbitati, et necdum experientia te movet, ut pestem fugias?

pestis enim est corruptio mentis multo magis, quam huius spiritus circumfusi intemperies quaedam et mutatio.

Haec enim animalibus pestis, quatenus animalia sunt, illa hominum, quatenus homines sunt.

3. Mortem noli contemnere, sed laeto animo eam excipe ut quae unum sit eorum, quae natura vult.

Therefore, whoever is not equally affected by death and life, by glory and infamy, which the nature of the universe equally employs, it is clear that he is impious.

However, I say that these things equally use the common nature, as if these things happen in the same way to those occurrences that take place through the necessary series of events and subsequently arise, according to an ancient plan of Providence, from which a certain design was laid down from the beginning for the construction of this order of the world. Certain reasons for future events were conceived, and selective generative forces of those things, which persist in this manner, change and succeed.

It would indeed be more elegant for a human being to depart from this life, having been free from falsehood, all pretense, luxury, and extravagance;

and by the fulfillment of these desires, to move from life with a satisfied mind, a second voyage.

But, do you choose to remain in the company of wickedness, and does not yet the experience urge you to flee, like a plague?

For a plague is the corruption of the mind much more than the instability and transformation of the air that surrounds this spirit.

This plague affects animals as they are animals, and humans as they are humans.

Do not despise death, but receive it with a joyful spirit as that which is one of those things that nature desires.

Cuiusmodi enim generis est, puerum esse, senescere, adolescere, vigere, dentire, pubescere, canescere, liberos procreare, utero ferre, parere et ceteri naturae effectus, quos vitae aetates adferunt, eiusmodi quoque est dissolvi.

For of such a kind it is, to be a child, to grow old, to reach adolescence, to thrive, to teethe, to reach puberty, to turn grey, to procreate offspring, to bear in the womb, to give birth, and the other effects of nature that the ages of life bring; likewise, it is also of this kind to be dissolved.

Est igitur hominis, qui rem reputavit, neque negligenter, neque violenter, neque fastuose adversus mortem se gerere, sed eam tanquam unam actionum naturalium exspectare;

So, it is the duty of a person who has considered the matter not to behave towards death carelessly, violently, or arrogantly, but to await it as one of the natural actions;

quemadmodum nunc exspectas, quando foetus ex utero uxoris tuae prodeat, sic tibi exspectanda hora, qua animula tua ex hoc involucro excidet.

just as you now await when the fetus will emerge from the womb of your wife, in the same way, the hour must be awaited when your soul will depart from this envelope.

Si populare vis praeceptum, quod cor tangat, facilem erga mortem te potissimum reddet, si consideraveris et, quales sint res subiectae, a quibus te divelli oportebit, et quales mores, quibuscum animus tuus non amplius commistus erit.

If you wish to follow a guiding principle that touches the heart, it will make you more amenable towards death if you consider what things are subject to separation from you and what habits your soul will no longer be intertwined with.

Iis tamen offendi neutiquam te oportet, sed eorum curam gerere, eosque placide ferre;

Nevertheless, you should not be offended by them, but rather concern yourself with them and bear them with equanimity;

nihilominus meminisse, tibi ab hominibus non idem tecum sentientibus esse discedendum:

nevertheless, you must remember that you must part ways with those who do not share the same views as you do:

hoc enim solum, si quidem forte, nos retraheret et in vita retineret, si cum hominibus eadem decreta probantibus vivere liceret.

for only this, perhaps, holds us back and keeps us in life, if we were permitted to live in agreement with those who approve the same decrees.

Nunc autem vides, quanta molestia ex dissensu eorum, quicum vivitur, oriatur, ut dicere libeat:

However, now you see how much annoyance arises from disagreement with those with whom you live, so that it is fitting to say:

"Citius veni, Mors, ne quando etiam mei ipsius obliviscar!"

"Come quickly, Death, lest I also forget myself!"

4 · Qui peccat, sibi peccat;

One who sins, sins against themselves;

qui iniuriam facit, sibi ipsi iniuriam facit, quippe se ipsum malum reddens.

one who does wrong, does wrong to themselves, as they make themselves into a source of harm.

5 · Saepe iniuste agit, qui nihil facit, non is modo, qui aliquid facit.

"Often acts uniustly, one who does nothing, not only he who does something.

6 · Sufficit, quae praesens est, comprehensibilis notio, et, quae praesens est, actio societati conveniens, et quae praesens est, animi affectio boni consulens, quidquid ex causa *externa* proficiscitur.

It suffices to have a clear understanding of what is present, and an action suitable for society, and an attitude of the mind which considers the common good, for whatever comes from an 'external' cause.

7 · Visum tollere:

To remove sight:

exstinguere animi impetum:

to quench the impulse of the mind:

principalem animi partem in sua potestate habere.

to have the principal part of the mind in one's power.

8 · In brutas animantes una divisa est anima;

In brute living beings, there is a single divided soul;

animalibus ratione praeditis unus animus rationalis distributus est, quemadmodum omnium terrenorum una est terra, et una luce cernimus unumque aerem spiramus, quotquot visus et animae participes sumus.

among creatures endowed with reason, there is a single rational mind, iust as there is one earth for all earthly things, and with a single light, we perceive and with a single air, we breathe, as many of us as are participants in sight and soul.

9 · Quaecunque aliquid commune habent, ad id, quod eiusdem generis est, tendunt.

Whatever things have something in common, tend towards that which is of the same kind.

Terrenum omne vergit ad terram, in idem confluit humidum omne et pariter aerium, ut opus sit rebus dirimentibns ac vi.

Every earthly thing inclines toward the earth; all that is humid flows together into the same [place] and likewise the aerial [flows], so that there is need for things that separate and force apart.

Ignis quidem sursum fertur;

Fire, indeed, moves upward;

omni tamen cum igne, qui hic est, tam promptus accendi, ut etiam materia quaevis, quae paulo siccior est, facile accendatur, quoniam minus habet admistum, quo incendium prohibeatur.

yet, with every fire present here, it is so readily ignited that even any drier material can be easily set ablaze, since it has less mixed in to prevent the blaze.

Itaque quidquid communis naturae rationalis particeps est, pariter ad cognatum tendit, vel magis etiam.

Therefore, whatever is a participant in the common rational nature, equally tends towards the related [elements], or even more so."

Quanto enim ceteris praestantius est, tanto paratius est, cum affinibus misceri et confundi.

The more excellent something is, the more readily it is prepared to blend and mix with its kind.

Hinc, ne longius abeam, in iis, quae ratione carent, reperiuntur examina, greges, pullorum nutricationes et quasi amores animae enim iam in his insunt, et in praestantiore reperitur intensius eongregandi studium, quale neque in plantis inest neque in lapidibus lignisve.

Hence, not to go further, among those lacking reason, there are swarms, herds, nurturing of offspring, and, as it were, the affections of the soul are already present in these things, and in the more excellent being, a more intense inclination to come together is found, a quality not present in plants, stones, or wood.

In animalibus vero ratione praeditis civitates, amicitiae, familiae, conventus atque in bellis foedera pacis atque induciae.

But in animals endowed with reason, there are cities, friendships, families, assemblies, and in times of war, treaties of peace and truces.

In iis, quae etiam praestantiora sunt, vel ex longe distantibus quodammodo unitas subsistit, ut in astris.

In those things that are even more excellent, a sort of unity exists, even among those that are far apart, as in the stars.

Sic adscensus ad id, quod praestantius est, etiam inter distantia mutuam affectionem efficere potest.

In this way, the ascent to what is more excellent can also create mutual affection among distant things.

Iam vide id, quod nunc fit.

Now see what is happening at present.

Sola enim animalia ratione praedita nunc mutui illius inter se studii et inclinationis oblita sunt, atque confluxus ille hic tautum non cernitur.

For only animals endowed with reason have now forgotten that mutual pursuit and inclination towards one another, and that gathering is not observed at all here.

Veruntamen, fugiant licet homines, undique occupantur;

Nevertheless, even if humans flee, they are occupied from all sides;

praevalet enim natura, atque diligenti contemplatione id, quod dico, comperies.

for nature prevails, and with careful contemplation, you will discover what I am saying.

Etenim facilius reperies terrenum aliquid nulli rei terrenae adiunctum, quam hominem ab homine prorsus avulsum.

Indeed, you will find it easier to discover an earthly thing not connected to any earthly thing than a human being completely detached from another human being.

10. Fert fructus et homo et deus et mundus, et suo quodvis tempore fert, nam quod usu loquendi hoc de vite aliisque huius generis tritum est, id nihil ad rem.

Both man and god and the world produce fruit, and they produce it at their respective times, for what is a well-worn saying about life and similar matters has no relevance here.

Ratio autem fructum habet et communem et proprium eiusmodi, cuiusmodi est ipsa ratio.

But reason also has its own kind of fruit, both common and individual, just like reason itself.

11. Si potes, meliora edoce:

If you can, teach me better things:

sin minus, memento, ad hoc tibi datam esse mansuetudinem.

but if not, remember that you have been given the capacity for gentleness for this purpose.

Etiam dii talibus propitii sunt iisque adeo ad quaedam consequenda, ut sanitatem, divitias, gloriam, opem ferunt.

Even the gods are favorable to those who pursue such things, and to the extent of helping them achieve certain things, such as health, wealth, glory, and assistance.

Idem tibi licet:

The same is possible for you:

aut dic, quis sit, qui te prohibeat.

either tell me who prevents you.

12. Laborem sustine neque ut miser, neque ut qui miserationem aut admirationem consequi velis, sed unum modo tibi sit propositum, moveri et motum sistere, prout ratio civilis exigit.

Endure labor, not as someone who is miserable, nor as someone who seeks pity or admiration, but let only one thing be your aim: to move and to come to a standstill as civil reason demands.

13. Hodie ex omni, in qua versabar, molestia evasi, vel potius omnem molestiam foras eieci;

Today, I have escaped from all the troubles I was involved in, or rather, I have cast out all trouble;

extra enim non erat, sed intra in opinionibus.

for it was not outside, but within in my opinions.

14. Omnia haec, familiaria usu, caduca tempore, sordida materia.

All these things, familiar through use, are fleeting in time, sordid in substance.

Omnia nunc talia, qualia sub iis, quos sepelivimus.

All things are now such as are beneath those whom we have buried.

15. Res foris consistunt, ipsae apud se, nec quidquam sui norunt nec pronunciant.

Things stand outside themselves, unaware and unpronounced.

Quid igitur de iis pronunciat?

What, then, does it pronounce about these things?

Principatus animi.

The rule of the mind.

16. Non in affectione sed in actione bonum et malum animalis ratione praediti et ad civitatem nati situm est quemadmodum virtus eius ac vitiositas non in affectione, sed in actione cernitur.

Good and evil in a creature endowed with reason and born into society are situated not in affection but in action, iust as its virtue and vice are perceived not in affection but in action.

17. Lapidi proiecto nec malum deorsum ferri, nec bonum, sursum ferri.

When a stone is thrown, neither evil descends nor good ascends.

18. Demitte te penitus in eorum mentes, et videbis, quales iudices metuas et quales in sua ipsorum causa sint iudices.

Proiect yourself deeply into their minds, and you will see what iudges you should fear and what kind of iudges they are in their own case.

19. Omnia in mutatione.

Everything is in flux.

Atque tu ipse in pervariatione et quodammodo corruptione, atque totus mundus.

And you yourself are in continual variation and, in a way, corruption, as is the entire world.

20. Alterius peccatum ibi relinquendum.

Another's wrongdoing should be left there.

21. Cessatio actionis, quies et, ut ita dicam, mors conatus et opinionis, nil mali.

The cessation of action, rest, and, so to speak, the death of effort and opinion—none of these are evil.

Transi iam ad aetates, pueritiam puta, adolescentiam, iuventutem, senectutem, etiam harum omnis mutatio inors, sed numquid mali?

Now move on to the ages, consider childhood, adolescence, youth, old age; likewise, every change in these is without evil, but is there any evil?

Transi porro ad vitam sub avo, deinde sub matre, post sub patre transactam, et quum multas alias vicissitudines ac mutationes et cessationes deprehendis, te ipse interroga, "Numquid mali?

"Sic igitur neque totius vitae cessatio et quies et mutatio.

22. Recurrito ad mentem et tuam ipsius et universi et huius hominis;

ad tuam, ut iustitiae studiosam eam reddas;

ad universi, ut recorderis, cuius sis pars;

ad alterius, ut intelligas, num ignorantia sit an consilium, et simul cogites, esse tibi cognatam.

23. Ut tu ipse ad corpus quoddam civile complendum natus es, sic singulae actiones tuae ad vitam civilem complendam faciant.

Quaecunque igitur actio tua nec propiorem nec remotiorem rationem ad communem illum finem habet, ea vitam tuam divellit, neque eam unam esse patitur, sed seditiosa est instar eius, qui in populo suae factionis homines a tali consensu dirimit.

24. Puerorum rixae et ludicra, et animulae cadavera gestantes, ita ut vehementius nos afficiat illud Nekuias.

25. Accede ad qualitatem formae eamque a materia secretam contemplare:

deinde longissimum tempus definito, quod res huius singularis qualitatis per naturam suam durare possit.

Furthermore, move on to a life under a grandfather, then under a mother, afterward under a father; and when you observe many other changes, alterations, and cessations, ask yourself, "Is there any evil?"

Therefore, neither the cessation, rest, nor change of a whole life is evil.

I turn to your own mind and to that of the universe and this individual;

to your own mind, so that you may render it devoted to justice;

to that of the universe, so that you may remember of what you are a part;

to that of the other, so that you may understand whether it is ignorance or intention, and at the same time reflect that it is connected to you.

Just as you were born to complete a certain civic body, so should your individual actions contribute to fulfilling the civic life.

Therefore, any action of yours that lacks a closer or more distant connection to that common purpose tears apart your life; it does not allow it to be whole, but is divisive like someone who, within their own faction, separates people from such agreement.

Children's quarrels and playful games, and bearing the remains of small animals, so that the story of the 'Nekyia' more deeply affects us.

Approach the quality of form and contemplate it separate from matter;

then define the very long period that this particular thing's quality can naturally endure.

26.

Perpessus es innumerabilia idcirco, quod non eras contenta mente tua faciente ea, ad quae comparata est.

You have endured countless things because your mind was not content doing what was in accordance with its nature.

Verum satis!

Enough of this!

27.

Ubi alii te reprehendunt aut oderunt aut tales contra te clamores tollunt, adi animulas eorum, penitus te intus in eas demitte, et vide, quales quidam sint.

When others criticize you, hate you, or raise such accusations against you, approach their souls, immerse yourself deeply within them, and see what kind of people they are.

Videbis, non oportere te angi, ut illis nescio quae opinio de te sit.

You will see that you should not be distressed by needing to know what their opinion of you might be.

Bene tamen iis velle debes:

Nevertheless, you should wish them well:

natura enim amici estis.

for you are in harmony with nature.

Quin etiam dii iis omni ratione consulunt per somnia, per vaticinia, in iis tamen rebus, quae iis curae sunt.

Indeed, the gods even consult them in every way through dreams, through oracles, in those matters that concern them.

28.

Eaedem sunt mundi vicissitudines in orbem redeuntes sursum, deorsum, a saeculo in saeculum.

The same are the cycles of the world, returning in a circle, upwards and downwards, from age to age.

Atque aut ad singula quaeque consilium capit universi mens;

And either the universal mind takes counsel for each particular thing;

quod si est, excipe id, quod ex eius consilio proficiscitur;

if so, accept that which proceeds from its counsel;

aut semel consilium cepit, reliqua autem per consequentiam fiunt et unum quodammodo conficiunt ;

or it takes counsel once, and the rest follow by consequence and somehow accomplish one thing;

aut atomi et corpora individua.

or atoms and individual bodies.

Summa autem rei:

The essence of the matter is this:

si deus est, omnia bene habent;

if there is a god, all is well;

si omnia consilio carent, noli tu sine consilio agere.

if all is without purpose, do not act without purpose.

Iamiam terra nos omnes occultabit;

Soon the earth will hide us all;

mox et ipsa mutabitur, et illa mutabuntur in infinitum, et rursus haec in infinitum.

soon it will also change itself, and they will change infinitely, and again these will change infinitely.

Nam si quis hos mutationum et vicissitudinum fluctus eorumque celeritatem consideraverit, omnia mortalia contemnet.

For if someone considers these waves of changes and the swiftness with which they occur, they will despise all mortal things.

29. Torrens est rerum omnium natura:

The nature of all things is like a torrent:

omnia rapit.

it sweeps away everything.

Quam viles quoque civilis peritiae studiosi et, ut opinantur, ex philosophiae praescriptis negotia gerentes homunciones! quam plena muco! Mi homo, quid tandem?

How cheap also are those who eagerly pursue civil expertise and, as they think, engage in affairs according to the precepts of philosophy! How full of mucus! My dear fellow, what now?

fac quod nunc natura abs te postulat.

Do what nature demands of you at this moment.

Aggredere rem, si tibi datur, neque circumspice, an quis cogniturus sit;

Engage with the task, if it is given to you, and do not consider whether anyone will recognize you;

et noli sperare Platonis rempublicam, sed sufficiat tibi, si vel minimum res procedit, et cogita, hunc ipsum eventum non parvi quid esse.

and do not hope for Plato's Republic, but let it be enough for you if even the smallest progress is made, and consider that this very outcome is not insignificant.

Decreta enim eorum quis mutare potest?

For who can change their decrees?

sine horum autem mutatione, quid aliud, quam servitus ingemiscentium et persuasum habere simulantium?

But without a change in these, what is there but the servitude of those groaning and pretending to be persuaded?

I nunc, et Alexandrum, Philippum, Demetrium Phalereum mihi narra! Viderint, an, quid natura communis vellet, intellexerint et se ipsi sub disciplina tenuerint.

Go on then, tell me about Alexander, Philip, Demetrius of Phalerum! Let them see whether they have understood what the common nature desired and whether they have held themselves in discipline.

Si vero tragicorum more egerunt, nemo me, ut eos imitarer, damnavit.

But if they have acted in the manner of tragic poets, no one has condemned me to imitate them.

Simplex est et verecundum philosophiae opus:

noli me ad fastum gravitate tectum abducere.

30. E superiore loco intueri greges innumerabiles, caerimonias innumerabiles et navigationis genus omne in tempestatibus et maris tranquillitate, et rerum praeteritarum praesentium et decedentium differitates.

Contemplare vero etiam vitam dudum sub aliis transactam, et post te transigendam eamque, quae nunc in barbaris gentibus degitur, et quam multi sint, qui ne nomen quidem tuum norint, quam multi, qui eius mox obliviscentur, quam multi, qui quum nunc fortasse te laudent, mox vituperaturi sint, atque nec memoriam, nec gloriam neque aliud quidvis ullius pretii esse.

31. Tranquillitas mentis in iis, quae ab externa causa proficiscuntur.

Iustitia in iis actionibus, quarum tu ipse es in causa, hoc est, agendi impetus et actio, quibus hic tantum finis propositus est, ut id, quod societati prosit, facias, ut quod naturae tuae consentaneum sit.

32. Ex iis, quae tibi molestiam creant, multa supervacanea tollere potes, quippe quae tota in opinione tua sita sint:

The work of philosophy is simple and unassuming:

do not draw me away from modesty to arrogance.

From a higher perspective, observe the countless herds, countless ceremonies, every type of navigation in storms and calm seas, and the differences between past, present, and future events.

But also contemplate the life that has been lived under others long ago, and the life to be lived after you, the life currently being lived in barbaric nations, and how many there are who may not even know your name, how many will soon forget it, how many who might praise you now will soon criticize you, and that neither memory, nor glory, nor anything of value will remain.

Tranquility of mind when dealing with things that originate from external causes.

Justice in those actions for which you yourself are the cause, meaning the impulse to act and the action itself, in which the sole purpose is to do what benefits society, what is in line with your own nature.

Out of the things that cause you distress, you can eliminate many that are unnecessary, since they are entirely based on your own opinion.

atque amplum liberumque spatium tibi comparabis, si totum mundum mente complexus fueris et aeternum aevum consideraveris et singulatim celerrimam omniam rerum mutationem contemplatus fueris, quam breve sit inter ortum et dissolutionem temporis spatium, quam immensum contra, quod ortum praecessit, quam infinitum pariter id, quod dissolutionem sequetur.

And you will attain a vast and free space for yourself if you have embraced the entire world in your mind, considered the eternal age, and observed individually the swiftest change of all things, how brief is the interval between the birth and dissolution of time, how immense, in contrast, the span that precedes birth, how equally infinite the span that follows dissolution.

33. Omnia, quae vides, brevi corrumpentur, et haec qui corrumpi vident, et ipsi brevi corrumpentur, et qui extrema confectus senectute moritur, in idem redigetur cum eo, qui immaturus obiit.

Everything you see will soon be corrupted, and those who see this corruption will also be corrupted shortly, and those who die in extreme old age will be reduced to the same state as those who died prematurely.

34. Quales sunt horum mentes! quibus rebus studuerunt quas ob causas diligunt et eolunt! Nudas eorum animulas intueri adsuesce.

What minds these people have! What things have they striven for, which causes they love and pursue! Accustom yourself to see their souls stripped bare.

Quando vel vituperando nocere vel laudando prodesse sibi videntur, quanta opinatio!

When they seem to themselves to harm by blaming or benefit by praising, what a delusion!

35. Amissio nihil aliud est, nisi mutatio.

Loss is nothing but change.

Hac autem gaudet universi natura, secundum quam omnia bene fiunt, ab aeterno eadem ratione facta sunt et in infinitum alia eiusdem generis erunt.

Yet universal nature rejoices in this, in which all things are well made; they were made by the same reason from eternity, and infinitely more of the same kind will follow.

Quid igitur dicis?

So what do you say?

Omnia facta esse, omniaque semper futura esse male, et nullam in tot diis unquam facultatem ease repertam, quae ea corrigeret, sed mundum eius infelicitatis damnatum esse, ut perpetuis malis affligatur?

That all things have been done, and that all things will always be done badly, and that no power has ever been found among the gods that could correct them, but that the world has been condemned to this misfortune, to be afflicted by perpetual evils?

36. Putredo materiae cuique rei substratae:

Decay is the underlying material for each thing:

aqua, pulvis, ossicula, foetor:	water, dust, little bones, stench:
rursus caili terrae, marmora;	again fertile earth, marbles;
aurum et argentum, faeces;	gold and silver, dregs;
pili, vestis;	hair, clothing;
sanguis, purpura et reliqua omnia eiusdem generis.	blood, purple dye, and all the rest of the same kind.
Etiam animula aliud eiusmodi, ex aliis in alia transiens.	Even the soul, of a similar nature, transitions from one thing to another.

37. Iam satis miserae vitae est et murmurationis et scurrlitatis! Quid perturbaris?

Life of misery is now enough, with its grumbling and mockery! Why are you disturbed?

quid in his novi?

What's new in these things?

Quid te percellit?

What agitates you?

num forma?

Is it your appearance, by chance?

vide eam! num materia?

Look at it! Is it your material possessions?

vide eam! Praeter has autem nihil est.

Look at them! Apart from these, there is nothing else.

Quin etiam erga deos fac tandem aliquando simplicior fias ac melior.

Indeed, also strive to become simpler and better in your attitude towards the gods.

Perinde est centum ac tribus annis haec contemplari.

It's the same as spending a hundred and three years contemplating these things.

38. Si quis peccavit, ibi malum est;

If someone has sinned, there is evil there;

fortasse tamen non peccavit.

perhaps, however, they have not sinned.

39. Vel ab una mente, quasi fonte communi, tanquam uni corpori eveniunt omnia, nec par est, partem queri de iis, quae in commodum totius eveniunt, vel atomi et nihil aliud nisi confusio et dissipatio fortuita.

Even from one mind, as if from a common source, everything comes together as if to one body. It's not right to complain about the things that happen for the benefit of the whole, or about atoms and nothing else but random confusion and dispersion.

Quid igitur perturbaris?

So why are you disturbed?

Menti* dic:

Say to yourself:

Mortua es, corrupta es, simulas, efferata es, pecudis more congrederis et pasceris.

40. Aut nihil possunt dii aut possunt.

Si igitur nihil possunt, cur precaris?

si possunt, cur non potius eos precibus rogas, ut tibi dent, ne quid horum extimescas aut cupias neque tali re doleas, quam ut horum aliquid vel absit vel adsit?

Omnino enim, si hominibus auxilium praestare possunt, in talibus quoque id possunt.

Verum fortasse dices:

"Haec dii in mea potestate posuere.

" Itane vero praestat, iis, quae tui sunt arbitrii, cum libertate uti, quam ea, quae tui arbitrii non sunt, animo servili et abiecto curare?

Quis tamen tibi dixit, deos nobis non ad ea quoque, quae in nostra potestate sunt, opem ferre?

Haec igitur ab iis precari incipe, et videbis.

Alius precatur:

utinam mihi contingat concubitus cum illa! Tu:

utinam non appetam illius concubitum!

Alius:

utinam eo priver! Tu:

utinam non opus habeam eo privari!

"You are dead, corrupted, pretending, senseless, behaving like a beast, mating and grazing."

Either the gods are powerless, or they are powerful.

If they are powerless, why do you pray?

If they are powerful, why don't you rather ask them with prayers to grant you that you neither fear nor desire any of these things, nor suffer in such a way that either something of these things is absent or present?

Indeed, if they can provide assistance to humans, they can also do so in such matters.

But perhaps you will say:

"The gods have placed these things in my power.

"Is it truly preferable, to make use of the things that are within your control with freedom, and to concern yourself with those that are not within your control with a servile and debased mind?

However, who told you that the gods do not offer help to us even for those things which are in our power?

Therefore, begin to ask these things of them, and you will see.

Another person prays:

"May I have a sexual encounter with her!"; and you:

"May I not desire that sexual encounter with her!", Another.

Another:

"May I obtain that thing!" You:

"May I not have a need to obtain that thing!"

Alius:

utinam filiolum non amittam! Tu:

utinam uon metuam amittere! Huc omnino verte vota tua, et vide, quid futurum sit.

41. Epicurus, Quum aegrotarem, inquit, non sermones mihi erant cum iis, qui me invisebant, de corporis affectionibus neque de rebus istiusmodi cum iis, ait, colloquebar;

sed perpetuo ea, quae coepta erant, de natura rerum disserebam, et in eo ipso occupatus eram, quomodo mens, quamquam istiusmodi in corpusculo motuum particeps, tamen, suum bonum servans, imperturbata staret;

neque medicis, inquit, occasionem praebebam sese iactandi, quasi magni quid facerent, sed vita et bene et beate agebatur.

Eadem, quae ille, tu quoque fac in morbo, cnm aegrotas, et in quacunque alia molestia:

nam a philosophia non deficere neque cum indocto et naturae rerum ignaro garrire, id omnibus philosophorum sectis commune est, sed in ea tantum re, quae nunc in manibus est, occupari atque instrumento, quo haec res perficitur.

42. Quum alicuius impudentia offenderis, statim te interroga, "fierine igitur potest, ut in mundo non sint impudentes?

"non potest.

Noli ergo postulare, quod fieri nequit:

Another:

"May I not lose my little child!" You:

"May I not fear losing him!" Certainly, turn all your desires towards this, and see what will happen.

Epicurus said, "When I was sick, there were no discussions to me about bodily ailments nor did I engage in conversations of that sort with those who visited me," he said.

However, I was constantly discussing the nature of things, which I had begun, and I was absorbed in the very thing itself, how the mind, although participating in the motions of the body, nevertheless, by preserving its own good, remained undisturbed;

Nor did I provide an opportunity for the doctors to boast, as if they were accomplishing something great, but life was being lived well and happily.

Do the same things in illness that he did, when you are sick, and in whatever other discomfort:

For not to abandon philosophy, not to converse with the unlearned and ignorant of the nature of things, this is common to all the schools of philosophy, but to be engaged only in that matter which is now in your hands and to be occupied with the tool by which this matter is accomplished, that is the peculiar mark.

When you are offended by someone's impudence, immediately ask yourself, "Can it be, then, that there are no impudent people in the world?

"It cannot be.

Therefore, do not demand what cannot happen:

nam hic quoque unus est illorum impudentium, quos in mundo esse necesse est.

For here too is one of those impudent people, whom it is necessary to exist in the world.

Idem vero et de versuto et infido et quolibet vitioso in promptu tibi sit;

And the same should be ready for you regarding the cunning, the untrustworthy, and any other vicious person;

simulatque enim recordatus fueris, fieri non posse, quin talium hominum genus sit, singulis eorum te aequiorem praebebis.

For as soon as you remember that it is impossible for there not to be such types of people, you will make yourself more equitable to each of them.

Utile vero etiam illud est, statim cogitare, quam natura homini virtutem dederit contra hoc peccatum;

But it is also useful to immediately consider what virtue nature has given to humans against this fault;

nam dedit, tanquam remedium, contra ingratum mansuetudinem, contra alium aliam quandam facultatem.

for it has given, as a remedy, gentleness against ingratitude, and against each particular fault, another corresponding capability.

Omnino autem tibi licet, meliora edocere eum, qui deceptus est;

However, it is entirely within your right to instruct him who has been deceived in better ways;

quisquis enim peccat, a fine sibi proposito aberrat et deceptus est.

for whoever sins, deviates from their intended end and is deceived.

Quidnam vero damni tibi illatum est?

But what harm has been done to you?

neminem enim eorum, quibus irasceris, quidquam fecisse reperies, quo mens tua peior reddatur;

Indeed, you will find that none of those against whom you are angry has done anything by which your mind would be made worse;

atque in eo tamen omne malum ac damnum tuum consistit.

and yet all your evil and harm consist in this.

Quid vero novi aut insoliti fit, ubi indoctus id, quod indocti est, facit.

But what is new or unusual when an ignorant person does what ignorant people do?

Vide, ne potius te ipsum reprehendere debeas, qui non exspectaveris,fore, ut is hoc peccatum committeret.

See whether you shouldn't rather blame yourself for not expecting that he would commit this fault.

Nam tu, quamquam ratione nactus eras occasiones cogitandi, credibile esse, hunc ita esse peccaturum, tamen eius oblitus eum deliquisse miraris.

For though you had the opportunity to think by reasoning, you still marvel that he has erred, even though it was credible that he would act thus.

Potissimum autem ubi aliquem ut infidum aut ingratum accusas, in te ipsum descende.

Especially when you accuse someone of being untrustworthy or ungrateful, turn your focus inward.

Manifesto enim peccatum tuum est, sive, quoniam hominem ita affectum fidem tibi servaturum esse credidisti, sive, quoniam, beneficium quum dares, non simpliciter dedisti, nec tanquam qui ex ipsa actione omnem eius fructum perciperes.

For indeed, your fault lies in this: whether because you believed that the person would maintain faithfulness to you once affected in such a way, or because, when you bestowed a favor, you did not give it simply, nor as if you were to reap all its fruit from the action itself.

Quid vero, beneficio in alterum collato, plus requiris?

What indeed, when a benefit is bestowed upon another, do you require more?

nonne sufficit tibi, quod naturae tua;

Is it not sufficient for you that by your nature...

convenienter aliquid egisti, sed huius mercedem postulas?

...you have done something fitting, but you seek reward for it?

perinde atque si oculus idcirco, quod videt, mercedem postularet, aut pedes, quod ambulant.

...as if the eye were to demand payment for seeing, or the feet for walking.

Quemadmodum enim haec facta sunt ad munus aliquod, quo quum pro naturae suae conditione funguntur, habent, quod ipsorum est:

For just as these things are done for some function, in which they function according to their nature and have what belongs to them:

sic etiam homo, utpote ad bene faciendum natus, si in alios beneficiun contulit, aut iisdem auxilium praestitit in rebus mediis, fecit id, ad quod natus est, et, quod suum est, obtinuit.

So also a human being, born for doing good, if he has conferred a benefit on others or provided help to them in ordinary matters, has done what he was born to do and has obtained what is his own.

LIBER X

CONTEMPLANS
MORTALITATEM ET VIRTUTEM

1.

Erisne tandem, aliquando, mi anime, bonus, et simplex et unus, et nudus, et corpore, quod te circumdat, perlucidior?

Will you, at last, my soul, become good, simple, unified, and pure, and more translucent than the body that surrounds you?

gustabisne tandem affectionem ad amorem et pietatem proclivem?

Will you, at last, experience an inclination towards love and affection, and a disposition towards love and compassion?

Erisne tandem plenus et nullius rei indigens et nihil ulterius desiderans, nihili amplius appetens neque animati neque inanimati, quo voluptatibus fruaris?

Will you, at last, be full and lacking nothing, desiring nothing further, not seeking anything more, neither of the living nor the lifeless, to satisfy your pleasures?

nec temporis, in quo diutius fruaris, nec loci, aut regionis aut blandae aeris temperiei, aut hominum consensus?

Neither the passage of time during which you may continue to enjoy, nor the place, the region, the gentle temperature of the air, nor the approval of others?

sed ea, quae nunc est, conditione contentus delectaberis praesentibus ac persuasum habebis, omnia quae tibi adsunt, bene tibi habere et a diis profecta esse et bene habitura esse, quaecunque illis visa erunt et quaecunque daturi sunt ad salutem illius vivae natura perfectae et bonae et iustae et honestae et omnia gignentis et continentis et ambientis et complectentis, quae, ut alia similia inde oriantur, dissolvuntur?

But will you, content with your current state, delight in what is present, and be convinced that everything that is present is for your own good, emanating from the gods and destined to be beneficial, whatever they shall appear to them and whatever they will give for the well-being of that living nature that is perfect, good, iust, honorable, generating and containing all things, surrounding and embracing them, which, as other similar things arise from it, will eventually dissolve?

Erisne tandem talis, qui cum diis hominibusque in tali societatis communione vivas, ut neque quidquam in iis reprehendas neque ab iis condemneris?

Will you, at last, become such a person who lives in such a shared community with both gods and humans that you neither find fault in them nor pass iudgment upon them?

2 .

Observa, quid natura tua requirat, quatenus natura tantum regitur:

Observe what your nature requires, as far as it is governed by nature alone;

id deinde fac et admitte, nisi, natura tua, qua animal es, eo deterius se habitura ait.

then do that and accept it, unless your nature, as an animal, predicts that it would be worse off as a result.

Deinceps observandum, quid natura tua, qua animal es, requirat.

Next, observe what your nature as an animal requires.

Atque id omne admittendum, nisi natura tua, qua animal es ratione praeditum, eo deterius se habitura sit.

And all of that should be accepted, unless your nature as a reasoning animal predicts that it would be worse off as a result.

Quod autem naturae, idem quoque civitati convenit.

What applies to nature also applies to the city-state.

His iam regulis utens ne ulla in re curiosius agas.

Using these rules, do not engage in anything too inquisitively.

3 .

Quidquid contingit, ita contingit, ut tu id ferre natus es, aut ut non natus es id ferre.

Whatever happens, happens in such a way that you were born to endure it, or that you were not born to endure it.

Quod si tibi contingit, ut natus es ferre, noli indignari, sed, ut natus es, perfer;

And if it happens to you that you were born to endure it, do not be indignant, but endure it as you were born to do;

sin, ut non natus es ferre, noli gravari;

but if it is something you were not born to endure, do not be weighed down;

peribit enim quum te consumpserit.

for it will pass away when it has consumed you.

Memento tamen, te natum esse ad quidvis ferendum, quod ut tolerabite facias, in tua opinione situm est, si cogitaveris, id tibi conducere aut tui esse officii, ut id facias.

However, remember that you were born to endure anything, and whether to bear it nobly is in your power, if you consider whether it is in your best interest or within your duty to do so.

4. Si quis fallitur, benevole eum doce et errorem indica.

If someone is mistaken, kindly teach them and point out their error.

Si non potes, te culpa ipsum, aut ne te ipsum quidem.

If you cannot, blame yourself, or not even yourself.

5. Quidquid tibi contingit, id tibi ab aeterno destinatum erat, et complexa causarum series ab infinito hoc coniunxerat, ut et tu esses et hoc tibi contingeret.

Whatever happens to you, was destined for you from eternity, and an interconnected series of causes had linked it from infinity, so that both you would exist and this would happen to you.

6. Sive atomi, sive natura, primum positum sit, me partem esse universi a natura administrati;

Whether atoms or nature is the primary source, I am a part of the universe governed by nature;

deinde, me familiari quadam ratione cum partibus eiusdem generis coniunctum esse.

then, I am united with parts of the same kind in a familiar way.

Horum enim memor, quatenus pars sum, nihil aegre feram eorum, quae mihi ab universo tributa sunt;

Keeping these things in mind, as I am a part, I will bear without complaint whatever is assigned to me by the universe;

nihil enim parti nocet, quod universo prodest.

for what benefits the whole does not harm the part.

Non enim habet quidquam universum, quod ei non prosit, quum et omnes, naturae id commune habeant, et praeterea universi natura id acceperit, ut non ab ulla causa externa cogatur ad id gignendum, quod ipsi noceat.

The universe does not possess anything that does not benefit it, since all things share this in common by nature, and moreover, the nature of the universe has received this, that it is not compelled by any external cause to generate anything harmful to itself.

Itaque quatenus recordabor, me huiusmodi universi partem esse, quidquid obtigerit, id gratum acceptumque habebo.

Thus, as long as I remember that I am a part of such a universe, whatever happens, I will consider it pleasing and welcome.

Quatenus autem familiari quadam ratione cum partibus eiusdem generis coniunctus sum, nihil faciam communioni contrarium, sed consulam cognatis et omnem conatum ad id;

But insofar as I am united in a familiar way with parts of the same kind, I will not act contrary to that union, but I will consult with my fellow members and make every effort towards that;

quod societati communi prosit, dirigam et a contrario avertam.

I will direct what benefits the common fellowship and turn away from the opposite.

His ita peractis, vita prospere mihi fluat necesse est, quemadmodum vitam illius civis prospere fluere existimaris, qui per actiones civibus utiles procedit, et quodcunque civitas ei tribuat, libenter amplectitur.

With these things accomplished in this manner, it is necessary that life flows favorably for me, just as you would think the life of that citizen flows favorably who acts in ways beneficial to his fellow citizens and embraces willingly whatever the city bestows upon him.

7 ·

Partibus universi iis omnibus, quae natura tantum in mundo continentur, necesse est corrumpi.

It is necessary for all those parts of the universe, which are only contained in nature in the world, to be corrupted.

Dixeris sic ad graviter significandum "aliud atque aliud fieri.

You may use it in this manner to express something seriously "one thing happening after another."

" Si autem natura et malum et necessarium iis hoc esset, universum non bene regeretur, partibus eius in aliud atque aliud transeuntibus et ad corrumpendum varia ratione comparatis.

But if both evil and necessity were natural for them in this matter, the universe would not be governed well, as its parts transition to different things and are arranged in various ways to cause corruption.

Utrum vero natura ipsa consilium cepit, partibus suis damnum inferendi easque tales efficiendi, ut et fortuito et ex necessitate in malum incidant, an eam latuit, tales eas factas esse?

Did nature itself decide to cause harm to its own parts and to render them in such a way that they would inadvertently and necessarily fall into evil, or was she ignorant that she had made them such?

utrumque enim incredibile.

For both scenarios are unbelievable.

Quod si quis, etiam nulla naturae ratione habita, id inde explicaret, quod hae semel ita comparatae essent, vel sic ridiculum foret dicere, partes universi ita comparatas esse, ut mutarentur, simulque id, quasi aliquid, quod contra naturam eveniret, mirari aut id aegre ferre;

But if someone were to explain even without considering the nature of things, that they were arranged in such a way because they were made that way, it would be just as absurd to say that the parts of the universe were arranged in a way that they would change, and at the same time, to marvel or be displeased at it as if it were something happening against nature.

quum praesertim in eadem dissolvantur singula, e quibus sunt composita;

Especially since each of these parts dissolves into the very things of which they are composed;

aut enim dissipatio atomorum est, aut mutatio et solidi quidem in terram, et spiritus in aerem, ita ut haec quoque recipiantur in rationem universi, sive hoc intra certum temporis circuitum conflagrat sive perpetuis vicissitudinibus renovatur.

For either it is the dispersal of atoms, or the transformation, indeed, of solids into earth and spirits into air, so that these things also are incorporated into the order of the universe, whether this occurs within a certain cycle of time through conflagration or is renewed through perpetual alternations.

Quin ipsum illud solidum et spirabile noli putare idem, quod ab ortu fuit.

Moreover, don't think that the very same solid and breathable thing remains which existed from its origin.

Hoc enim quidquid est, heri et nudius tertius ex alimentis et aere, quem spiritus hausit, influxit.

For whatever it is, yesterday and the day before, it flowed in from nourishments and air, which the spirit inhaled.

Id igitur, quod recepit, mutatur, non id, quod mater genuit.

Therefore, that which it received changes, not that which the mother gave birth to.

Fac autem, id te nimis annectere illi singulari modo affecto, nihil id revera obstare arbitror ei, quod nunc dixi.

However, be careful not to attach yourself too much to that particular mode of affection. I believe that nothing truly opposes what I have just said.

8. Nomina adeptus viri boni, verecundi, veritatis studiosi, prudentis, concordis, magnanimi, cave ne aliis nominibus appelleris, et si haec nomina amiseris, celeriter ad ea redi.

Having acquired the names of a good man, one who is modest, devoted to truth, prudent, harmonious, and magnanimous, be cautious not to be addressed by other names. And if you lose these names, return to them quickly.

Memento autem prudentiae nomine tibi significari sedulam singularum rerum considerationem et diligenter institutam;

Moreover, remember that the name of prudence signifies to you diligent consideration of individual matters and careful discernment.

concordiae nomine spontaneam eorum receptionem, quae a natura communi assignantur;

The name of harmony signifies the spontaneous acceptance of those things assigned by the common nature.

magnanimitatis nomine intentionem partis intelligentis eiusque elationem supra levem asperumve carnis motum et gloriolam et mortem et alia eiusmodi.

The name of magnanimity implies the intention of the intelligent part and its elevation above the light or rough movement of the flesh, as well as vanity, death, and other similar things.

Haec igitur nomina si tibi servaveris, neque tamen admodum appetens, ut alii te illis appellent, alius eris et aliam inibis vitam.

Therefore, if you preserve these names for yourself, not desiring excessively that others address you by them, you will be different and you will embark on a different life.

Talem enim esse, qualis adhuc fuisti, et in eiusmodi vita raptari et inquinari, hominis est prorsus sensu carentis et vitae avidi et istorum bestiariorum similis, qui, quamquam vulneribus sc sanie repleti, ut in crastinum diem serventur, orant, utpote eodem in statu iisdem unguibus et morsibus obiiciendi.

For to be such as you have been thus far, and to be swept away and tainted in such a life, is characteristic of a person entirely devoid of reason, greedy for existence, and similar to those beasts. They, though filled with wounds and pus, plead to be preserved for the next day, so that in the same state, with the same claws and bites, they may be subjected to the same wounds and bites.

In haec igitur pauca nomina te recipe, et, si fieri potest, ut in iis maneas, mane, quasi in aliquas beatorum insulas traiectus;

In these few names, therefore, find yourself, and if possible, if you can remain in them, remain, as if you were transported to some islands of the blessed.

si iis te excidere easque non tueri te sentis, audacter abi in angulum aliquem, ubi ea tuearis, aut omnino e vita abi, neque tamen iratus, sed simplici, libero ac modesto animo, ut qui hoc anum saltem in vita egeris, quod ita decessisti.

If you feel that you are falling away from them and not protecting them, boldly withdraw to a corner where you can protect them, or depart from life altogether, yet not in anger, but with a simple, free, and modest mind, as someone who has lived at least this long, departing as you have.

Ut autem illorum nominum memineris, utique magnum tibi erit auxilium, si deorum memor fueris, atque eos nolle, animalia ratione praedita ipsos adulari, sed velle, ut ea omnia sibi quam simillima fiant, ac ficum esse, quae faciat, quae ficus sint, et canem, quae canis, et apem, quae apis, et hominem, quae hominis.

However, in order to remember those names, it will certainly be of great help to you if you remember the gods and understand that they do not wish rational creatures to flatter them themselves. Instead, they desire that all those creatures become as similar to themselves as possible, like a fig tree producing what a fig tree produces, a dog producing what a dog produces, a bee producing what a bee produces, and a human producing what a human produces.

9.
Mimus, bellum, terror, torpor, servitus quotidie delebunt illa sancta tua decreta.

Playfulness, war, fear, laziness, and daily slavery will erase those sacred decrees of yours.

Atque quam multa ratione a naturae studio aliena imaginaris aut praetermittis!

And how many things contrary to the pursuit of nature do you imagine or let go unnoticed!

Omnia autem sic considerare et facere te oportet, ut et, quod praesens necessitas postulat, perficiatur, et facultas contemplandi exerceatur, et fiducia ex certa rei cuiusque scientia orta conservetur, latens quidem, nec vero abscondita.

But you should consider and handle all things in such a way that both what present necessity demands is accomplished, and the faculty of contemplation is exercised, and confidence arising from the certain knowledge of each thing is maintained—concealed indeed, but not concealed.

Quando enim simplicitate frueris?

When will you experience simplicity?

quando gravitate?

When seriousness?

quando cuiusque rei cognitione, qualis per naturam suam sit, et quem locum in mundo occupet, et quamdiu pro natura sua perdurare possit, et e quibus conflata sit, et quibus subesse possit, et quinam eam et dare et auferre possint.

When the understanding of the nature of each thing, what its place is in the world, how long it can endure according to its own nature, from what elements it is composed, under what influences it can fall, and by what means it can be given or taken away?

10.
Aranea, musca capta, se effert;

A spider, upon capturing a fly, rejoices.

alius, ubi lepusculum, alius, quum reticulo apuam, alius, quum apros, alius, quum ursos, alius, quum Sarmatas cepit.

Another, when he catches a little hare. Another, when he captures a partridge. Another, when boars. Another, when bears. Another, when Sarmatians.

Nonne enim etiam hi latrones, si decreta spectaveris?

For don't even these robbers, if you examine their decisions, do the same?

11

Viam ac rationem contemplandi, quo modo cuncta inter se mutentur, comparatam habe, et semper iis adhibe atque in hac parte te exerce;

Have a method and rationale of contemplating how all things change into one another, and apply it always and practice this aspect of yourself.

nihil enim est, quod perinde magnum animum efficiat.

For there is nothing that can so magnify the soul.

Exuit corpus et quum reputaverit, iamiam ab hominibus discessurum se haec omnia relinquere debere, totum se permisit iustitiae in iis rebus, quas ipse agit, et in iis, quae accidunt, naturae universi.

Strip off your body; when you have considered that you must soon leave human affairs and that everything will be left behind, wholly entrust yourself to iustice in the actions you undertake and in what happens, in the universe of nature.

Quid autem alii de ipso dicant aut opinentur aut contra ipsum faciant, id ne cogitat quidem, quippe his duobus contentus, ut id, quod nunc agat, iuste agat, et id, quod nunc obtingat, libenter amplectatur:

But what others may say or think about him, or do against him, he does not even consider. He is content with these two things: that he acts iustly in what he does at present and that he embraces with pleasure whatever happens at present.

reliqua omnia negotia ac studia omisit nihilque aliud cupit quam ut recta via legi convenienter progrediatur et deum sequatur recta progredientem.

He has cast off all other interests and pursuits, desiring nothing else but to proceed rightly according to reason, following God as He makes progress along the right path.

12

Quid suspicione opus est, quum considerare tibi liceat, quid sit agendum, et, quum id perspexeris, placide et constanter hac progredi;

Why is suspicion necessary when you are free to consider what must be done? And when you have understood it, to proceed calmly and consistently along this path.

si non perspexeris, assensum sustinere et optimos quosque in consilium adhibere;

If you haven't understood it, to withhold assent and consult the wisest people.

si alia aliqua his obstiterint, pro iis, quae nunc sunt, rerum opportunitatibus considerate progredi, ei, quod iustum videtur, firmiter adhaerentem.

If any obstacles arise, to continue making decisions based on the present circumstances, while firmly adhering to what seems iust.

Optimum enim est, hoc consequi, quum certo ab hoc aberrare sit turpissimum.

For the best thing is to achieve this: to deviate as little as possible from this path is the most honorable.

Quietus autem simul et agilis, alacris simul et compositus est, quisquis rationi in omnibus obsequitur.

He who is at once calm and quick, cheerful and well-composed, follows reason in all things.

13. Quamprimum e somno expergefactus es, te percontare numquid tua intersit, ut ab alio iusta et honesta fiant.

As soon as you wake up from sleep, ask yourself if it is in your interest that someone else does what is iust and honorable. It makes no difference.

Nil interest.

Numquid oblitus es, istos, qui aliis vel laudandis vel vituperandis tantopere se iactant, tales in lecto esse, tales ad mensam, qualia faciant, qualia fugiant, qualia sectentur, qualia furentur, qualia rapiant, non manibus pedibusque, sed pretiosissima sui ipsorum parte, qua, si quis velit, fides acquiratur, verecundia veritas, lex, genius bonus?

Have you forgotten those individuals who boast so much about either praising or criticizing others, yet in private, are the very same people as they appear in public? They act in their beds and at their tables exactly as they advise others to do or avoid. They pursue and condemn the very things they advocate or disparage, not with their hands and feet, but with the most precious part of themselves. In that aspect, if anyone desires, trustworthiness can be acquired, honesty resides, law, good character, and morality find their place.

14. Naturae pariter omnia danti ac recipienti probe institutus et verecundus homo:

A person properly attuned to both giving and receiving from nature, and modest, says: "Give whatever you want; take away whatever you want!" He doesn't assert this arrogantly, but complies with it, and does so willingly.

"da, inquit, quidquid vis;

"Give," he says, "whatever you want;

aufer quidquid vis!"

take away, whatever you want!"

Neque hoc dicit ferocia elatus, sed illi obtemperans et bene volens.

He doesn't say this boastfully, but complying with it and having goodwill towards it.

15. Parvum est, quod reliquum est.

What remains is small.

Vive ut in monte.

Live as if on a mountain.

Nihil enim refert, hic an illic, modo ubique, tanquam in urbe, sic in mundo.

For it makes no difference whether you live here or there, as long as you live everywhere, iust as in a city, so in the world.

Videant, contemplentur homines hominem verum naturae convenienter viventem.

Let people see, let them contemplate a true human being living in harmony with nature.

Si eum nos ferunt, occidant nam id satius, quam sic vivere.

If they drive him to death, let him die, for it's better than living like that.

16. Omnino non amplius, de eo, qualem, oporteat esse bonum virum;

Indeed, no longer should you discuss what kind of person a good man should be;

disserere, sed talem esse.

instead, be that person.

Totius aevi ac totius naturae cogitatio crebro tibi occurrat, et omnia singulatim spectata, quod ad materiam attinet, granum, quod ad tempus, terebrae circum actionem.

Let the thought of the entire span of time and the entire scope of nature frequently come to your mind, and as you contemplate each thing individually in terms of its material aspect—a grain of sand—and in terms of its duration, the movement of the drill around it.

18. Ad unamquamque rem animum advertens, eam considera ut iam dissolutam, et in mutatione et quasi putredine et dissipatione versantem, aut quatenus quasi ad moriendum nata sit.

Direct your attention to each thing, and consider it as already dissolved, in a state of change, almost in decay and dispersion, or insofar as it is almost naturally inclined towards death.

19. Quales sint vescentes, dormientes;

Consider the nature of those who eat and sleep;

coeuntes, excernentes, reliqua.

Coming together, producing, and so on.

Deinde quales, ubi inflantur, efferantur, irascantur et quasi ex sublimiore loco increpent;

Then consider the nature of things—how they inflate, how they are carried away, how they become angry, as if scolding from a higher place; a little while before, how they were subservient to many things and why.

paulo ante autem quam multis servirent et ob quas res.

But a little while before, when they served many things and for what reasons.

Et paulo post inter tales erunt.

And shortly after, they will be among such things.

20. Confert cuique, quod cuique fert natura universi, et tum confert, quam illa fert.

Nature of the universe provides to each thing what is suitable, and then, confers what that very thing offers.

21. "Amat imbrem terra, amat sanctus aether.

"The earth loves the rain, the sacred air loves."

"Amat mundus facere, quidquid futurum est ut fiat.

The world loves to make whatever will happen to happen.

Dico igitur mundo:

Therefore, I say to the world:

"idem, quod tu, ego amo.

I love the same as you love.

"Numquid etiam sic dicitur illud, "amat hoc fieri?"

Is it also said this way, 'He loves that this happens?'

22. Aut hic vivis et adsuevisti:

Either you live in accordance with this principle and have become accustomed to it

aut foras abisti et hoc volebas:

or you have gone away from it and desired something else

aut moreris et munere defunctus es.

Or you die and have fulfilled your role.

Praeter haec nihil est.

Besides these things, there is nothing.

Esto igitur bono animo.

Therefore, be of good cheer.

23. Semper tibi evidens sit, huiuscemodi aliquid esse agrum:

Always keep in mind that life is like this: a field of such things.

et ut omnia hic eadem sint, quae in vertice montis aut in littore aut ubicumque demum vis.

and that everything here is the same as at the summit of a mountain or at the shore or wherever you may be.

Omnino enim vera reperies haec Platonis:

For indeed, you will find these statements of Plato to be true:

"ut septo, inquit, in monte moenibus circumdatus" et "mulgens pecudem."

"like cattle in a pen, he says, surrounded by walls on a mountain," and "milking the cow."

24. Quidnam mihi est pars mea principalis?

What then is my principal role?

qualem ego eam nunc praesto?

What character am I displaying now?

quam ad rem ea nunc utor?

For what purpose am I using it right now?

numquid intelligentia caret?

Is it lacking in understanding?

num a communi societate soluta est et divulsa?

Is it separated and torn from the common society?

num carunculae ita adfixa et admixta, ut simul cum ea convertatur?

Are its attachments and mixtures in such a way that they are turned together with it?

25. Qui dominum fugit, fugitivus est:

One who flees from their master is a runaway;

dominus autem est lex, et, hanc qui transgreditur, fugitivus.

and the master is the law, and whoever transgresses it is a fugitive.

Neque vero minus qui dolet aut irascitur aut metuit, * quippe qui aversetur, factum essse aut fieri aut futurum esse aliquid eorum quae ab universitatis administratore constituta sunt, qui ipse lex est, cuique, quod suum est, tribuens.

And surely no less is one who grieves or becomes angry or fears, for such a person turns away from the constitution established by the ruler of the universe, who is the law itself, and who assigns to each person their rightful place.

Ergo:

Therefore:

qui aut metuit aut dolet aut irascitur, fugitivus est.

He who either fears, grieves, or becomes angry is a runaway.

26. Hic discedit misso in uterum semine:

Such a person departs after casting the seed into the womb.

id deinde alia natura excipiens excolit et absolvit foetum - ex quali qualem!

Then, another nature receives it, nurtures and completes the fetus—out of what material and into what form!

Alimentum rursus per gulam demisit, quod alia deinceps causa excipiens sensum inde et motum et omnino vitam ac vires - quot et quales res!

Once again, it sends nourishment through the throat, which another nature subsequently takes up for various reasons, extracting sensation, movement, and altogether life and power—how many and what kinds of things!

efficit.

it achieves this!.

Haec igitur, quae tanta caligine involuta fiunt, contemplari oportet, et vim illam sic cernere, ut eam, qua res vel deorsum vel sursum feruntur, cernimus, non oculis quidem, nec tamen minus clare.

Therefore, one should contemplate these things that are enveloped in such darkness and perceive that force in such a way that we perceive the force by which things are borne either downward or upward—not with our eyes, yet no less clearly.

27. Semper considerare, quomodo, qualia nunc fiunt, talia etiam antea facta esse omnia, et considerare, talia esse futura.

Always consider how things of the same kind as those now occurring have also occurred before, and consider that such things will be in the future as well.

Atque totas fabulas et scenas eiusdem generis, quas vel per experientiam tuam vel ex antiqua historia cognovisti;

And all the stories and scenes of the same kind, which you have known either through your own experience or from ancient history;

ob oculos ponere, veluti totam Hadriani aulam, totam Antonini aulam, totam aulam Alexandri, Philippi, Croesi;

to place them before your eyes, as if the entire court of Hadrian, the entire court of Antoninus, the entire court of Alexander, Philip, Croesus;

omnia enim illa eiusdem generis fuerunt, modo per alios.

for all of those were of the same kind, only through others.

28. Hominem quemcunque ulla de re dolentem aut eam indigne ferentem similem animo tibi finge porcello, qui, dum mactatur, calcitrat et grunit - huius etiam similis est is, qui solus in lectulo decumbens tacite alligationem nostram deplorat - et animali duntaxat rationi praedito datum esse, ut iis, quae fiunt, sponte obsequatur;

Imagine any person who is hurt or angered by anything, or bears it indignantly, as similar in nature to a pig. Just as a pig, when it is being sacrificed, squeals and struggles—so too, such a person is similar to that pig, who, when alone in bed, silently laments out bondage. It has been given only to an animal endowed with reason to willingly obey what happens; to simply follow is necessary for all.

simpliciter autem sequi omnibus necessarium.

to simply follow is necessary for all.

29. Singulatim ad res, quas agis, singulas animum advertens te ipse interroga, num mors horrenda sit idcirco, quod te hac re privat.

Individually, focusing your mind on the things you do, question yourself: Is death dreadful for this reason, because it separates you from this thing?

30. Quum peccato alicuius offenderis, statim transiens tecum perpende, quid simile ipse pecces, ut, quod argentum pro bono habes aut voluptatem aut gloriosam et quae huius sunt generis.

When you are annoyed by someone's mistake, immediately reflect that you might be making a similar mistake yourself, valuing money, pleasure, or a glory belonging to this kind. .

Huic enim rei intentus mox irae oblivisceris, si etiam illud tibi succurrerit, eum vi coactum agere - quid enim faciet?

For being focused on this matter, you will soon forget your anger if it also occurs to you that he is compelled by force—what else can he do?—

- aut, si potes, libera eum vi illa cogente.

or, if you can, free him from that compulsion

31. Satyronem ubi vides, Socraticum tibi finge Eutychem aut Hymena;

When you see a Satyr, imagine to yourself that you see Eutyches or Hymen;

et Euphratem quum vides, Eutychionem cogita aut Silvanum;

and when you see Euphrates, think of Eutychion or Sylvanus;

Alciphrone viso, animo tuo obversetur Tropaeophorus, et, viso Xenophonte, Crito aut Severus;

when you see Alciphron, let Tropaeophorus be present in your mind, and when you see Xenophon, think of Crito or Severus;

et te quum adspicis, Caesarum aliquem cogita, et sic in quolibet geminum ei aliquem.

And when you look at yourself, imagine someone like the Caesars, and so with anyone in any case.

Tum tibi succurrat:

Then let this come to your mind: Where are those people now? Nowhere, or anywhere.

ubi nunc sunt illi?

nusquam aut ubicunque.

Nowhere, or anywhere.

Sic enim semper spectabis res humanas ut fumi ac nihili instar, praesertim quum simul recordatus fueris, id, quod semel mutatum sit, non per infinitum tempus esse duraturum.

For in this way, you will always regard human affairs as smoke and nothing, especially when you remember at the same time that whatever has changed once will not endure for an infinite amount of time.

Tu autem, quamdiu?

But as for you, how long?

cur vero tibi non sufficit, spatium hoc tam breve, prout decet, transigere?

Why indeed is this brief span not enough for you to live as you should?

Qualem materiam, qualem rem, in qua elabores, fugis?

What kind of material, what kind of task that you are struggling with, are you fleeing from?

Quid enim haec omnia sunt, nisi exercitia rationis, quae accurate, et, ut naturae scrutatorem decet, ea, quae in vita sunt, perspecta habet?

For what are all these things but exercises of reason, which, just as it is fitting for a student of nature, has thoroughly understood those things that exist in life?

Persiste igitur, donec etiam haec tibi familiaria reddideris, quemadmodum bonus stomachus cuncta sibi reddit familiaria et ignis validus, quidquid inieceris, inde flammam et splendorem edit.

Persist, therefore, until you have made these things familiar to yourself, just as a healthy stomach renders all things familiar to itself and a strong fire, whatever you put into it, produces from there flame and brightness.

32. Nemini liceat, id, quod verum est, loquenti, te dicere non esse simplicem aut bonum, sed mentiatur, quisquis horum aliquid de te opinatur.

Let no one be allowed to speak the truth, saying that you are not simple or good, but whoever thinks anything of these things about you is deceiving themselves.

Quidquid autem huius generis est, id in tua situm est potestate.

But whatever is of this kind, it is within your power.

Quis enim est, qui te prohibeat, quominus bonus et simplex sis?

For who is there to prevent you from being good and simple?

tu tantum certo statue, non diutius vivere, nisi talis sis futurus.

You only need to firmly resolve not to live any longer, unless you are going to be such.

Neque enim ratio te iubet, si non talis sis, diutius vivere.

For reason does not require you to live any longer if you are not going to be such.

33. Quid est, quod hac in re optime vel agi vel dici possit?

What is there that can be done or said in this matter most excellently?

nam quodcunque fuerit, id ipsum facere vel dicere licet, neque causari, te impediri.

For whatever it may be, you are allowed to do or say it, and nothing can cause you to be hindered.

Non gemere desines, priusquam ita affectus fueris, ut quod voluptariis deliciae, idem tibi sit, in quavis materia subiecta tibique oblata ea facere, quae propriae hominis constitutioni consentanea sunt:

You will not cease to groan before you have become so affected that what delights the hedonist is also the same for you, and you can do those things that are in accordance with your own nature in any matter presented to you:

fructus enim loco habendum est, quidquid secundum tuam naturam agere tibi licet.

For whatever you are allowed to do according to your nature, that should be regarded as a reward.

Ubique autem id licet.

And everywhere, this is permissible.

Cylindro quidem non datur, ut proprio suo ex motu ubique feratur neque aquae, neque igni, nec reliquis, quae a natura aut anima ratione carente reguntur;

However, it is not granted to a cylinder to move everywhere by its own motion, nor to water, nor to fire, nor to other things that are governed by nature or a soul lacking reason;

multa enim sunt, quae haec coercent iisque resistunt.

For many things indeed constrain these and resist them.

157

Mens autem et ratio per omne quae obsistunt, secundum naturam et voluntatem suam procedere potest.

However, the mind and reason can proceed through all obstacles according to their nature and will.

Hanc facilitatem, qua ratio per omnis ferri potest, ut ignis sursuro, lapis deorsum, cylindrus per declive, ob oculos tibi ponens, nihil amplius require.

This ease, through which reason can be carried through all things, like fire ascending, a stone descending, a cylinder on a slope, by setting before your eyes, requires nothing more.

Reliqua enim omnia impedimenta aut corporei sunt cadaveris, aut sine opinione et ipsius rationis remissione nec vulnerant nec minimum quidem mali efficiunt;

For all other obstacles are either the body's remains or without opinion, and the relaxation of reason itself neither wounds nor even causes the slightest harm;

alioquin qui hoc pateretur, statim deterior fieret.

otherwise, whoever would undergo this would immediately become worse.

In aliis quidem operibus, quidcunque alicui contingat mali, eo ipso redditur deterius id, quod patitur;

In other works, whatever misfortune happens to someone, by that very fact, what they suffer becomes worse;

hic autem, si ita dicere licet etiam melior fit homo et laude dignior, si iis, quae ipsi obiiciuntur, recte utitur.

but here, if it is permissible to say so, a person becomes even better and more worthy of praise if they make proper use of the things that are presented to them.

Omnino autem memento, civem indigenam nihil laedere, quod civitatem non laedat, nihil autem civitatem laedere, quod legem non violet;

However, always remember not to harm a fellow citizen in a way that does not harm the city, and not to harm the city in a way that does not violate the law;

eorum autem, quae infortunia dicuntur, nihil violat legem.

but those things that are called misfortunes do not violate the law.

Quod igitur legem non violat, id neque civitatem neque civem laedit.

Therefore, what does not violate the law does not harm either the city or the citizen.

34. Ei, qui veris decretis* acutus est, brevissimum et in medio positum sufficit, quo admoneatur de moerore et metu abiiciendis, ut "Sternit humi frondes alias vis aspera venti"...

For someone who is discerning with true judgments, a brief and moderate reminder is sufficient, by which they are prompted to discard grief and fear, just as "A rough force of wind scatters leaves to the ground"...

"sic hominum genus est."

so is the human race."

Foliola et liberi tui;

Your little leaves and children;

foliola et ii, qui maximo sublato clamore, ut fidem dictis faciant, alios celebrant, aut e contrario diris devovent, aut clam vituperant et rideat;

Leaves and those individuals, who, with the greatest uproar, either celebrate others to establish their trustworthiness, or on the contrary, condemn them with curses, or they mock and deride in secret;

foliola pariter, qui famam posthumam excipient.

likewise, leaves, who will receive posthumous reputation.

Omnia enim haec "veris nascuntur in hora.

For all these things "are born true at the right time."

" Post ventus ea humum sternit;

After the wind, it lays them on the ground;

deinde silva alia in ipsorum locum profert.

Then another forest brings forth in their place.

Brevitas autem temporis communis est omnibus;

However, the brevity of time is common to all;

tu vero omnia perinde atque aeterna forent, fugis et sectaris.

but you, imagining that all things are the same as eternal, flee from them and pursue them.

Mox etiam tui claudentur oculi, et eum, qui te extulit, mox alius lugebit.

Soon your eyes will also close, and the one who praised you will soon mourn another.

35. Sani oculi est videre omnia, quae sub visum cadunt nec dicere:

To have healthy eyes is to see all things that fall within sight and not to say,

"viridia volo.

"I want green."

" Hoc enim eius est, qui oculis laborat.

For this is the concern of someone who struggles with their eyes.

Sanum porro auditum et olfactum oportet ad omnia, quae auditu aut olfactu percipi possunt, esse paratum.

Furthermore, a healthy sense of hearing and smell must be ready for all things that can be perceived by hearing or smell.

Bene valentis porro stomachi eat, ad omnia alimenta pariter se habere, ac mola se habet ad omnia, ad quae molenda fabricata est.

For a well-functioning stomach, all foods are digestible in the same way that a mill is suited for grinding everything it was made to grind.

Atque sic etiam mentis sanae est, ad omnia, quae eveniant, esse paratam.

Similarly, a healthy mind is prepared for all things that happen.

Illa vero, quae "Liberos," inquit, "mihi salvos esse volo", aut, "omnes quidquid faciam laudare volo," oculi instar est, qui viridia poscit, et dentium qui mollia.

Indeed, the desire for "I want my children to be safe" or "I want everyone to praise whatever I do" is like having eyes that crave green things or teeth that crave soft things.

36. Nemo adeo felix est, cui morienti non adstituri sint quidam, qui malo, quod accidit, laetantur.

No one is so fortunate that, as they die, there won't be some standing by who are pleased by the misfortune that befalls them.

Bonus et sapiens fuerit:

Even if they have been good and wise:

nonne tamen ad extremum erit, qui secum dicat:

Won't there still be, in the end, someone who says to themselves:

"Respirabimus tandem aliquando ab hoc paedagogo:

"We will finally breathe free from this tutor:

nemini quidem nostrum gravis ac molestus fuit, sed sensi, eum nos tacite damnare.

Not one of us was heavy or troublesome, but I sensed that we secretly condemn him.

Haec igitur de viro probo.

These things, therefore, about a virtuous man.

In nobis autem quam multa alia sunt, propter quae a nobis liberari cupiant haud pauci?

But in us, how many other things are there for which not a few desire to be liberated from us?"

Haec igitur moribundus contemplaberis et libentius discedes, haec tecum reputans:

Therefore, as you are dying, you will contemplate these things and depart more willingly, reflecting within yourself:

"discedo e tali vita, in qua ipsi vitae socii, quorum gratia tantos suscepi labores, tot fudi preces, tantas sustinui curas, me migrare volunt, quod inde aliud quid levaminis sibi fore sperant.

"I depart from such a life, in which the very companions of life, for whose sake I undertook so many labors, poured forth so many prayers, endured so many cares, wish me to migrate, because they hope that something else may bring relief to them from there.

Quid igitur est, cur quis diutius hic morari cupiat?

What, then, is the reason why anyone would wish to linger here any longer?"

Nec tamen propterea illis minus benevolus hinc discede, sed mores tuos servans, amicus, benevolus, mitis;

However, do not depart from them with any less goodwill; but maintaining your own character, be a friend, be benevolent, be gentle.

neque tamen contra quasi vi avellaris, verum, quemadmodum in eo, cui facilis mors contingit, animula facile corpore exsolvitur, talem etiam tuam ab his secessionem esse oportet;

cum his enim natura te copulavit et coniunxit.

Verum nunc dissolvit?

Dissolvor igitur tanquam familiaribus, nec tamen reluctans, sed nulla vi coactus discedens:

nam hoc quoque unum est eorum, quae naturae conveniunt.

37. Solemne tibi sit, in singulis cuiusvis actionibus, quoad fieri potest, tecum reputare:

"Quorsum haec eius actio spectat?

"A te ipso autem fac initium teque primum explora.

38. Memento, illud, quod te quasi fidiculis huc illuc impellat, id esse, quod intus absconditum est;

hoc est suadela, hoc vita, hoc, si verum volumus, homo.

Noli igitur unquam cum eo mente complecti circumiectum tibi vas et instrumenta illa undique tibi afficta:

nam dolabrae sunt similia, abs qua eo tantum differunt, quod adnata sunt.

Nam profecto non magis cuiusquam harum partium tibi usus est sine illa causa, quae ea movet eorumque motum retinet, quam radii textrici, aut calami scribenti, aut flagelli currus rectori.

Certainly, indeed, you have no more use for any of these parts without the cause that sets them in motion and sustains their movement than a weaver's shuttle has without the weaver, or a pen without the writer, or a whip without the charioteer.

LIBER XI

HUMILITATEM ET
GRATITUDINEM COLENS

I . Haec sunt propria animo ratione praedito: se ipse videt, se effingit, se, qualem vult esse, reddit, et fructus, quos fert, ipse percipit - plantarum enim fructus et quae his in animalibus respondent, alii percipiunt - finem suum consequitur, ubicunque vitae terminus immineat. Non;

quemadmodum in saltatione et actione fabularum, manca et mutila redditur tota actio, si quid inciderit, sed in quacunque parte, et ubicunque deprehensus fuerit, id, quod sibi proposuit, perfectum et omnibus numeris absolutum reddit, ut dicere possit, "ego quae mea sunt, habeo."

These are the unique attributes of a mind endowed with reason: it sees itself, imagines itself, molds itself into whatever form it wishes, and reaps the fruits it bears – for the fruits of plants and the corresponding functions in animals are perceived by others. It achieves its purpose, wherever the end of life approaches. No

iust as in a dance or a play, the whole performance is spoiled and incomplete if anything goes wrong, whether in a particular part or at any point, yet wherever it is detected, it perfects and completes what it set out to do, as if saying, "I have what is mine."

Totum praeterea mundum contemplando pervagatur, et, quod hunc ambit, vacuum, et figuram eius, atque in aevi immensitatem se extendit et omnium rerum regenerationem certis temporum periodis circumscriptam complectitur et considerat, atque intelligit, nihil novi visuros esse posteros nostros, nihilque maius vidisse maiores nostros, sed eum, qui quadraginta vixerit annos, si vel minimum mentis habuerit, quodammodo et praeterita et futura vidisse omnia, quum eiusdem speciei sint omnia.

Moreover, it ranges through the entire world by contemplating, perceiving the universe that encircles it as empty, grasping its form, extending itself into the vastness of time, embracing the cycle of all things bounded by specific periods, and comprehending that our descendants will see nothing new, and that our ancestors saw nothing greater. Instead, a person who has lived forty years and possessed even a modicum of reason has, in a sense, seen both past and future, since all things belong to the same nature.

Proprium quoque est animo ratione praedito, amare proximos, et veritas, et verecundia et summa sui ipsius aestimatio, quae etiam legi propria est.

It is also characteristic of a rational mind to love one's fellow beings, truth, and modesty, as well as to have a high estimation of oneself, which is also consistent with the law.

Sic igitur non differt recta ratio a ratione legis.

Thus, true reason is not different from the reason of law.

2 . Cantilenam iucundam, et saltationem et pancratium contemnes, si voce concinna in singulos sonos divisa, de his singulatim te interrogaveris, num hoc inferior sis;

You will despise pleasant songs, dances, and wrestling if, with a melodious voice divided into distinct sounds, you question yourself about each of these separately, asking whether you are inferior in any of them.

nam te id confiteri puderet;

For you would be ashamed to admit it,

et vero, si simile quid feceris in saltatione, quod ad singulos motus et gestus attinet, idemque in pancratio.

and indeed, if you have done something similar in dancing, concerning each individual movement and gesture, the same goes for wrestling.

In omnibus igitur omnino rebus, excepta virtute et iis, quae e virtute proficiscuntur, ad singulas earum partes recurrere memento et per earum divisionem ad ipsas contemnendas abire.

Therefore, in all things without exception, except for virtue and its derivatives, remember to analyze each of their parts and through their division, proceed to dismiss them.

Idem ad totam vitam, fac, transferas.

Similarly, apply this approach to your entire life.

3.

Qualis, est animus paratus, si iam debeat a corpore solvi et vel exstingui vel dissolvi vel permanere?

What kind of mind is prepared, if it must now be separated from the body, either extinguished or dissolved or continue to exist?

Haec tamen promptitudo ut a singulari iudicio proficiscatur, nequaquam e mera obstinatione, ut in Christianis, sed re bene deliberata, et cum gravitate et, ut etiam alit id persuadere possis, sine fastu tragico.

However, let this readiness arise not from blind stubbornness, as is the case with Christians, but from well-considered reasoning, with seriousness, and without bombastic show, so that you may even persuade others without theatricality.

4.

Feci aliquid quod societati prodest?

Have I done something that benefits society?

Igitur utilitatem consecutus sum:

Therefore, I have achieved utility.

hoc, ut semper tibi in promptu sit et occurrat! Nunquam desine.

May this be always at your disposal and readily available to you! Never cease.

5.

Quaenam est ars tua?

What is your craft?

Bonum esse.

To be good.

Hoc autem qua alia ratione fit, nisi per praecepta tum ad naturam universi tum ad propriam hominis conditionem spectantia?

But how is this achieved by any other means than through principles that pertain both to the nature of the universe and to the condition of humanity itself?

6.

Primum tragoediae sunt institutae, quae monerent de iis, quae accidant, eamque esse rerum naturam, ut haec sic eveniant, atque ne, quibus in scena delectamini, iisdem in maiore scena offendamini.

First, tragedies were instituted to warn us about the things that happen. The nature of events is such that they occur in this manner, and those things that delight you in the theater shouldn't offend you on a larger stage.

Nam videtis, non posse fieri, quin haec non accidant, eaque etiam illos sustinere, qui, "Eheu, Cithaeron!" exclamant.

For you see, it's not possible for these things not to happen, and even those who cry out "Alas, Cithaeron!" have to endure them.

Atque dicunturque quaedam ab iis, qui fabulas composuerunt, utiliter, velut potissimum hoc :

And certain things are said by those who composed the plays, and they are said for a useful purpose, most notably this:

"Si me meosque liberos di negligunt, huius etiam constat ratio,"

"And if the gods neglect me and my children, the same reasoning applies,"

Et rursus

"Nam neutiquam hominem rebus irasci decet."

Et: "Spicas ut frugiferas, sic vitam metere;"

et quae id genus sunt alia.

Post tragoediam vetus comoedia in medium prolata est, quae paedagogicam usurpabat libertatem et ipsa sermonis licentia ad homines de fastu vitando admonendos non inutilis erat;

quo consilio etiam Diogenes quaedam hinc suscepit.

Deinde quaenam fuerit media comoedia et quo consilio nova sit instituta quae paulatim in artificiosum imitationis studium abiit, considera.

Nam etiam ab his dici quaedam utilia, nemo ignorat;

verum totum huius poesis et fabularum institutum quorsum spectat?

7. Quam liquido compertum habes, nullum aliud, vitae genus ad philosophandum tam idoneum, quam hoc, quo forte versaris

8. Ramus a ramo cohaerente amputatus non potest non a tota arbore abscissus esse.

Sic igitur etiam homo ab uno homine avulsus, tota societate excidit.

Ac ramum quidem alius amputat;

And again:

"For it is by no means fitting for a man to be angry with things."

And: "As you gather fruit-bearing crops, so should you reap life;"

and other similar sayings of that kind.

After tragedy, the old comedy was introduced, which utilized a pedagogical freedom and even the license of speech was not useless in admonishing people to avoid arrogance;

With this intention, even Diogenes took up certain things from here.

Then consider what the middle comedy was and for what purpose the new comedy was established, which gradually moved towards a skillful pursuit of imitation.

For even some useful things are said by them, as no one is ignorant;

but what is the entire purpose of this poetry and the structure of these stories?

Which you have clearly found out, that no other way of life is so well suited to philosophical inquiry as the one in which you happen to be engaged.

A branch severed from a tree while still connected to a branch cannot help but be cut off from the entire tree.

In the same way, a person separated from one human being is cut off from the whole society.

And one person, indeed, cuts off a branch;

homo autem se ipse a proximo separat, dum eum odit et aversatur, ignorat autem, se simul a tota civitate sese abscidisse.

But a person separates themselves from their neighbor when they hate and turn away from them, yet they are unaware that they have at the same time cut themselves off from the entire community.

Veruntamen illud munus est eius, qui hanc societatem condidit, Iovis, quod nobis licet rursus cum eo, cui antea adhaesimus, coalescere ac rursus partem necessariam ad totius integritatem fieri.

However, this is the gift of the one who established this society, Iupiter, that we are allowed to once again merge with the person whom we previously adhered to, and once more become a necessary part of the integrity of the whole.

Quod tamen saepe in illa separatione versatur, facit, ut id quod abscessit, haud facile uniri et in pristinum locum restitui possit.

However, what often happens in that separation is that what has departed is not easily reunited and restored to its original place.

Omnino ramus, qui ab initio cum arbore germinavit et cum ea constanter quasi conspiravit, non similis est ei, qui, postquam abscissus erat, iterum insertus est, quidquid dicant hortulani:

Indeed, a branch that initially sprouted with the tree and consistently acted as if in harmony with it is not the same as one that, after being severed, is reattached, no matter what gardeners might say:

Una quidem fruticari, verum non una probare eadem decreta.

Indeed, it is one thing to grow together, but not the same to approve the same decisions.

9. Qui tibi secundum rectam rationem procedenti impedimento sunt, sicut a sana agendi ratione te depellere non possunt, ita neque benevolentiam erga ipsos tibi excutiant;

Those who are obstacles to your proceeding according to right reason, just as they cannot divert you from sound principles of action, likewise cannot shake your goodwill toward them.

sed utrumque pariter tuere, constantiam in iudicando et agendo, et mansuetudinem erga eos, qui te impedire aut alia ratione molesti esse conantur.

But defend both equally: the steadfastness in judgment and action, and the gentleness towards those who try to hinder or trouble you by other means.

Etenim non minus imbecilli animi est, iis succensere, quam ab actione desistere et consternatum succumbere;

For it is a sign of a weak mind to be provoked by them, just as it is to give up action and yield to discouragement;

uterque enim pariter desertae stationis reus est et qui metu perculsus eat et qui cognatum sibi natura et amicum aversatus est.

for in both cases, one is guilty of deserting his post, whether driven away by fear or estranged from his kin and friend by his own disposition.

10. Nulla natura inferior est arte;

No nature is inferior to skill;

nam etiam artes naturam imitantur.

for even arts imitate nature.

Quod si est, natura omnium praestantissima et ceteras omnes complectens artium solertiae neutiquam cesserit.

And if this is the case, then nature, which embraces all the other arts, is by far the most excellent, and no skill can surpass it.

Omnes autem artes praestantiorum gratia deteriora efficiunt:

However, all arts, for the sake of achieving excellence, make things worse.

igitur etiam communis natura.

Therefore, even common human nature.

Atque hinc sane iustitiae origo, ex hac autem reliquae virtutes oriuntur:

And truly, from this arises the origin of iustice, and from this, other virtues are born.

non enim servari poterit id, quod iustum est, si aut medias res ad nos pertinere putamus, aut nos facile decipi patimur, aut in assentiendo temerarii et inconstantes sumus.

For that which is iust cannot be preserved if we either believe that external events concern us directly, or if we are easily deceived, or if we are reckless and inconsistent in our iudgments.

11. Non veniunt ad te res, quarum cupido et aversatio te conturbant, verum quodammodo ipse ad eas accedis.

External circumstances do not come to you causing your desires and aversions, but rather you approach them in a certain manner.

Proinde tuum de iis iudicium quiescat;

Therefore, let your iudgment about them be at rest;

quo facto etiam illae manebunt immotae et ut eas neque sectans neque fugiens videberis.

by doing this, they will also remain undisturbed, and you will appear neither to pursue nor to avoid them.

12. Sphaera animi sui similis, quando se neque extendit ad aliquid, neque intro se contrahit, neque dilatatur, neque subsidit, sed lumine collustratur, quo veram et omnium rerum et suam ipsius naturam perspiciat.

The sphere of one's own mind is like this, when it neither extends itself to something external, nor contracts itself inwardly, nor expands, nor subsides, but is illuminated by its own light, by which it perceives the true nature of all things and its own nature as well.

13. Contemnit me aliquis?

Does someone despise me?

ipse viderit.

Let them decide for themselves.

Ego vero cavebo, ne quid contemptu dignum agere aut dicere deprehendar.

But I will take care not to be caught doing or saying anything deserving of contempt.

Odit me?

Does someone hate me?

ipse viderit.

Let them decide for themselves.

Ego vero omnibus sum mitis et benevolus et paratus, qui huic errorem ostendam suum, neque tamen exprobrandi causa, neque ut ostentem, me tolerare, sed ingenue et benigne, ut ille Phocion fuit, nisi quidem id simulavit.

I, on the other hand, am gentle, benevolent, and ready to show their error to anyone, not with the intention of rebuking or displaying that I can tolerate it, but openly and kindly, as Phocion was, unless of course he pretended to be so.

Intus enim ea eiusmodi esse oportet, et a diis conspici hominem nullam rem aegre ferentem aut quiritantem.

For such qualities must reside within a person, and the gods must observe a person enduring or complaining about nothing.

Quid enim mali tibi est, si ipse nunc id agis, quod naturae tuae proprium est?

For what harm is there to you if you yourself are now doing what is consistent with your own nature?

et excipis id, quod nunc universi naturae tempestivum est, quippe constitutus homo, qui per omnia, qualiacunque demum sunt, societatis saluti consulas?

And you also embrace what is timely according to the nature of the universe at this moment, since you are a human being placed in it, so that in all your actions, no matter what they may be, you contribute to the welfare of society.

14. Qui mutuo se contemnunt, iidem alter alteri assentantur, et qui id agunt, ut alios superent, iidem aliis, se submittunt.

Those who mutually despise each other will also agree with each other, and those who strive to surpass others will submit themselves to others.

15

Quam putidus et fucatus est, qui, "Ego," inquit, "aperte tecum agere constitui"?

How shallow and insincere is the one who says, "I have resolved to speak openly with you."

Quid agis, homo?

What are you doing, man?

hoc praefari te non oportet.

You don't need to announce this beforehand.

Illico apparebit;

It will become evident immediately;

in fronte inscripta esse debet haec vox, "Ita se res habet," statimque ex oculis apparere, quemadmodum in amantis oculis statim omnia intelligit is, qui amatur.

On the front, the phrase "Ita se res habet" should be inscribed, and it should immediately appear from the eyes, just as in the eyes of a lover, everything is immediately understood by the one who is loved.

Talem omnino oportet esse vi rum simplicem ac probum, qualis est, qui hircum olet, ut qui ei adstat, simulatque accedit, velit nolit, sentiat.

A man should be genuinely straightforward and honest, like someone who smells a goat, so that whoever approaches him, whether they like it or not, perceives it.

Affectatio autem simplicitatis instar pugionis est.

However, affectation of simplicity is like a dagger.

Nil turpius amicitia lupina.

Nothing is more disgraceful than wolfish friendship.

Maxime omnium hoc fuge.

Above all, avoid this as much as possible.

Vir bonus, simplex et benevolus haec omnia in oculis habet, nec latent.

A good, simple, and benevolent person keeps all these things in their eyes and nothing is hidden.

16

Optime vitam transigendi facultas ipsa in animo sita est, si res indifferentes in nullo discrimino ponit;

The best ability to live life is situated within the mind itself if it places indifferent things in no distinction;

id autem faciet, si earum unamquamque seiunctim et ex omni parte spectaverit et meminerit, illarum nullam nos cogere, ut hoc vel illud de iis opinemur, neque ad nos accedere, sed illas quietas consistere, nos autem esse, qui iudicia de iis proferamus easque in nobis ipsis depingamus, quum liceat non depingere, adeoque liceat, si forte clam irrepserint, statim delere:

it will achieve this if it examines and recalls each of them separately and from all sides, not compelling us to form any particular opinion about them, nor approaching us itself, but letting them remain calm, while we are the ones who pronounce judgments about them and paint them within ourselves, even though it is permissible not to paint them, and thus permissible, if they happen to creep in secretly, to immediately erase them:

brevi tantum tempore hac cautione opus fore, tum vitae finem instare.

This caution will be needed only for a short time, then the end of life will approach.

Quid tamen in his omnino difficile est?

However, what is altogether difficult in these things?

Si enim naturae conveniunt, iis laetare et facilia tibi sunto;

If they agree with nature, reioice in them and let them be easy for you;

si contra naturam, quaere, quid tibi secundum tuam naturam sit et ad hoc contende, etiamsi non gloriosum sit.

if they go against nature, seek what is in line with your own nature and strive for it, even if it's not glorious.

Venia enim cuique est, qui bonum suum sectatur.

For everyone is granted the privilege who pursues their own good.

17. Unde prodierint singula, quibus ex materiis substratis singula constent, in quid mutentur, mutata qualia sint futura, et ut nihil mali patiantur.

From where individual things come forth, from what underlying materials they consist individually, into what they change, what qualities they will have changed, and how they might suffer no harm.

18, Ac primum:

And first:

quaenam mihi ad eos sit ratio, et nos, alterum alterius causa, natos esse, me alio quodam respectu iis esse praefectum, ut gregi aries, ut armento taurus.

what reason do I have towards them, and we, born for the sake of one another, I being assigned to them in some other respect, like a ram to the flock, like a bull to the herd.

Altius vero rem repete, ex hoc:

But let's delve deeper into the matter, starting from this point:

si non atomi, natura est, quae res administrat;

if not atoms, then there is a nature that governs things;

quod si est, deteriora sunt praestantiorum causa, haec autem, alterum alterius causa.

But if there is, the lesser things exist for the sake of the superior, and these, for the sake of one another.

Deinde, quales sint ad mensam, in lectulo, reliqua;

Then, what they are like at the dining table, on the bed, and the rest;

potissimum vero, quibus decretorum necessitatibus cogantur, et haec ipsa quanto cum fastu agant.

especially, the circumstances by which they are compelled to act according to their iudgments, and how extravagantly they conduct themselves in such matters.

Tum, si recte haec faciant, non esse aegre ferenda;

Then, if they perform these actions properly, they are not difficult to tolerate;

sin minus, eos manifesto nolentes et ignorantes agere.

but if not, they openly act unwillingly and unknowingly.

Omnis enim animus, ut veritate, sic etiam ea virtute, quae suum cuique pro dignitate tribuit, invitas privatur;

For every soul, as it is deprived of the truth, so it is deprived of that virtue which accords each its due;

hinc quoque dolore afficiuntur, quum iniusti, ingrati, avari, omninoque in alios peccantes audiunt.

hence, they are also affected by pain when they hear about the uniust, ungrateful, greedy, and those who sin against others in every way.

Porro, te quoque ipsum multa peccare et alium eiusdem generis esse;

Moreover, you yourself also make many mistakes and are of the same kind as others;

atque, si quibusdam abstineas peccatis, tamen tibi esse habitum, ex quo proficiscantur, etsi ignavia aut gloriae cupiditate aut alia mala de causa similibus abstineas.

and, even if you refrain from certain sins, you still have a disposition from which they arise, although you may abstain out of laziness, the desire for glory, or other similar misguided motives.

Porro, te, an peccaverint, ne satis quidem intelligere multa enim etiam ex prudenti dispensatione fiunt;

Moreover, whether they have sinned or not, you cannot even fully understand, for many things are also done through prudent discretion;

atque omnino multa explorata haberi oportere, priusquam de aliorum actionibus certi aliquid statuas.

and certainly, many things should be thoroughly examined before you make any definite iudgment about the actions of others.

Porro, quando maxime stomacharis et inique fers, puncti instar esse vitam humanam et brevi nos omnes vita esse excessuros.

Moreover, at the very times when you are most annoyed and bear things uniustly, consider human life as a mere point, and that we will all depart from life in a short time.

Porro, non eorum actiones nobis molestiam creare, quippe, quae in illorum mentibus insint, sed nostras opiniones.

Moreover, it is not their actions that create trouble for us, for those actions reside in their minds, but it is our iudgments.

Tolle igitur et missum fac iudicium illud, quasi malum esset, et abiit ira.

Therefore, remove and dismiss that iudgment, as if it were an evil, and let go of your anger.

Quomodo vero tollas?

Reputans tecum, non esse inhonestum:

nisi enim sola turpitudo esset malum, necesse esset, te quoque multa peccare et latronem et quid non fieri.?

Porro, quanto molestiora nobis adferant, ira et dolor qui ex iis oriuntur, quam res ipsm, propter quas irascimur et dolemus.

Denique, benevolentiam, si genuina, non simulata aut fucata sit, invictam esse.

Quid enim tibi faciet, qui vel maxime contmeliosus est, si benevolus ei esse perrexeris, et, si occasio ita tulerit, eum placide adhorlatus fueris, et eo tempore, quo te laedere conatur, quietus sic admonueris;

"Absit, mi fili! ad aliam rem nati sumus:

ego quidem neutiquam laesus ero, sed tu laederis, mi fili!"

Atque quam lenissime et universim ei ostendere, rem sic se habere, neque apes id facere, neque alias animantes, quae natura gregatim vivant.

Oportet vero hoc neque irridendi neque exprobrandi causa te facere, sed cum sincero amoris affectu atque animo non irritato, neque vero tanquam in schola, neque ut alius, qui adstat, te admiretur, sed aut ei soli id dici oportet, aut, si forte alii adsint...

But how can you do that?

By reflecting within yourself that it is not dishonorable:

for if only disgrace were evil, you would necessarily have to admit that you also commit many wrongs and become a thief and whatnot.

Moreover, how much more troublesome to us are anger and the pain arising from them, than the things themselves for which we become angry and grieve over.

Certainly, if genuine, not pretended or feigned, goodwill is invincible.

For what will it do to you, even if someone is extremely insulting, if you choose to be kind towards them and, if the opportunity arises, greet them calmly, and at the moment they attempt to harm you, admonish them quietly in this way:

"Far from it, my friend! We are born for something else: I certainly will not be harmed, but you are harming yourself, my friend!"

And to show them as gently and universally as possible, to explain to them that the situation is thus, neither do bees do it, nor other creatures that live in groups according to their nature.

But you must do this without the intention of mocking or reproaching, but with a sincere feeling of love and a calm mind, neither as if in a school, nor like someone else who is present, admiring you. Instead, it should be said to them alone, or if others happen to be present...

Horum novem capitum memento, quasi dona ea a Musis accepisses;

Remember these nine principles as if you have received them as gifts from the Muses;

et incipe tandem homo esse, dum vivis.

and finally, start being a true human being while you live.

Pariter vero cavendum, ne aduleris eos, quam ne irascaris:

Equally, be cautious not to flatter them, as well as not to become angry with them;

utrumque enim a societatis commmunione alienum est et damnum adfert.

for both of these behaviors are foreign to the bonds of society and bring harm.

Accedente autem ira, in promptu sit, non irasci esse viri, sed lenitatem ac mansuetudinem, ut humaniorem, ita viro digniorem esse;

But when anger arises, it should be readily evident that a man is not prone to anger, but rather to show kindness and gentleness, so as to become more humane and more worthy as a man; strength and dignity should be present in him, not in one who becomes indignant and offended.

huic robur et nervos et fortitudinem inesse, non ei, qui indignatur et offenditur.

To this person, strength, vigor, and courage belong, not to the one who becomes indignant and offended.

Quanto enim propinquius hoc est affectuum vacuitati, tanto etiam potentiae propius est.

For the closer this is to the absence of emotional disturbances, the closer it is to power. And just as sadness, so too is anger a trait of a weak human; both are wounded and surrender themselves.

Atque ut tristitia, ita etiam ira infirmi hominis est;

If you like, also accept a tenth gift from the leader of the Muses:

nam uterque vulneratus est et sese dedit.

For both have been wounded and have given in to themselves.

Si lubet, etiam decimum a Musarum praeside donum accipe:

It is unjust and tyrannical to allow others to be like that toward you as long as they do not wrong you.

nolle peccare pravos homines, esse insanum;

To wish that wicked people not sin is insane;

quoniam appetit id, quod fieri non potest.

since it desires what cannot be accomplished.

Concedere, ut erga alios tales sint, modo non in te peccent, iniquum esse et tyrannicum.

To grant that others be such, as long as they do not harm you, is unjust and tyrannical.

19.

Quattuor potissimum mentis aberrationes perpetuo cavendae, et si quando eas in te deprehenderis, tollendae eo, quod de singulis sic tecum loqueris:

Four particular deviations of the mind must always be guarded against, and if you ever detect them within yourself, you should dismiss them with these reflections:

Haec opinio non est necessaria:

This belief is not necessary;

hoc societatis vinculum solvit:

this loosens the bonds of society;

hoc non a te dicturus es;

this you will not say;

non autem a te dicere ineptissimum habeto.

but consider it extremely foolish to say such things.

Quartum est, in quo tibi ipse exprobras, proficisci id a parte tui diviniore devicta et succumbente parti corporis viliori ac mortali eiusque crassis voluptatibus.

The fourth is when you blame yourself for something; proceed by calming your higher self and overpowering the inferior and mortal part of your body, along with its coarse pleasures.

20.

Animula tua omneque igneum, quantum commistum est, quamquam natura sursum feruntur, tamen universi dispositioni obtemperantia, hic in hac massa commixta detinentur.

Your soul, and everything fiery within you, though naturally inclined upwards, still adheres to the harmony of the universe; it is confined here in this compound mass.

Quidquid porro in te terrenum et humidum est, quamquam deorsum fertur, tamen sursum attollitur et statum occupat sum ipsius naturae non proprium.

Whatever, furthermore, is earthly and watery within you, though it tends downwards, is yet lifted upwards and assumes a position that does not belong to its own nature.

Sic igitur ipsa elementa universo obtemperant et postquam alicubi per vim collocata sunt, ibi permanent, donec iterum dissolutionis signum datur.

Thus, the elements themselves obey the order of the universe and, once placed somewhere by force, remain there until the signal for dissolution is given.

Nonne igitur turpissimum est, solam tui partem ratione praeditam esse immorigeram et locum suum indigne ferre?

Is it not then extremely disgraceful for the rational part within you to be unruly and to resist its proper place?

quamquam ei nihil quidem per vim imponitur, sed ea tantum, quae naturae eius conveniunt - et tamen non sustinet, sed in adversam fertur partem:

Although nothing is forcibly imposed on it, but only what is in accordance with its nature, it still does not endure, but is carried to the opposite side:

motus enim, quo ad iniurias, voluptatum blanditias, iram, dolorem, metum fertur, nihil aliud est, nisi defectio a natura.

The movement by which it is carried toward iniuries, the allurements of pleasures, anger, pain, and fear, is nothing but a departure from its nature.

Quin etiam mens, quum aliquid eorum, quae accidunt, aegre fert, stationem suam deserit:

Furthermore, when the mind resents something that happens, it abandons its post:

ad pietatem enim et deorum venerationem non minus nata est, quam ad iustitiam.

Indeed, iust as it is not born any less for devotion to duty and reverence for the gods than for iustice.

Nam haec quoque in eorum numero sunt, quae ad societatem servandam faciunt, immo vero iustis actionibus antiquiora.

For these things are also among those that contribute to the preservation of society, indeed even more ancient than iust actions.

21. Cui non unum idemque vitae consilium est, is unus idemque per totam vitam esse non potest.

To him who does not have one and the same plan of life, it is not possible to be one and the same throughout life.

Neque vero sufficit, quod dictum est, nisi etiam id addideris, quale hoc consilium esse debeat.

Nor is it enough, what has been said, unless you also add this, what kind of plan it ought to be.

Quemadmodum enim non eadem est opinio de bonis, quae quoquo modo bona esse videntur multitudini, sed de certis quibusdam, hoc est, de communibus;

For iust as the opinion about goods is not the same, which in any way seem good to the multitude, but about certain specific ones, that is, about common ones;

ita etiam id consilium nobis proponendum quod societati communi et civitati accommodatum est.

Likewise, the same kind of plan must be proposed to us, which is adapted to the common society and the state.

Ad hoc enim qui omnes suos conatus dirigit, is actiones sibi similes praestabit, et hac ratione semper unus idemque erit.

For he who directs all his efforts toward this goal will consistently perform actions similar to his purpose, and by this means, he will always be the same and consistent.

22. Murem montanum et domesticum, et huius pavorem et trepidationem.

As for the mountain and domestic mouse and their fear and trembling;

23. Socrates etiam vulgi placita Lamias appelabat, puerulorum terriculamenta.

Socrates also called the opinions of the masses "Lamias," the bugaboos of children.

24. Lacedaemonii peregrinis sub umbra sedem, assignabant in spectaculis:

The Spartans assigned seats in the shade to foreigners during the spectacles;

ipsi, ubi fors ferebat, considebant.

they themselves would sit wherever chance led them.

25. Socrates Perdiccae, quod ad coenam non veniebat, "Ne pessimo" inquit, "interitu peream" hoc est, ne gratiam in me collatam referre nequeam.

Socrates, regarding his absence from dinner at Perdiccas's, said, "I am not dying a most wretched death" - that is, lest I be unable to repay the favor shown to me.

26. In literis Ephesiorum praeceptum erat, ut semper alicuius ex antiquis, qui virtuti operam dederant, reminiscerentur.

Among the instructions of the Ephesians in their teachings, there was a precept to always remember someone from the ancients who had devoted themselves to virtue.

27. Pythagorei mane oculos ad coelum tollere nos iubent, ut eorum recordemur, quae in iisdem et eadem ratione suum opus perficiunt, et ordinis ac puritatis nudaeque simplicitatis:

The Pythagoreans instruct us to lift our eyes to the sky in the morning, so that we may remember those things which in the same and consistent manner accomplish their own work - things of order, purity, and straightforward simplicity.

nullum enim velamentum astri.

For there is no covering of a star.

28. Qualis fuerit Socrates, quum Xanthippe pallio eius sumpto foras exisset;

What kind of person Socrates was when Xanthippe went outside with his cloak on?

et quid familiaribus suis dixerit pudore suffusis ac recedentibus, quum eum sic indutum viderent.

and what he said to his friends, blushing and withdrawing, when they saw him dressed like that.

29. Nunquam scribendi et legendi praecepta dabis, nisi prius ipse didiceris.

and what he said to his friends, blushing and withdrawing, when they saw him dressed like that.

Id multo magis in vita.

This is much more applicable in life.

30. "Quum liber haud sis, ius loquendi non habes."

"When you are not free, you have no right to speak."

31. "Cor meum mihi risit."

"My heart laughed at myself."

32. "Virtuti gravibus facient convicia verbis."

"Insults will not harm true virtue."

33. Ficum hieme quaerere, insani est:

To seek a fig in winter is madness:

talis est, qui liberos optat, quando non amplius datur.

similar is one who wishes for children when it is no longer possible.

34. Filiolum exosculanti praecepit Epictetus, ut intus diceret:

Epictetus advised someone kissing his little son to say inwardly:

"Cras fortasse morieris."

Perhaps you will die tomorrow.

- At hoc mali ominis.

But this is an evil omen.

- Nihil, inquit, mali ominis est, quod opus aliquod naturae significat, aut etiam "spicas demeti" mali ominis.

"There is no evil omen," he said, "in anything that signifies a natural occurrence, or even 'harvest the figs,' is an evil omen."

35. Uva acerba, matura, passa, omnes mutationes non in nihilum, sed in id, quod nunc non est.

Unripe grape, ripe grape, raisin—every change is not into nothing, but into that which does not exist at the present moment.

36. Liberi arbitrii latro nullus est.

There is no robber of free will.

Hoc Epicteti.

This is from Epictetus.

37. Artem vero assensum praebendi monebat esse reperiendam et in loco de appetitionibus cautionem servandam, ut sint cum exceptione, ut sint societati utiles, ut cuiusque rei dignitatem sequantur, atque appetentia prorsus abstinendum, aversatione autem ad nihil eorum utendum, quae non sint in nostra potestate.

He also taught that the art of giving assent should be cultivated and caution should be exercised in relation to desires, ensuring that they are with reservation, useful for society, following the dignity of each thing, and one should completely abstain from desire, while using aversion only toward those things which are not in our power.

38. Non igitur, inquit, certamen est de re vulgari, sed de eo, utrum insaniamus, necne.

Therefore, he says, the contest is not about a common matter, but about whether we become insane or not.

39. Socrates:

Socrates:

"Quid, inquit, vultis, utrum animas habere eorum, qui ratione praediti sunt, an eorum, qui ratione carent?"

"What, he says, do you want, whether to have the souls of those who are endowed with reason or those who lack reason?"

- Eorum, qui ratione sunt praediti.

- Those who are endowed with reason.

-Quorumnam ratione praeditorum? sanorum an pravorum?

- Of those endowed with reason, which ones? The sound-minded or the unsound-minded?

-Sanorum.

- The sound-minded.

-Quare igitur eas non quaeritis?

- Then why don't you seek them?

-Quoniam habemus.

- Because we have them.

-Quamobrem igitur pugnatis et contenditis?

- Then why do you fight and argue?

LIBER XII

Stoicam Resistentiam Amplexans

I.

Omnia illa, quae per ambages assequi cupis, iam nunc habere potes, nisi tibi ipse invides, hoc est, si, omisso eo, quod praeteriit, et eo, quod futurum est, commisso providentiae, id duntaxat, quod praesens est, ad sanctitatem et iustitiam dirigis

ad sanctitatem, ut diligas ea, quae tibi destinantur;

tibi enim hoc tulit natura et te huic ad iustitiam, ut libere et sine ambagibus veritatem, loquaris atque secundum legem et pro cuiusque dignitate agas.

Therefore, you can have all those things which you desire to achieve through circuitous paths right now, unless you sabotage yourself, that is, if you set aside what is past and what is to come, entrusting them to providence, and focus only on what is present, directing yourself towards sanctity and iustice

towards sanctity, to love what is allotted to you;

for nature has inclined you to this, and it has directed you to iustice, so that you may speak truth freely and without ambiguity, and act according to law and the dignity of each.

Ne vero te impediat neque alterius malitia, neque opinio, neque vox, nec vero sensus carunculae tibl circumdatae nam viderit id, quod patitur.

But do not let yourself be hindered by the malice of others, or by opinion, or by speech, nor even by the sensation of the little fleshy mass that surrounds you, for it sees what it endures.

Si igitur, quocunque tandem tempore in exitu futurus sis, ceteris omnibus missis;

Therefore, if at any time you are to reach your end, leaving aside all else;

principalem tui partem et divinam particulam magni aestimaveris neque hoc metueris, ne vivere aliquando desinas, sed ne nunquam naturae convenienter vivere incipias, homo eris mundo, qui te protulit,

- and if you esteem the principal part of yourself and the divine spark within you highly, and do not fear this, that you may one day cease to live, but rather that you may never begin to live in accordance with nature, you will be a man in harmony with the universe that brought you forth;

dignus et desines in patria tua peregrinus esse eaque, quae quotidie fiunt, tanquam inopinata admirari et ab hoc vel illo pendere.

worthy and you will cease to be a stranger in your homeland, and you will marvel at the things that happen every day as if unexpected, and you will not depend on this or that.

2 .

Deus mentes omnes hisce corporeis vasis, corticibus, sordibus denudatas videt.

God sees all minds stripped of these corporeal vessels, husks, and filth.

Sola enim sua ipsius intelligentia ea tantum attingit, quae ab ipso in illas derivata ac delibata sunt.

For only through his own understanding does he touch those things that have been derived and distilled from himself into them.

Quod ipsum si tu quoque facere adsueveris, multa temet molestia liberabis.

And if you also become accustomed to doing this, you will free yourself from many troubles.

Qui enim carnem sibi circumdatam non respicit, is multo minus in veste, domo, gloria et alio huiusmodi cultu et apparatu contemplandis occupabitur.

For he who does not regard the flesh that surrounds him will be much less occupied with contemplating clothes, houses, glory, and other such attire and decoration.

Tria sunt, ex quibus constas:

There are three things from which you are composed:

corpusculum, animula, mens.

a little body, a little soul, and a mind.

Horum reliqua, quatenus eorum cura tibi demandata est, tua sunt, tertium autem solum proprie tuum.

The rest of these, as far as their care is entrusted to you, are yours, but the third is solely your own.

Quamobrem si a te ipso, hoc est, a mente tua separaveris quaecumque alii dicunt et faciunt, et quaecumque ipse dixisti et fecisti

Therefore, if you separate from yourself, that is, from your mind, whatever others say and do, and whatever you yourself have said and done,

et quocunque ut futura, conturbant et quaecumque vel circumdati corpusculi vel huic congenitae animulae non tui sunt arbitrii, et quocunque extrinsecus circumfluens vertigo volvit,

And being disturbed by neither worrying about the future nor by whatever concerns the tiny particles that surround us or the innate soul within us, which are not under our control, and by whatever external distractions come and go.

ita ut vis intelligendi rebus a fato obvenientibus exempta, pura ac libera apud se ipsam vivat, iusta agens;

So that the power of understanding, exempt from the events imposed by fate, lives within itself, pure and free, acting justly.

ea, quae accidunt, libenter accipiens et, quae vera sunt, loquens;

accepting willingly whatever happens and speaking what is true;

si, inquam, a mente haec separaveris, quae e communi cum corpore affectione ei adhaerent et temporis id, quod futurum est, et id, quod praeteriit, teque ipse feceris talem, qualis est globus Empedocleus:

f, I say, you separate these things from your mind, which cling to it in common with the body and are connected by time, both future and past, and you make yourself such as the Empedoclean sphere:

"Orbis teres mansione laetifica gaudens."

"A round globe reioicing in its happy abode."

atque id tantum temporis, quod vivis, hoc est praesens, bene ut vivas studueris, poteris id, quod usque ad mortem relinquitur vitae, tranquillus, generosus et genio tuo propitius transigere.

And if you strive only for the present time, which is the time you live, to live well, you will be able to spend the time that remains in life, until death, tranquilly, generously, and in harmony with your own nature.

4.

Saepenumero mirari soles, quomodo fiat, ut, quum sese magis quam alios quisque diligat, suam tamen ipsius de se opinionem minoris faciat, quam aliorum.

"Often you wonder how it happens that, while each person loves themselves more than others, they still hold a lower opinion of themselves than of others."

Igitur si cui deus aut prudens praeceptor adstans ei praeciperet;

So, if a god or wise teacher were standing by someone and commanding them;"

ne quidquam cogitaret aut animo conciperet, quod non, simulatque conceperit, proferre posset;

"that they would think or conceive in their mind anything which they couldn't, as soon as they conceived it, express."

ne unum quidem diem id sustineret.

nor would they be able to endure it for even one day.

Adeo magis alios, quid de nobis sentiant, veremur, quam nos ipsos.

So much more do we fear what others think of us than what we think of ourselves.

5.

Quomodo fit, ut dii, qui pulcre et cum singulari erga genus humanum amore omnia disposuerunt, hoc neglexerint, quod inter homines etiam ii, qui admodum probi sunt, qui quasi plurima cum diis commercia habent iisque per opera pia et sacra ministeria maxime familiares exstiterunt, postquam semel defuncti sunt, non amplius reducuntur, prorsus exstinguuntur?

How is it that the gods, who have arranged everything beautifully and with a special love for the human race, have neglected this matter? Among humans, even those who are highly virtuous and have a close relationship with the gods through their pious deeds and sacred services, once they have died, are no longer brought back, and are completely extinguished?

Hoc si quidem sic se habet, certo scito, si aliter se habere deberet, deos sic res instituturos fuisse.

If this is indeed the case, know for certain, if it should be otherwise, the gods would have arranged things so.

Nam si iustum esset, fieri quoque posset, et si naturae consentaneum esset, natura id ferret.

For if it were just, it could also happen, and if it were in accordance with nature, nature would bear it.

Ex eo igitur, quod non ita se habet, si quidem non ita habet, persuasum habe, non oportuisse id fieri.

Therefore, based on the fact that it is not so, if indeed it is not so, understand that it was not necessary for it to happen.

Ipse quoque intelligis, te in hac rei indagatione cum deo de iure disceptare, cum diis vero non ita ageremus, nisi optimi et iustissimi essent.

You yourself also understand that you would not engage in this investigation with a god about justice, but we would not act in such a way with the gods unless they were the best and most just.

Quod si ita est, nihil contra iustitiae ac rationis legem in mundi dispositione neglectum praetermiserint.

But if it is so, they would have neglected nothing contrary to the law of justice and reason in the arrangement of the world.

6. Adsuesce etiam iis, quae fieri posse desperas:

Also, become accustomed to those things which you despair of being possible:

nam etiam sinistra manus, quum ad alia opera ob desuetudinem,

for even the left hand, when it comes to other tasks due to lack of practice.

iners sit, frenum tamen validius, quam dextra, tenet;

It may be weak, but it still holds the reins more firmly than the right hand;

ei enim rei adsueta est.

for it is accustomed to that task.

7. Qualem oporteat deprehendi a morte tum corpore tum animo;

Consider what kind of state should be found in both body and soul at the time of death;

brevitatem vitae, immensitatem aevi praeteriti ac futuri et omnis materiae imbecillitatem considera.

reflect on the brevity of life, the immensity of the past and future ages, and the frailty of all matter.

8. Nudatas corticibus contemplari formas;

Contemplate forms stripped of their outer shells;

et quo referantur actiones;

and to what end actions lead;

quid dolor;

what is pain;

quid voluptas;

what is pleasure;

quid mors;

what is death;

quid gloria;

what is glory.

quis sibi ipse molestiarum auctor;

He himself is the author of his own troubles;

quomodo nemo ab alio quoquam impediatur;

no one is hindered by anyone else;

omnia in opinione sita.

everything is based on opinion.

9. Similem esse oportet in decretorum usu pancratiastae, non gladiatori;

In the use of decrees, one should resemble a pancratiast, not a gladiator;

hic enim gladium, quo utitur, deponit et interficitur;

for the gladiator lays down and is killed by the sword he uses;

ille vero manum semper praesto habet, neque alia re opus habet, quam ut manum contorqueat.

but the pancratiast always keeps his hand ready, and he needs nothing else but to twist his hand.

10. Quales sint res ipsae intueri, divisione facta in materiam, formam et rationem, in qua sunt ad alias res.

Observe the nature of things themselves, after dividing them into matter, form, and reason, in which they exist for other things.

11. Quanta homini est potentia, ut nihil aliud faciat, nisi quod Deus probaturus sit, et libenter accipiat, quidquid Deus illi assignarit.

How great is the power of man, that he does nothing except what God would approve and willingly accept whatever God assigns to him.

12. Quidquid naturae consequens est, de eo nec dii sunt accusandi, quippe qui nihil nec sponte neque inviti peccent, neque homines;

Whatever follows from nature, the gods are not to be accused, since they do nothing wrong willingly or unwillingly, nor are humans;

hi enim nihil non inviti peccant.

for humans do nothing but unwillingly commit wrong.

Ergo nihil accusandum.

Therefore, nothing should be accused.

13. Quam ridiculus ac peregrinus, qui quidquid est eorum, quae in mundo fiunt, admiratur!

How ridiculous and foreign is the one who admires whatever happens in the world!

14. Aut necessitas fatalis et ordo inviolabilis, aut providentia placabilis, aut confusio temeraria sine summo aliquo rectore.

Either there is fatal necessity and inviolable order, or there is a placable providence, or there is reckless confusion without any supreme director.

Si igitur necessitas inviolabilis, cur reluctaris?

If, therefore, there is an inviolable necessity, why do you resist?

si vero providentia, quae placari possit, auxilio divino dignum te praesta;

But if there is a providence that can be appeased, present yourself worthy of divine assistance;

si mera confusio, quae rectore caret, eo contentus esto, quod in tanto rerum fluctu in te ipso mentem aliquam rectricem habes.

If it is mere confusion without a ruler, be content with the fact that amidst such a tumult of events, you have a guiding principle within yourself.

Quodsi aestus ille te corripuerit, carunculam, animulam et reliqua abripiat! mentem enim non abripiet.

But if that surge overwhelms you, let it snatch away your flesh, your breath, and everything else! For it will not snatch away your mind.

15. An vero erit, ut lucernae lumen, donec exstinguatur, luceat, et splendorem non amittat;

Or will it be like the light of a lamp that continues to shine until it is extinguished, without losing its brightness;

in te autem veritas et iustitia et temperantia prius exstinguantur?

But in you, will truth, justice, and temperance be extinguished before that?

16. Si quis opinionem tibi excitet, quasi peccavit, tu tecum:

If someone arouses in you the opinion that you have committed a fault, consider with yourself:

Num certo mihi constat, an hoc sit peccatum?

Am I really certain whether this is a fault?

aut si peccaverit, an se ipse peccati reum non damnaverit?

Or if I have indeed committed a fault, has he not already condemned himself as guilty of the same fault?

Hoc enim perinde est ac si suum ipsius vultum dilaceret.

For it is as if he were tearing apart his own countenance.

Eum, qui nolit, improbum peccare, similem esse ei, qui nolit ficum in fructibus succum ferre, et infantes vagire et equum hinnire et quae alia sunt necessaria.

To refuse to commit wrongdoing is similar to someone refusing to produce iuice from figs, or infants crying, or a horse neighing, or any other necessary action.

Quid enim aliud facere potuit, quum talem habitum habeat?

For what else could he do, given his nature?

Si igitur strenuus es, hunc habitum sana.

Therefore, if you are diligent, heal this nature.

17. Si non convenit, noli id facere;

If it is not fitting, do not do it;

si non est verum, noli id dicere.

If it is not true, do not say it.

Tuus enim esto impetus.

Let your impulse be your own.

18. Universum semper intueri, quid sit ipsum illud, quod opinionem in te excitat, idque diligenter explicare dividendo in causam et materiam et consilium, quo exstiterit, et tempus, intra quod finem sit habiturum.

Always contemplate the whole, what that very thing is that stirs opinion within you, and carefully analyze it by dividing it into cause, matter, and the intention from which it arose, and the time within which it will come to an end.

19. Sentias fac tandem aliquando, esse aliquid in te praestantius et divinius, quam ea, quae affectus movent atque omnino tanquam fidiculis te trahunt.

Finally, realize that there is something in you more excellent and divine than those things which stir your emotions and pull you like puppet strings.

Quid mihi nunc est mens?

What is my mind now?

num metus?

Is it fear?

num suspicio?

Is it suspicion?

num libido?

Is it desire?

num aliud quid eiusmodi?

Is it anything else of that sort?

20. Primum, ne quid temere aut sine certo consilio.

First, do nothing rashly or without definite purpose.

Deinde, ut non alio, nisi ad societatis salutem referatur.

Then, let everything be directed towards the well-being of society and nothing else.

21. Brevi neque ipse ullus usquam eris, nec quidquam eorum, quae vides, neque eorum, qui nunc vivunt, quisquam.

Soon, neither you nor any of the things you see, nor any of those who are currently alive, will exist.

Omnia enim ita nata sunt, ut mutentur, vertantur, intereant, ut inde alia sua quaeque serie oriantur.

For everything is born to change, to transform, to perish, so that new things may arise in their own series.

22. Omnia, opinio;

Everything is a matter of opinion;

et haec in te sita est.

and this lies within you.

Tolle igitur, quando libet, opinionem, atque, ut promontorium praetervecto maris tranquillitas, sic tibi omnia serena et portus aestu vacans.

Therefore, whenever you wish, dismiss opinion, and just as after passing a promontory, the sea becomes calm, may everything be serene for you and free from turmoil.

23. Una aliqua quaecumque demum est actio, quae suo tempore desiit, nihil mali patitur eo, quod desiit;

Whatever action, finally, it may be, that ceases at its appointed time, suffers no harm from ceasing;

neque is, qui illius actionis auctor est, eo, quod illa desiit, mali quid patitur.

nor does the author of that action suffer any harm because it ceased.

Eodem igitur modo omnium actionum complexus, qui vita dicitur, si tempore suo desinet, nihil inde mali patitur, quod desiit, nec qui suo tempore huic seriei finem fecit, male affectus est.

In the same way, the totality of all actions, which is called life, suffers no harm from ceasing at its appointed time, and the one who has brought an end to this series in due time is not adversely affected.

Tempus autem ac terminum natura constituit, interdum propria, ut in senectute, omnino autem universi natura, cuius partibus sese mutantibus, novus semper ac vegetus totus mundus permanet.

However, nature establishes both the time and limit, sometimes individually, as in old age, but always universally, as the whole world remains perpetually new and vibrant, with its parts constantly changing.

Pulcrum autem semper et tempestivum, quod universo prodest.

But what is beautiful and timely is always beneficial for the universe.

Cessatio igitur vitae singulis quidem non est malum, quia neque inhonesta est, siquidem neque a potestate nostra pendet nec societati repugnat;

Therefore, the cessation of life is not inherently evil for individuals, as it is neither dishonorable, since it does not depend on our power nor does it contradict society;

bonum autem, si quidem universo tempestiva et commoda est et cum eo fertur.

Rather, it is beneficial if it is timely and in harmony with the universe.

Ita enim etiam numine divino fertur, qui eadem, qua deus, via fertur et mente sua ad eadem fertur.

In this way, it is also in accord with the divine will, as it follows the same path as God and is carried by its own mind towards the same destination.

24. Haec tria in promptu haberi oportet:

These three things should be kept in mind:

in iis, quae agis ne quid temere agas aut secus, quam ipsa iustitia egisset;

In your actions, ensure that you do nothing rashly or contrary to what iustice itself would have done;

in iis vero, quae extrinsecus accidunt, ea vel casu fortuito vel providentia evenire, et neque fortunam culpandam, neque de providentia querendum.

Regarding external events, recognize that they may occur either by chance or by providence, and do not blame fortune or complain about providence.

Secundum, quale unumquodque sit a semente usque ad animationem, ab animatione usque dum animam reddit, ex qualibus conflatum sit, et in qualia dissolvatur.

Secondly, consider the nature of each thing from its seed to its animation, from animation until it returns the soul, what it is composed of, and into what it dissolves.

Tertium, si repente in sublime elatus res humanas cerneres, earumque , quanta esset, varietatem considerares, eodem conspectu comprehendens quantum undique aeriorum et aetheriorum sedes suas habet, te, quotiescunque evectus esses, eadem semper visurum esse eiusdemque generis res, easque ad breve tempus duraturas.

Thirdly, if you were suddenly lifted up and could behold human affairs and contemplate their vast variety, encompassing the extent of the heavens and the celestial realms, you would realize that whenever you were elevated, you would always see the same things and that they would endure for a brief time.

De his fastus!

Regarding these matters, cast away your pride!

25. Eiice foras opinionem, salvus eris.

Reiect the opinion, and you will be safe.

Quis igitur prohibet, quominus eam eiicias?

Who, then, prevents you from discarding it?

26. Quando aliquid moleste fers, oblitus es, omnia secundum naturam universitatis fieri;

When you bear something with difficulty, you have forgotten that everything happens according to the nature of the universe;

tum vero, alterius peccatum a te alienum esse;

Moreover, that the wrongdoing of others does not concern you;

praeterea, omnia, quae nunc fiant, semper ita facta esse et futura esse et nunc ubique fieri;

Furthermore, that everything that is happening now has always happened, will always happen, and is happening everywhere;

porro, quam sancta sit hominis cum universo hominum genere cognatio, non enim sanguinis et seminis, sed mentis communio est.

Furthermore, consider how sacred is the kinship of human beings with the whole human race, for it is not a matter of blood or seed, but a communion of minds.

Oblitus vero etiam es huius, quod animus uniuscuiusque ratione praeditus deus est et inde fluxit;

Yet, you have forgotten that the mind of each person is a god-like faculty and has originated from there;

tum porro, nihil cuiquam esse proprium, sed et filiolum et corpusculum et ipsam animulam inde fluxisse;

Moreover, that nothing belongs exclusively to anyone, but that every little child, body, and soul has flowed from there;

porro, omnia in opinione sita esse, denique, unumquemque id tantum temporis, quod praesens est, et vivere et amittere.

Moreover, that everything is based on opinion, and finally, that each person has only the present moment to live and to lose.

27.

Continuo recolere memoriam eorum, qui aliqua de re vehementer indignati sunt, qui summis honoribus aut calamitatibus aut inimicitiis aliave quacunque fortuna nobilitati sunt, deinde reputare, ubi nunc illa omnia?

Recall immediately the memory of those who have been vehemently indignant about something, those who have been elevated by the highest honors, calamities, enmities, or any other fortune, and then consider: where are all those things now?

Fumus et cinis et fabula aut ne fabula quidem.

Smoke, ashes, and a mere story, or not even a story.

Succurrant tibi porro quae huius generis sunt omnia, ut Fabius Catullinus rure, Lucius Lupus in hortis, Stertinius Baiis, Tiberius Capreis, Velius (?

Therefore, let all things of this kind come to your aid, such as Fabius Catullinus in the countryside, Lucius Lupus in the gardens, Stertinius in Baiae, Tiberius in Capri, Velius (?

) Rufus, et quidquid est huiusmodi vehementis studii, quod opinione nititur;

) Rufus, and whatever else there may be of such intense pursuits that rely on opinion;

et quam vile omne, quod intenditur, quanto magis philosophum deceat, in quavis data materia iustum, temperantem et diis simpliciter obedientem se praestare.

And how trivial is everything that is pursued, how much more fitting it is for a philosopher to present himself as iust, moderate, and simply obedient to the gods in any given matter.

Fastus enim sub modestia gliscens omnium maxime intolerabilis.

For pride, when it grows under the guise of modesty, is most intolerable of all.

28. Interrogantibus, "Ubi deos conspicatus aut, unde compertum habens, eos esse, eos ita veneraris?

" primum etiam visu percipi possunt;

deinde vero , neque animum meum vidi et tamen eum in honore habeo.

Sic igitur etiam deos ex iis, quibus quoquo tempore eorum vim experior, et esse intelligo et eos veneror.

29. Vitae salus, res singulas ex omni parte, quid sint, intueri, quae earum sit materia, quae forma:

toto ex animo, quae iusta sunt, facere;

quae vera sunt, dicere.

Quid reliquum est?

quam ut vita fruaris, bonum alii bono ita adnectens, ut ne minimum quidem spatium relinquatur.

30. Unum lumen solis, etiamsi muris, montibus, aliisque innumerabilibus dividatur.

Una communis materia, etiamsi innumeris corporibus certo modo constitutis dividatur.

Una anima, etiamsi naturis innumerabilibus et propriis limitibus dividatur.

Unus animus ratione praeditus, etiamsi diremptus esse videatur.

When someone asks, "Where have you seen the gods, or from where do you know that they exist, and why do you worship them in such a manner?"

Firstly, they can be perceived even by sight;

Furthermore, I have not seen my own mind, and yet I hold it in high regard.

In the same way, I understand the existence of the gods from the effects I experience at any given time, and I both acknowledge and worship them.

To contemplate the nature of things, to understand what they are from every perspective, what their substance is, what their form is;

To act in accordance with what is just from the depth of one's soul;

To speak what is true.

What remains?

To enjoy life, attaching your own good to the good of others in such a way that not even the smallest space is left vacant.

Just as the light of the sun, even if divided among walls, mountains, and countless other objects, remains one.

Just as the common matter, even if divided into numerous bodies arranged in a certain way, remains one.

Just as the soul, even if divided into countless individual natures and distinct boundaries, remains one.

Just as the mind, endowed with reason, even if it appears to be separated, is still connected;

Ceterae vero rerum, quas dixi, partes, ut spiritus et materiae substratae, sensus expertes et a communionis studio alienae :

The other parts of things that I mentioned, such as spirits and underlying matter, devoid of senses and alienated from the pursuit of communion:

quamquam etiam has mens continet, et gravitas, quae eas in eundem locum cogit.

However, the mind contains even these, and gravity, which brings them together in the same place.

Mens autem singulari quodam modo ad naturas eiusdem generis fertur, neque divellitur ab ea societatis studium.

Yet, the mind is inclined in a special way towards the natures of its own kind and is not disconnected from the pursuit of fellowship.

31. Quid praeterea expetis?

What else do you desire?

diutius in vita esse?

To exist longer in life?

an vero sentire?

Or to feel?

animo moveri?

To be moved in the soul?

crescere?

To grow?

rursus denasci?

To be born again?

voce uti?

To use your voice?

cogitare?

To think?

Ecquid horum tibi videtur desiderio dignum Quodsi haec singula satis vilia sunt, progredere ad ultimum, Deum et rationem sequi.

Do any of these seem worthy of desire to you? But if each of these is quite insignificant, then proceed to the ultimate goal, to follow God and reason.

Horum autem cultui repugnat, inique ferre, si quis per mortem his cariturus sit.

However, it is contrary to the worship of these things and unjust to complain if someone is deprived of them through death.

32. Quantula pars infiniti et immensi aevi unicuique assignata est?

How small a part of infinite and immense eternity is assigned to each individual?

celerrime enim in aeternitate evanescit.

For it swiftly vanishes in the vastness of eternity.

Quantula totius materiae?

How small a part of the entire matter?

quantula totius animm?

How small a part of the entire soul?

in quantula totius terrae glebula repis?

In how small a patch of land on Earth do you crawl?

Haec omnia tecum reputans nihil magni facias, nisi hoc, ut agas, quemadmodum natura tua iubet, et feras, ut communis natura fert.

Considering all these things, you should not think anything of great importance, except this: to act as your nature commands and to bear what common nature brings.

33. Quomodo mens se ipsa utitur?

How does the mind use itself?

In hoc enim sita sunt;

For that is where everything is situated;

omnia.

everything.

Reliqua non tui sunt arbitrii;

The rest is not within your control;

si non tui arbitrii, cadavera et fumus.

if not within your control, they are corpses and smoke.

34. Maximam vim ad mortis contemptum excitandum habet hoc, quod etiam ii, qui dolorem pro malo et voluptatem pro bono habebant, eam contempserunt.

This has the greatest power to arouse contempt for death, that even those who considered pain as evil and pleasure as good have despised it.

35. Cui id tantum, quod tempestivum, bonum est, et cui perinde est, plures an pauciores secundum rectam rationem actiones exegerit, et cuius nihil refert utrum longiore an breviore temporis spatio mundum contemplatus sit, huic mors quoque non est formidini.

For whomsoever it is good, only as long as it is timely, and for whom it makes no difference whether they have performed more or fewer actions in accordance with right reason, and for whom it matters not whether they have contemplated the world for a longer or shorter span of time, death is also not to be feared.

36. Homo, civis fuisti in magna hac civitate.

You were a citizen in this great city.

Quid tua interest, utrum quinque annis, an tribus?

What does it matter to you, whether for five years or for three?

Quod enim fit secundum legem, id aequum est unicuique.

For what is done according to law is fair to each individual.

Quid igitur adeo grave est, si hac civitate te emittit, non tyrannus, non iniustus iudex, sed natura, qum te in eam induxit?

So why is it so grave, if this city releases you, not a tyrant, not an uniust iudge, but nature, which brought you into it?

perinde ac si histrionem idem praetor, qui eum conduxit, e scena dimittit.

Iust as if the praetor, who hired the actor, dismisses him from the stage.

Verum quinque actus fabulae non peregi, sed tres tantum.

True, I have not completed all five acts of the play, but only three.

Recte dicis;

You speak rightly;

in vita tamen etiam tres actus totam fabulam constituunt.

however, in life, even three acts constitute the whole play.

Finem enim determinat is, qui olim concretionis auctor fuit, et nunc dissolutionis auctor est;

For its end is determined by the one who was once the author of its composition and is now the author of its dissolution;

tu vero neutrius auctor es.

but you are the author of neither.

Abi igitur propitius;

Therefore, go forth in a favorable manner;

nam is quoque, qui te exsolvit, propitius est.

for he who releases you is also favorable.

Made in the USA
Columbia, SC
05 July 2024

467f887a-32ef-48ec-81d5-74fe6ba938b6R01